The Succession Bridge

Key Manager Succession Alternatives for Family-Owned Businesses

by
Loyd H. Rawls

CLU, ChFC, MSFS

Published and distributed exclusively by:
The Family Business Resource Center
2420 Martin Road, Suite 300
Fairfield, CA 94533
www.seekingsuccession.com

Senior Editor, Layout and Cover Design: Ricci M. Victorio, MA
Second Edition Editor: Michael Ludden
Technical Legal Advisor: Jonathon H. Green, Esq.
Additional Editing and Graphic Design: Peter Sander, MBA, CFP

For information or reprint permission contact:
The Family Business Resource Center

Printed in the United States of America

Dedication & Acknowledgments

Contrary to conventional thinking and the glitzy contentions of the media, modern business success is not about the great leader. No doubt, leadership is critical, but the demands of business are such that optimum execution is not realistic unless there is a strong, dedicated management support staff.

Business today is about the management team implementing the mission while the big cheese is doing the hob-knobbing, TV interviews or just taking it easy. The hard core fact is that key management is critical to both success and succession. And, as history continually affirms, key managers who can do the right thing when no one is looking, carry weight beyond expectations and can move the needle of productivity are hard to find.

Anyone who believes the 80/20 rule is an optimist. From my perspective as a family business succession planner, 10% of the employees -- the key managers -- account for 80% of the businesses productivity.

Having set this foundation, I am pleased to dedicate this book to the key managers who have worked with me over the last 20 years to confirm the concept of the Succession Bridge. These dedicated, management stalwarts did not win the sperm lottery and were not the frog kissed by the owner's daughter. They have been fixtures of success from dark-thirty to dark-thirty; continually looking to improve and stay one step ahead of rapidly changing circumstances.

Sometimes the impact of these key managers has been special and on occasion even very special. But, always, these management pillars have bought into the dream and have taken spiritual ownership of the family business into which the sovereign wisdom of God has placed them.

To name just a notable few of this group, specific appreciation is expressed to: *Dan Thill, Ricci Victorio, Denise Ware, Joe Jankowski, Ron Feldner, Richard Young, Todd Huber, Wayne Davis, Rick Wiler, Bart Gulvas, Ron Mulholland, Bill Drees, Michelle Proctor, Donna Jo Matracea, James Johnson, Philip Wright, Bobby Johnson, George Pong, Bradley Francis, Ellen Vega, Michael Moorhead, Michael Mamic, James Ng, Robert Cira, Robin Edmond, Robert Selff, Candice Miller, Deborah Davis, Milissa Ehrig, Michael Coughlin, Calvin Leiser, Hanley Dawson IV, John Leanardi, Michael Lensink, Dominic Marino, Dean Petersen, Louis Scaramuzzo, Martin Stilwell, Denise Valentin, Timothy Gadomski, Glenn Gilbert, Roland Jewett, William*

Keyes, Peter Brandwein, Peggy Busby, Thomas Ostrowski, Charles Saneman, Jack Saneman, John Rooney, Charles Cramer, Thomas Lorden, Larry Culver, Jeri Heckman, Michael LaLoggia, Tommy Lorden, Danny Lorden, Jere Wood, Mark Chasey, Patrick Eads, Richard Pladna, Thomas Vani, Tom Vacca, Billy Mayhew, Harriet Smith, Julie Coates, Ken Shepherd, Richard Llewellyn, David Furlow, Danny Braden, John Lucas, Dan Umansky, David Ellis, Mark David, Jacob Lopez, Frank Rivera and others who are beyond our ability to mention.

It is my hope that the forthcoming description of the experiences I have had with this group will provide encouragement for the greater utilization of key managers in the succession of the family owned business.

And I dedicate this book to the family members who have supported and encouraged me to proclaim my passion: my wife and dear friend Pat; our eternal blessings afoot; Amy, Kendall and Champ; my parents, Loyd and Flora; my sister, Dora and her beloved husband Richard Majer; my in-laws, Tom, Judy, Brian, Deb, Gary, Patti, Dale and Susanne; our friends, Ernie and Susan Kelly. I also extend appreciation to my editor and friend Mike Ludden, technical advisor, Jonathan Green and my mentors, Paul Kuck and Louis Bachrodt, III.

And, primal to any good that may come from this humble servant, thanks be to Jesus Christ, my Lord and Savior.

About the Author

Loyd H. Rawls has a passion for keeping the family business in the family and helping business owners achieve their succession goals. He has conveyed his theories and passion to an impressive group of business consultants and professional educators, and together they have developed The Rawls Succession Planning Group, which addresses the financial planning issues of business succession; and The Family Business Resource Center, dedicated to promoting the success and succession of family owned businesses through training family principals, successors, key personnel and family members in the three most significant factors effecting business succession: leadership development, management team enhancement, and communication.

Advisors often ask what the secret is to Loyd Rawls' success as a succession planner. The answer is that Loyd provides significant services that support his clients in maximizing their business productivity and for the ultimate succession of the family business legacy. Loyd's unique concepts of "Succession Success$_{SM}$" and "Succession Certification$_{SM}$" add recognizable value to these businesses. Loyd and his associates are known for their core operating goal: to exceed the expectations of their clients by addressing any and all critical issues that impact the achievement of family business succession.

"The Rawls Company has given us advice and guidance concerning day-to-day operations and especially in establishing the road map for family succession of our four corporations."
B.W. Simpkins, Chairman, S&S Enterprises, Inc.

"What appeared to be a straightforward estate planning issue in my eyes grew into a successful effort to tie all these larger issues together. While it seemed overwhelming at first, I am excited that we stayed with it, and did some much needed strategic planning and addressed head-on many related areas as well. It was worth every penny we spent."
Jim Graham, President, Santa Margarita Ford

Table of Contents

1 Business Succession: How, What and Why?

"Mr. Rawls, I told you that you would be wasting your time. You should realize that this is not my favorite subject. If you had not invited me to this wonderful golf club and agreed to give me strokes, trust me, I would walk of the room at the mention of the subject."

"Whoa Bob, give you strokes? Jack told me you were a notorious sandbagger and here you are already begging strokes! Don't you have any pride?"

We were sitting in the grill enjoying a continental breakfast before challenging the fabulous Lake Nona Golf Course. Bob sipped his coffee and responded with a big smile, "If you want me to listen to your sales pitch, you had better give me two a side and do it from a golf cart because I am not ready to talk about my retirement this early in the morning."

"Oh, man, you are the master of cynicism. Tell me, what made you so negative on succession?"

"It's real simple, Loyd," he responded resolutely, "a divorce, a pushy daughter and two worthless sons.

"The divorce speaks for itself. My ex-wife contends that I am a natural at making everyone around me miserable. Unfortunately, she owns a third of the business and spares no opportunity to remind me that, in addition to being a disappointing husband for our 28 years, I was a lousy dad."

"Thank goodness I no longer live with her or my pushy daughter. However, my daughter does work in the business. I'm surprised I have not seen her in here because all she does is play golf. And my two sons are great examples of the dark side of money. One is a career drug addict and the other is an artist. At 37 and 33 years old, neither has ever supported himself.

"About 25 years ago, I met an estate planning genius just like you who convinced me to transfer some stock and real estate into trusts for my kids, to avoid estate taxes. Little did I know I was going to be creating worthless bums."

Oh, yes, Bob was intense and cynical. And the double espresso did not help. I quickly led him out to the course and he proceeded to take out his frustration on me. When we returned to the grill for lunch, he drank two beers before I could read the menu. As he sipped his third, he began to relax. Assuming it was now or never, I asked, "In light of your unfortunate family circumstances, what are your succession plans?"

"Well sonny boy," he responded, "I am going to ride the beast until it dies or I die. If I get bored or senile on the way, I am just going to sell it."

"So is it reasonable for me to assume that you really don't care what happens to this business?"

"Do I care? The reason I don't like to talk about succession is that I care too much! My grandfather started this business. My heart is in my feet because I have screwed up my sons and spoiled my daughter and now my family's succession chain is going to be broken."

From this turbulent experience began a relationship with a good friend and client. And from the beer-assisted opening, we initiated a relationship that continues today. And from that preliminary talk, we would begin a process of evaluation that would lead to the development of a new management team for Bob, with nine key managers involved in a fabulous multi-level Succession Bridge program. We have established a win/win relationship between Bob and some fast-moving, hard-charging managers that has assured the continuity of Bob's business as security for his children and a career opportunity for his grandchildren. I share this story to high-light the purpose of this book, to explain how key managers can take an active and even critical role in family business succession.

The use of these key managers is a powerful concept that has substantially influenced my perspective on family business succession. And it has substantially increased the number of families that I am able to impact.

The reason is quite simple. Based upon my experience, 25 percent of all family-owned businesses are legitimately not interested in succession for a variety of reasons. Another 50 percent have no qualified, committed successors. Only the remaining 25% have family members who are candidates to take over the reins. When I began as a business succession specialist 30 years ago, this 25 percent was the only market I cultivated.

My epiphany was the recognition that succession still could be achieved for that remaining 50 percent, through the use of key managers.

And that brings us to the decision to publish this book. The Succession Bridge concepts we are going to discuss have tripled the number of qualified succession planning candidates.

I am excited about succession and excited to share these concepts with you. To get this process moving and be sure there is no confusion, we'll review a few concepts about the family business that were discussed in detail in my earlier book, "Seeking Succession."

What is a family business all about? First and foremost, it is more than just a business. The family works for much more than money. The pride and self-esteem of a family in business creates something that is far more powerful. Owning a family business creates feelings of significance, pride, notoriety and a sense of control over one's destiny. Participating in the conversion of sweat, tears, anxiety, creativity and countless time into a self sustaining entity that impacts employees, vendors and customers is a unique and profoundly gratifying experience.

This ability to create value, security and prosperity for your family drives a unique, intense level of productivity. That pride in the family and the appreciation for its financial resources creates a strong motivation to ensure the continuity and the succession of the business.

Unfortunately, combining family and business also has its dark side and a special set of potential conflicts.

I have continually affirmed an early observation that you cannot run a family like a business and you can not run a business like a family. The only realistic hope of dealing with naturally conflicting dynamics is an ever mindful and prayerful pursuit of balance between family and business issues.

In fact, the term "family business," is a contradiction. "Family" ideally describes an institution in which membership carries unconditional acceptance. Families are about emotions and kinship. They provide protection, mentoring and support for meeting the challenges of life. There is acceptance based simply upon who you are, a member of the family by birth, adoption or marriage.

Businesses, on the other hand, are institutions in which membership is based upon highly conditional acceptance. And the conditions are always the same -- performance, productivity, profits and net worth.

And so family and business are bizarre bedfellows. From a positive perspective, the combination of acceptance, togetherness and support of family, along with the organization, commitment and accountability of business, can create a marvelous hyper-productive enterprise.

However, this same combination can create frustration, friction, anxiety and resentment, which, in turn, compound the negative by profoundly handicapping productive capability. While family members united in a business can show an amazing resilience and commitment, only a few families show the harmony, teamwork and commitment required for long-term planning.

This book, then, will help you navigate this challenge by first helping you recognize that Succession Success of the contemporary family business is dependent upon more than family. Succession Success of a family business is dependent upon the emotional buy-in and commitment of key managers.

By picking up this book, you've shown that you already recognize the unique value and power of a family business. You recognize how difficult it can be to develop a strategy and implement the structures necessary to perpetuate a family enterprise through the next generation.

Let's first acknowledge this obvious premise:

Business continuity alone is not too difficult. Just execute estate plans, begin transferring stock and maintain sufficient liquidity to pay tax on the assets you decide to hold until your death.

Business succession is an altogether different undertaking. In the chapters to come, I will show family business owners, key managers and less experienced supporting advisers how to enhance the probability of family business succession by being more business minded.

We'll be discussing how to assess your family leadership and management assets and how to enhance the probability of achieving personal business succession goals though a variety of progressive structures that help you recognize, retain, motivate and more favorably position the key managers who are critical to business operations.

This book will increase your practical awareness of concepts and structures that can help you with the unfortunate unavailability or inherent weaknesses of family successor resources.

In some cases, the issues discussed are technical and will require professional help. Don't let that scare you. In every chapter, you'll find practical examples of companies that have successfully applied the concepts and structures, often despite serious challenges.

We'll also take a careful look at the most important retention and motivation tool available to you, the drafting of agreements that spell out how businesses will be operated and managed. We will describe the process of achieving these spiritual agreements -- Covenants -- that set down in black and white the philosophical understanding that owners and managers need for optimum management of a family business. Covenants are all about trust, about having the company's best interests - and the management team's best interests - at heart.

We'll focus on covenants in Chapter 14. In the meantime, let's begin to examine the fundamental issues.

The key to succession is preparation and a willingness to confront tough issues. Let's get started by making sure we understand how to define the problem.

Our focus is family business succession, not family business continuity. These terms are commonly confused, so let's look at what they mean.

Business continuity planning addresses the physical issues involved in transferring a business to the next owners. Hand over the keys to the front gate, transfer the stock, sign off on the bank accounts and you have initiated business continuity. The issues involved primarily are technical in nature, such as deciding which family members will continue to run the business, the valuation and legal considerations of a sale or gift; the administrative and tax issues of an estate transfer; the licensing and regulatory requirements of cities and state; and the commercial contingencies established by vendors, creditors, unions and franchisers. No doubt there are also a few non-technical issues, such as determining who will own the business and who will control the business.

However, if the admittedly challenging technical issues are conquered, business continuity planners believe they have accomplished their goal because of the default conclusion that the successor owners will work out the tough details.

Yet the lingering and haunting question is, "How long will the business continue?" If you are "lotto lucky," your children will be happy, harmonious and natural business managers as you pursue business continuity. If you are typical, however, the average business will begin to show cracks in the foundation within five years of the transfer.

The average survival rate of a "hand over the keys" business continuity effort is 5 to 10 years. It takes that long for the business to be scuttled by one or more of the six classic succession challenges: an insecure retiree, inept management, family dis-

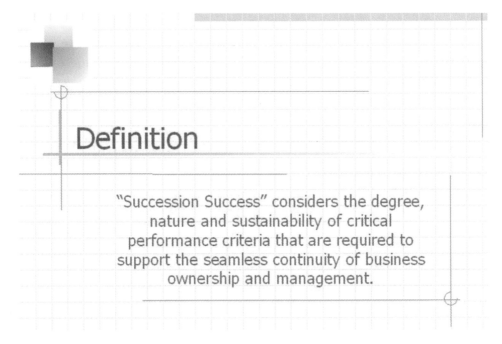

Definition

"Succession Success" considers the degree, nature and sustainability of critical performance criteria that are required to support the seamless continuity of business ownership and management.

sension, inadequate creditor/vendor confidence, ineffective business structuring or inadequate financial planning.

Planning for your business succession means recognizing the perils to family business continuity and working in advance to address them in a comprehensive way. Business succession planning assumes that, if those currently in control do not assert their power to reconcile the issues, the family's business will become "road kill."

We are going to start by helping you with a realistic assessment of whether you and your business have the qualifications for succession. If you have them, or if you can make the changes necessary to meet them, you'll have made a serious beginning. We will provide you with the tools to make that evaluation and, if you make the grade, we will affirm that you have the "Succession Success" foundation to assume that your family business goal can be achieved.

"Succession Success" means that your business shows a lasting -- and demonstrable -- succession capability. Crossing this major hurdle is a substantial distinction that will give family members, senior managers, vendors, lenders and franchisers peace of mind that the business will endure the predictable long-term challenges inherent with both family and business. This Peace of Mind is referred to as "Succession Success."

In contrast with what it takes to achieve business continuity, Succession Success is not exclusively based upon financial criteria. It is the result of a careful analysis of two-dozen factors, including your financial plan, your relationships with manufacturers and vendors and your capitalization and profitability. Most importantly, it deals with the dynamics of the family.

For many of you, that will mean a process of reorientation. Achieving the critical balance between the dynamics of family and business is essential to Succession Success. Just as each of us is inclined to be right handed or left handed, each of us approaches family issues from either a family or a business perspective. Therefore, depending upon our individual natural inclination, Succession Success requires some of us to be more business-minded and some to be more family-minded.

Succession Success Evaluation

You'll find the criteria for Succession Success in Appendix A. This evaluation is most effectively performed by a professional who understands the dynamics of succession planning and who has also had extensive experience working in the family business environment. You can certainly take a shot at self-evaluation. However, the exercise is most effective through an individual who understands your potential and who can also assess your current positioning.

This self-assessment will enable you to develop an understanding of all the issues that can impact the succession of your business and help you gain an initial view of the remedial improvements needed to enhance your peace of mind. Reaching Succession Success will bring strength and power to a business through high achievement across a broad base of performance factors.

Succession Success is a realistic achievement of every business. Yet you must understand that success cannot be described in mere dollars and cents. You'll have to be willing to do more than just pay lip service to issues that do not immediately impact the bottom line.

As you read further, you may find that many of the concepts we discuss in this book may not fit your sense of the conventional definitions of success. Please be patient, because, from a succession perspective, success is not defined solely in terms of continuity through the next generation. Trust me. With more than 30 years of practical experience, I guarantee that what we are going to talk about is just as important to the future as the bottom line is to the present.

The Toughest Decision

The first fundamental decision of succession is making the "Disposition Decision." Deciding what to do with the family jewels is never a simple decision. Even when the business is a real rag and there is little or no hope that change can be achieved, it is usually difficult for owners to conclude that it should be sold or liquidated. And even when the business seems an ideal candidate to achieve Succession Success, there are always lingering questions about children, managers or changing financial circumstances.

It all comes down to who will assume the mantle of leadership. Assuming financial conditions are favorable to succession, the assessment of the availability of capable, mature, and motivated management talent usually determines the outcome of the Disposition Decision. Reasonable logic concludes that there is no sense expending time, resources and effort in preparation for business succession if there are no capable successors.

The absence of family members who can operate the business is indeed the most frustrating hurdle to succession.

I have discovered the proverbial "poison pill" to succession planning has not been profitability, but the lack of confidence in successors or the physical absence of successors. I have witnessed immeasurable levels of frustration, disappointment and depression in business owners who concluded that there is no hope that their business legacy could continue after they retire.

We call it the "Succession Gap," a projected break in the critical continuity of competent management of a family business. This talent gap could be the product of several very common circumstances. There may be no children. There may be no children, in-laws or close relatives who have achieved the knowledge and experience necessary to assume management control and leadership. There may be no children actively employed in the business because of age or career preference. Or, in the most frustrating and complicated circumstance, parents may lack confidence that their children have the specific core competencies to run the business.

Let's assume for instance that you are the owner and operator of a very nice business. You have devoted your adult life to mixing the sweat of your brow with the grit of long days to build a solid, highly profitable enterprise. The wear and tear of long hours and constant stress has worn you down. The irony of your circumstances is that now, when you have built a great business, you have lost your heart for the hassle and the 12-hour workdays. You are ready to slow down and enjoy the cash flow your business is producing and the hobbies that you have been postponing for a lifetime.

You have talked to your kids about the benefits of continuing your business. But your experience-tempered counsel has not created a quantum change in their motivation. You have exposed them to as much training as they will tolerate and, although they have the knowledge, they lack the heart for the commitment required to manage the business. You have tried to mentor them and your close supervision only creates friction. Your children do not have the work ethic required to establish the essential role-model leadership.

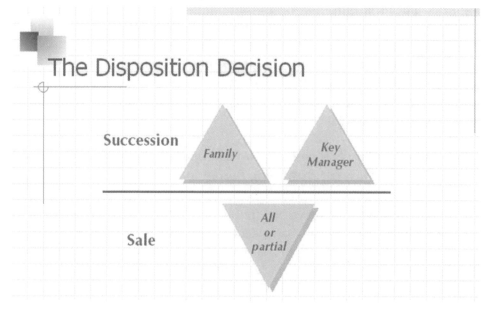

The Disposition Decision

Succession   Family   Key Manager

Sale   All or partial

The hard-core reality is that - regardless of the level of the success you have achieved, your commitment to business succession, the quality of your financial planning, the strength of your family unit, and the training of your kids - business succession is critically dependent upon motivated and capable successor managers.

As you assess the capability of your family successors, you recognize that the Disposition Decision carries stewardship responsibility. You want your children to enjoy the fruits of ownership. At the same time, you have concerns about your retirement peace of mind and security. And you have concerns regarding the high standing of your family's reputation, as well as long-standing loyal employees who would be negatively impacted by mismanagement or sale to a third party.

This is the stage where you begin to recognize the gravity of your situation. Commonly, all options appear negative. You could push on and transfer the business to your children in the spirit of business continuity planning, praying for the best. Your hope would be that you have either underestimated your children or that they will receive Divine Inspiration to run the business beyond your most ambitious expectation.

Your concerns aren't likely to go away.

Foremost, you know your children. Although you admit that you may be over-critical and biased, you also recognize that you did not get where you are by being a fool. So, you inherently trust your intuitive conclusion that your kids currently -- possibly permanently -- lack what it takes to run the business. With this heavy feeling in your chest, you realize that an abrupt change in the motivation, attitudes and/or acuity of your children would be a long stretch, even with Divine Intervention. And now you dwell on how the decline and eventual failure of the business would affect your reputation, financial security, family harmony and long-standing employees.

Your other option is to sell. This is an easier consideration if you do not have any children actively employed in the business. One of the toughest discussions is explaining to families why the business is being sold, rather than passed to them. Hopefully you feel a stewardship responsibility to find someone who can take care of your baby (the business) and your career employees.

Regardless of the circumstances, if your pragmatic business mind, accompanied by considerable second- guessing, confirms that selling is your best option, then it is a matter of determining the proper <u>circumstances to pull the trigger.</u>

Don't underestimate this decision.

Harvesting a lifetime of hard work to create sufficient liquid capital to meet your retirement income needs looks good on paper. However, giving up control, recurring cash flow, lucrative fringe benefits and cutting the ties to your first-born is no easy step.

If you decide to sell the business, your children's future careers will be seriously impacted. After all, one or more of your children will usually have devoted their career to the business in varying levels of productivity. Typically, within three years after a sale, a new owner seeking economies would cast your children and your higher-paid long-term managers adrift. Your children's income levels would surely drop. They are very likely to come to you to underwrite them in a new business.

From your perspective, there is no reasonable expectation that your children would be more motivated or more productive in a new venture. Having sold the "money machine," your resources would now have to be managed for both income and security. In the dubious world of the contemporary stock market, this could be a harrowing experience. There may be no room in your defensive investment posture for you to take risks trying to lock your children into a new business, so you are caught in the dilemma of what to do.

From a feelings perspective, you worry that your children will resent your decision to sell when they get a taste of the real world of employment. If you support their new business endeavor or share with them a sufficient amount of the sales proceeds to maintain their socio-economic standing, they may be more supportive of your lack of confidence in their ability to carry on the business. Unfortunately, either of these alternatives could cause palpitations if you are not totally convinced the sales proceeds can support you and your spouse in the manner that you had anticipated.

On the other hand, if sufficient cash is created from the sales proceeds to take care of everyone, and your children already own a significant portion of the business, sharing the wealth would be natural. The only potential problem would be witnessing your children squander what they received and then come to you wanting more.

Irrespective of how horrifying or appealing it may be to sell your business, most owners don't want to totally separate from it. Working less and avoiding hassles is ideal, but severing ties is another thing. In many cases, money is not the significant issue. Whether you sell the business or keep it will not significantly impact your lifestyle or spending habits.

It is not uncommon for a business owner to simply love his business. After all, it is usually the spiritual first born. A love for the business is the fundamental reason business owners do well. It's a success because you devoted your time and interest to it in lieu of having diverse hobbies and interests. The business was your hobby and in many cases your friends and your lover. Consequently, the thought of handing your creation over to a new owner and requiring your kids to start over in another career may be too depressing. For you, having no place to go to talk shop and maintain a sense of value and purpose can be frightening. Having something to do, even opening the mail, can be very important. You love your spouse, but spending your days as a retiree hanging around the house may be too much for you to handle.

This is what we call your "Succession Gap." To outsiders, this separation between where you are and confidence in the succession of your business may seem like an inconsequential crack in the sidewalk. However, the pressure in your chest reflects that your Succession Gap is more like the Grand Canyon. Your brain is compelling you to do the smart thing (sell it) and your heart is pulling you to do the right thing (keep it.) Is there no way to have your cake and eat it too?

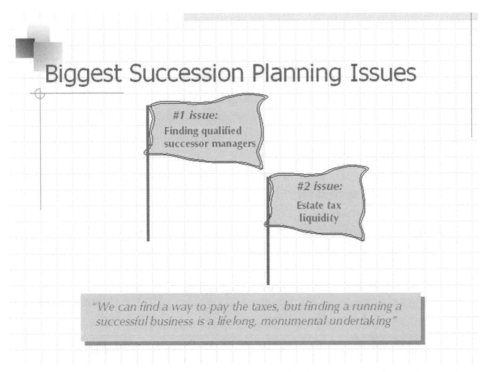

Biggest Succession Planning Issues

#1 issue:
Finding qualified
successor managers

#2 issue:
Estate tax
liquidity

"We can find a way to pay the taxes, but finding a running a successful business is a lifelong, monumental undertaking"

During the first 15 years of my career as a business succession planner, I was repeatedly charged with resolving "The Dilemma." My clients often were unwilling to pursue either of the classic disposition alternatives of selling their business or turning it over to their children with fingers crossed.

Needless to say, I had my own frustrations over futilely attempting to pound square pegs into round holes. In some of these unfortunate circumstances, my tenacity prevailed and I was successful in cornering my client and forcing them to make a decision to sell the darn thing or pray for Divine Inspiration in their children. In other, even more unfortunate circumstances, my clients grew weary of me pressing the "Disposition Decision" and told me to "chill out" or even "hit the road."

In all of these cases, my clients challenged me to find answers that would not force them to sell. When it was very apparent that Junior and/or Sis were not drawing adequate voltage to achieve succession, my classic response was that I was a planner, not a magician. I empathized with my client's dilemma and struggled with my inability to achieve their goals. I was frustrated professionally because I had worked frantically to acquire new clients, but only achieved the satisfaction of implementing succession plans for half of them.

Further, I recognized that I wasn't even touching 50% of the family business market, because so many owners had concluded there was no need to waste their time or money discussing succession when it was obvious that there were no family successors.

At the same time, the business environment was maturing. In my first book, "Seeking Succession: How to Continue the Family Business Legacy," (Second Edition, copyright 2003, The Family Business Resource Center), I identified estate tax liquidity as the most devastating issue to succession. It remains a huge issue for all owners. Yet, in today's business world, amid the confusion inflicted by the estate tax repeal, it is no longer the chief concern.

Business moves faster today. There is less room for error, less time to learn from mistakes and more competition.

Today, finding highly qualified, motivated managers, and capable successor management is, hands-down, the number one issue.

Most of my clients would gladly pay twice the "discounted" estate tax that ultimately would be levied upon their business just to have someone, in or out of the family, whom they totally trusted to continue the business through the next generation. We can find a way to pay taxes, but running a highly competitive, high velocity, capital-intensive business is a monumental undertaking.

Unfortunately, some families just do not have family members involved in the business or those involved cannot get the job done. As I repeatedly affirm, this is not an indictment of either the client or their children. It is the exception, not the norm, for a family successor to have the full complement of core competencies to operate a business. Although a child may win the sperm lottery, that does not necessarily mean that they were also blessed with the full package of business genes. Actually, from my perspective, it appears that God pursues balance between the good fortune of being born into a prosperous family and the endowment of motivation and management talent. The absence of capable family talent fractures the classic dream of succession, wherein family members lead and very capable support managers follow. The key question here is: How do I find someone who can keep the business going?

About 15 years ago I was fortunate to work for an outstanding civic and business leader we will call Mr. Distributor. He was the mayor of a major city in the South and the founder of an outstanding business that was and still is a leading air conditioner distributor in his state. Mr. Distributor was very happily retired from the day-to-day management of the company. The only activity he let interfere with hunting and fishing was a monthly board of directors meeting. Mr. D's son, Junior, was a very capable businessman and aspiring successor. However, Junior was a 35-year-old, impressive sales manager, not the president. Mr. D. had retired several years earlier, and at that time, he did not think Junior was ready to assume the leadership responsibility for a very competitive business that was being challenged by foreign manufacturing and quantum advances in technology.

But Mr. D. neither sold nor handed over the keys to his semi-qualified heir. Instead, he very wisely selected a seasoned 55 year-old key manager to be his successor as president and leader. The company was doing well under the leadership of this talented manager. Equally impressive, Junior understood. He was very aware of his inexperience. He was comfortable in the vice-president's role, reporting to a non-family member. It is wonderful when family members are willing and able to assume leadership of a business and key managers can follow with the core competencies to achieve the strategic mission. As this simple example illustrates, family business succession does not require a family member to assume the leadership responsibility.

Yet businesses fail this test time and again, Despite the dreams and aspirations of their owners, it is estimated that only one-fourth of all family businesses will achieve succession. This means that a staggering three-fourths of all family businesses will not find successful continuity through the managing hands of the next generation.

Two-thirds of this group never really had a prayer. Struggling profits, inadequate capitalization, outdated technology, family dissension, or another weakness made the concept of succession no more than an imaginative dream.

The long, frustrating years of fighting for profits, reconciling squabbles or futile efforts to teach the principles of business ultimately take their toll on those families that fail to build diverse strength in their business. One-fourth of all family businesses faces this perplexing dilemma.

This is both unfortunate and depressing when you fully grasp the immense implications of the termination of a successful business.

I believe in this basic premise: Family business succession is a once in a lifetime opportunity regardless of whether there is an heir with the "five M's" of succession: mentality, maturity, morals, management, and motivation.

I further believe that, in the absence of a qualified heir, there continues to be a viable opportunity for succession through key managers who can bridge any unfortunate gap.

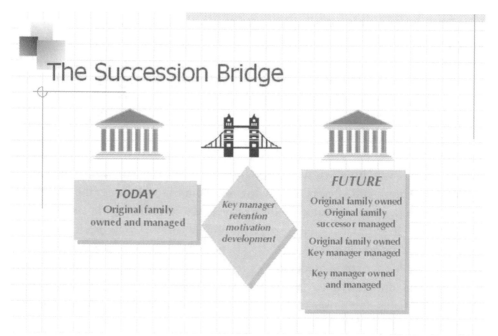

The Succession Bridge

TODAY
Original family
owned and managed

*Key manager
retention
motivation
development*

FUTURE
Original family owned
Original family
successor managed

Original family owned
Key manager managed

Key manager owned
and managed

I call this concept a "Succession Bridge." The potential spiritual and financial rewards of succession do not have to be put in jeopardy just because your children lack any one or more of the "five M's." The rewards of succession far exceed those of selling out, not only for your immediate family but also for the key managers who have helped you build a great business. Unless you have never had a heart for succession, the risk of pursuing succession for a vibrant thriving business is no greater than the risk that has been your companion throughout your entrepreneurial career and surely no greater than the systematic risk of financial markets, which will hold the proceeds of a sell-out. A substantial portion of the succession-handicapped segment of the family business community could discover a new world of gratifying opportunity by using a Succession Bridge.

The payoff for an open-minded adventurous attitude is that many family owned enterprises could continue as family assets. The significant legacies of many great business people and community leaders can be perpetuated as examples of those that will follow.

The purpose of this book is to help you understand the potential of a Succession Bridge and how one of these dynamic structures can help you overcome Succession handicaps and fulfill your business <u>*succession dreams.*</u>

A secondary purpose of this book is to offer encouragement to those key managers who have given up hope of being recognized for their contribution to the success of the business. And for those highly motivated managers, this book can serve as a base of creative thinking about how to overcome the ever-growing capital obstacles to becoming a partner or business owner.

Building a Succession Bridge is necessary whenever there are no family members ready, able or willing to begin assuming responsibility of business continuity at the time succession needs to begin. Building a Succession Bridge means identifying and developing non-family key managers - temporarily or permanently - to preserve and grow the business.

Building a Succession Bridge involves two specific tasks: selection and retention. Selection is just what the word implies - identifying the right people to carry the business forward to and through the next generation of ownership and/or management. Obviously, selection is critical, for the family legacy may be entrusted to these leaders for a good while, maybe forever. Selection is a delicate process, described further in Chapter 2. You will see that key managers can be a single individual or a group of individuals.

Retention is also a literal term. Once the key manager (or managers) is identified, they must be kept in the business. Their role will become as important as previous family owner/managers.

Given that these key managers are highly skilled and experienced in their own right, and may have entrepreneurial aspirations of their own, it is important to adequately motivate and compensate them to stick around.

Much of the remainder of this book explains key manager retention strategies and tactics, ranging from recognition with adequate compensation to motivation with ownership or even outright control.

A Succession Bridge can be a key factor in the succession process, as described in "Seeking Succession: How to Continue the Family Business Legacy." The availability of a Bridge may be the decisive difference in the Disposition Decision -

succession vs. sale. Once deciding on succession, for many businesses, executing an appropriate Bridge strategy through experienced leadership is critical for success.

Family Succession Criteria: The Five "M's"
- Mentality - Must be above average intelligence.
- Maturity - Must be fully matured with sound self-esteem.
- Morals - Must be a role model for honesty.
- Management - Must be a leader.
- Motivation - Must have pride and be determined to carry forward family legacy.

2 Assessing Managers

When an architect considers the construction of a bridge, there are critical engineering features, including the span, the foundation and the environment. With an understanding of these features, subordinate design issues can be addressed, which ultimately leads to a structure that safely, effectively, and efficiently bridges the gap.

Likewise there are also several critical engineering features to the construction of a Succession Bridge. Similar to the structures that carry mammoth eighteen-wheelers, as well as your precious fanny, the critical design considerations of a Succession Bridge are the time frame (span), supporting management (foundation), and the business dynamics (environment).

In this chapter, we will discuss the foundation of a Succession Bridge, supporting management.

This discussion assumes that you have recruited, cultivated, trained and empowered managers who have become instrumental to the success of your business.

It is worth mentioning that, if you have a valuable family business and you do not have trusted, loyal, supporting managers who enhance productivity, you are carrying an inordinate amount of operational weight. Fatigue, frustration and burnout may be stalking you. If you find yourself in this predicament, in lieu of wasting your time considering the dynamics of a Succession Bridge, you may want to look in the mirror and examine your management motives and methods.

The presence of trusted managers is a compliment to a business. Quality management creates business value. And, from a business succession perspective, quality management can indeed, sustain value. The presence of high quality managers shows that the principles of the owners have attracted and retained quality and commitment. The absence of trusted, operationally important managers may also mean that the owners are users, not developers. The owner could believe that current profits are more important than any current or future employee or customer. An absence of managers who share a passion for doing things right and doing the right thing may also indicate that owners do not acknowledge or respect the possibility that a non-family member could be the most valuable contributor to the success of your business.

Unfortunately, this myopic view of management is a fairly common condition in the closely held family business. The common ideology is: Why trust anyone but family? Unfortunately, far too many boneheads fail to recognize the obvious answer -- because family members may not have the goods to take you where you want to go.

What is the worst business succession situation? When the owner of a very successful business, who is teetering on burnout, realizes that there are no qualified family successors or key managers who can be trusted to relieve the pressure and keep the business afloat in the event of a death or disability.

This pathetic situation is generally the reflection of a cultural gap, showcased by irrational frugality, micro management and paralyzing insecurity. Although the blaring absence of qualified succession management may appear to be ignorance, these circumstances are generally evidence of a complex situation that demands a major paradigm shift. This is not an impossible undertaking, but one that dictates a protracted process that goes beyond the scope of this book.

Assuming the business owner has a created management culture and takes pleasure both in his success and the success of supporting management, the task at hand is to establish a reliable method of assessing managers to determine who could be part of the foundation of a Succession Bridge. No doubt there are scientific methods of selecting someone who has the technical expertise and leadership capability to be a manager. However, I haven't encountered any scientific process in 30 years of succession planning that can predict the managers who can assume the responsibility of a Succession Bridge.

The vast majority of managers are selected based upon their experience, instincts and prayers of the owners. "He looks like a conscientious guy, so let's give him a shot." The results compare to a very good major-league batting average, about one in three. Over a reasonable period of time, through trial and error, the more productive managers are identified and positioned to maximize the impact of their skill sets on the company. However, in the realm of a Succession Bridge, we are dealing with the family jewels, the protection of legacies and the fulfillment of dreams. It is therefore prudent that you approach the selection of Succession Bridge candidates conscientiously, realizing that you may not have the luxury of being wrong twice before you are right.

With a Succession Bridge, business continuity THROUGH the next generation can be achieved under less than optimum circumstances. As I discussed in "Seeking Succession," management resources are very important to business succession when qualified family members are on board. And you don't have to be a brain surgeon to acknowledge that management resources are critical to the development and implementation of a Succession Bridge.

As a fundamental component of succession planning, I am called upon regularly to evaluate managers. After countless experiences with memorable bumps and scrapes, I have become confident in this role. However, I can recall being frantic the first time I was put on the burner as a presumed management consultant. I sat in front of Joe Jankowski, one of the premier management minds in the automobile business, babbling as I searched for a response to his request that I assess his managers. It was not uncommon for me to develop concepts that exceeded my qualifications or experience. However, here was a highly skilled, very successful manager, asking me to evaluate his team who, from my perspective, already were kicking butt and taking names. Joe even had a PhD in industrial psychology on retainer. How could I improve on this situation? So with more of a gift for gab than a background in management science, I was forced to render my opinions and hope that I would not embarrass myself.

After frantically reading a book by one of the self professed management experts, I was even more confused and frenzied. As my scheduled interviews approached, in desperation, I decided to develop a practical process that would help me fake it while I prayed that I could make it. As I was driving to my first interview, I concluded that I would interview each manager, directing questions at or around five management characteristics: Competency, Confidence, Character, Commitment, and Community. In subsequent interviews, I endeavored to confirm or refine an opinion by soliciting comments and opinions from the manager's subordinates, associates and supervisors. The process boiled down to an objective search for a consensus opinion based upon feedback in these five management criteria.

If a manager "whiffs" in one area or is considered weak in a couple of areas, he is at best journeyman who cannot be relied upon to do anything out of the ordinary. If a manager is solid in most criteria and only weak in one or two, he could be relied upon as a key player. If a manager is solid in all criteria, and excelled in one or two, he was special.

If I could not find a weakness in any criteria and recognized profound strengths in most, I figure I had just met superman. Fortunately, I did not humiliate myself. When I later shared this frantic experience with Joe, he replied, "Loyd, you may not be a management consultant, but you are a good actor, because you had me fooled." I'll pause here for a point about style. Clearly gender has nothing to do with management ability. However, to avoid the monotony of constant "he or she" references, I'll simply use "he," with the expectation that readers will understand this refers to anyone.

Most important, this practical process has continued to provide outstanding results.

If you will use what management science makes available and also utilize an assessment of the "Five C's," to support your instincts, your management selection batting average will blow away baseball statistics and become more compatible to the risks associated with a Succession Bridge.

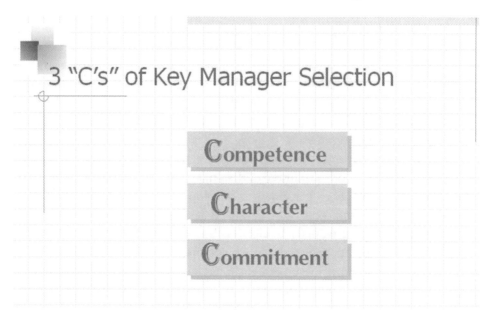

3 "C's" of Key Manager Selection

Competence

Character

Commitment

Allow me to potentially refine your instincts with these considerations about the "Five C's."

How do we judge competency? There is no substitute for the test of time. A manager has crossed the first hurdle to becoming a Succession Bridge candidate when he has illustrated the ability to excel at job performance over a prolonged period. Advancing through the ranks of mediocrity is prima fascia evidence that a manager is competent. However, be mindful that competency is represented by excellence, not just out performing contemporaries!

A Succession Bridge candidate will stand out as a role model for skill and professionalism.

Sure, while a competent manager predictably needs coaching along the way, rarely, if ever, do you have to show him or her something twice. Needless to say, a competent manager has proven through a history of quality performance that he does not need tight supervision. This individual illustrates time and again the unfortunately rare ability to learn through experience and listening.

History of performance should have a primary role in projecting competency for a particular position.

Forecasting competency in areas where there has been no opportunity for experience, is another issue. You, me, and all the esteemed industrial scientists have to instinctively judge growth potential based on how a manger has mastered previous challenges. In other words, we are flying by the seat of our pants. When answers to projected competency questions just do not come together, assistance from an experienced professional in Succession Bridge decisions, is well worth the investment.

Confidence is the leadership component. This term translates from Latin derivatives, meaning "with strength." Capable managers express themselves with strength and conviction in all aspects of their work. They will even tell you, their boss, where to get off if you try to push them in the wrong direction. They also project confidence in their dealings with subordinates, colleagues, and customers.

Interacting with strength distinguishes a manager as a leader.

We are not talking arrogance, which is self-serving at the expense of others. We are talking about the personal self-esteem that is required to help others do better, feel better, and be better. When necessary, confident managers even confidently express that they lack confidence. As I have personally illustrated for many years, a manager does not necessarily have to know what he is doing to be a leader.

Confidence is expressed by the managers who are consciously competent. The managers are humbly aware that he knows what he is doing and the profound impact his efforts have upon others.

The next criterion is character. Before you question what character has to do with management, remember that managers are delegated some of the power of ownership. If this power is abused or neglected, the owner pays. In a Succession Bridge environment, the owner will potentially be entrusting the family jewels with a manager. Evaluating character is essentially an x-ray of the morals and values that will be representing the family name. There is no questionnaire for this immense responsibility. Evaluating character is primarily experiential. Character appraisal is made over time, during which we watch and learn how the manager behaves when (they think) no one is looking, how they treat subordinates, and the shortcuts they take when circumstances allow.

Trust is essential. For a Succession Bridge candidate, this trust goes beyond the current generation of owners because it is the next generation that will have its neck on the table relying heavily upon a Succession Bridge for critical decisions. If there are questions about a manager's character, there is reason for concern. As an example, the candidate could be John Citizen by day and cheating on his spouse by night. Some would say what a manager does on his private time is his own business. That's reasonable thinking for a manager, but a Succession Bridge candidate must be held to a higher standard.

What a Succession Bridge candidate does away from work is crucial to how he may act when the current owner is no longer around.

The candidate's relationships with spouse, children, parents, in-laws, neighbors and church are often a revelation of true character. Would a key manager who cheats on his spouse cheat on you?

Do not overlook the obvious. When thinking about the selection of managers, think in terms of a statement that contradicts contemporary thinking - "It's the character, stupid." Feel grateful if you encounter a manager who puts you in your place, when he is asked to compromise ethics or take a short cut.

There is predictable gossip about an up and coming manager. Everyone in the spotlight or in a position of authority is the target of an occasional rumor. Continuous rumors from a variety of sources should be cause for caution. But when considering opinions of others, use common sense. Everyone including employees, managers, colleagues, friends and enemies, is skeptical and critical of senior managers and family members who appear to have been the benefactor of the sperm lottery" or an unprecedented advancement. My personal criterion is that I give no credence to rumors that have not been affirmed by two independent sources.

The next management criterion is commitment. Make no mistake, commitment and its first cousin, loyalty, are the fuel that powers Succession Success. I believe that over-achievers are the bedrock to success in private enterprise, even when the talent is thin. Business is a daily magnet for adversity. How managers deal with setbacks, disappointments and failure defines their commitment.

Through the course of time, we instinctively know who has a proprietary attitude, who serves beyond expectation and who puts the team's missions above personal gain. However, if there have been no defining challenges or profound learning experiences, a proprietary attitude is nothing but theoretical B.S.

If there is any question about whether a particular manager really has a commitment, ask yourself how this individual has handled adversity. Did pressure and disappointments make them stronger or weaker? If you have not observed a candidate deal with adversity, hold back your opinion until you do. Reflecting on their career will give an indication. If they have had lots of jobs and have shown easy mobility, they may be prone to bail out when the going gets tough.

I suggest that you listen to what the manager says about retirement, work hours, working conditions and recurring challenges. And listen very carefully to what they don't say. Watch the body language that may personify the villain of teamwork more commonly known as The Lone Ranger. Do they want to sit at the end of the table or can they be part of a group? Do they always have to drive or can they sit in the back seat? Listen for the enthusiasm they do not express, which speaks volumes about whether they buy in to the owner's goals, values, and dreams of business succession.

Endeavoring to implement a Succession Bridge is an expressed willingness to smack adversity right in the chops.

Consequently, before you embark on this mission it is imperative that you confirm which manager or managers have sufficient commitment to be relied upon as a critical support structure when the going gets tough.

The final criterion is community, the essence of teamwork. A manager is called to coordinate, direct, and supervise a community of employees who have a common purpose. In order to lead a group, a manager must become part of the group. It is unrealistic to achieve team synergy when a designated leader does not practice the concept. An important criterion for a manager is being community centric, as opposed to self-centric. This is a natural attitude for some and an impossible attitude for others. Ultimately, the upside potential of a manager will depend upon the degree to which he thinks in terms of the group and implements actions for the betterment of the group.

To have a sense of community or team simply means that a manager perceives himself, not only as the leader, but also as an integral member of a team.

The most effective managers realize that they are paid to assert direction. However, before painting the way, they search for the right decision for all concerned, the community. They recognize that both the owners and subordinates have delegated to them the responsibility for strategic decisions and administration.

Remember that teamwork depends upon each member agreeing to defer personal preference to group welfare. A manager who is community minded gives subordinates the peace of mind that their willingness to defer personal preferences will not be abused and their sacrifices will be rewarded. In contradiction to the presumed delegation of authority by a superior, achieving agreement to be identified as an integral part of a productive unit is the ultimate product of management.

In review, I hope that you have not found this practical approach to management assessment too heavy. It's really simple, but unfortunately anything reduced to writing can be confusing. To illustrate a practical application of some of The Five C's of Management, consider this interesting case history regarding the complexities of making Succession Bridge decisions regarding a son in law.

Case History: Mr. Caterpillar

The family owned several very successful Caterpillar heavy equipment franchises. My client, Mr. Cat, was an obsessive-compulsive micro-manager known to demand the highest level of productivity from every employee. He had two daughters, neither of whom was active in the business. One was a school teacher with no business interest. The other daughter, Martha, was bright, aggressive and well educated. She had started a career in the business as the accounting manager.

Dan, her husband, had entered the firm 10 years earlier to help out his father-in-law after his entire management team walked out. Dan quickly showed that he was a natural salesman. Contrary to expectations, Mr. Cat managed Dan's development very well, requiring him to start at a bottom sales position and work his way up. Dan's performance was nothing short of phenomenal. Defying the son-in-law stereotype, he was a workaholic. Within a year after being hired he was setting new records as a salesman. After two years he was transferred to credit and finance and quickly assumed the lead position in that department, which then led him to a used-equipment sales manager. After a couple of years of comparable success he moved to a new-equipment sales manager role. Everything he touched turned to gold.

When I met Mr. Cat, he presented me with a bizarre situation. "My son-in-law, who is now general sales manager, is a dream come true from a business perspective. He is the smartest salesman I have ever encountered. He may also be the very best sales manager in the nation.

'However, from a family perspective, his obsession with the business has become a disaster. Martha quit her job to be a full time mother and wife. Now she is openly resentful of his success and her relegation to changing diapers and cooking his dinner. Dan's problems with my daughter have driven a wedge between him and my wife. And because of this family dilemma, business performance is beginning to decline. With success and money, my humble son-in-law has become arrogant about his ideas and accomplishments, constantly pushing me for more money.

"As this has developed, my equally strong-willed daughter, who admittedly is self-centered and immature has accused him of seeing other women, doing drugs, and neglecting his family so he can be a business big shot.

"I would not tolerate this treatment of my daughter -- regardless of being real or imagined -- for one second, but I just cannot bring myself to fire my most productive manager in our history. I am 60 years old and ready to begin throttling back.

I now find myself in a brutal crossfire between my only hope for succession and the father of three grandchildren, my oldest daughter and my wife."

Here was a client who found comfort only in working and now his work was hell. In amazement, I offered my common response to yet another ever-amazing family business situation: *"More resounding evidence that facts are stranger than fiction."*

I counseled Mr. Cat to play it cool and stay out of the crossfire between his son-in-law and daughter. I advised him that he was a sure loser in any initiative with either Dan or his daughter. If one of them did not throw him under the bus, his wife would surely drop him in the grease. I recommended that he encourage them to take care of their marriage and, until this dilemma was reconciled, he should refrain from any succession discussions.

Although Dan may appear to be a phenomenal manager, he was not a candidate as a Succession Bridge if he did not have the character to hold his marriage to the boss' daughter a higher priority than his career. Furthermore, if he did not get off his high horse he would ultimately flame out as a leader and team builder. No doubt Dan was in a delicate position with Martha, but he was the only one who could work this out.

The only situation worse than his current dilemma was for his daughter to get a divorce, which would then make him dependent upon an ex-son-in-law who would predictably utilize his grandchildren as leverage in legal warfare with his daughter.

Just as the family dynamics were approaching critical mass, the economy began to soften. Unwilling to reconcile that the Fed was on a mission to cool off the economy, Dan charged ahead. He expanded inventories and opened up a new used-equipment location. He was boldly confident that he could make money regardless of the state of the economy.

But, as fate would have it, Dan was not the gunslinger he thought he was, nor was he good at grasping the obvious. Inventory credit costs skyrocketed. The factories offered big time incentives to reduce inventories, effectively killing the used equipment business. Dan's used-equipment site was a resounding flop. Embarrassed by the failure, Mr. Cat seized the opportunity/excuse to come back into the day-to-day operation, just looking for a reason to give Dan the hot poker. Almost overnight, Dan digressed from a modern day management phenomenon to dumb son-in-law.

As if this turmoil was not enough, Dan also lost his magic touch as a sales manager. Apparently, with the reduction in sales volume, the major diver of his bonus, Dan started penciling pay plans. In retaliation, about a third of the sales force walked out and engaged an attorney to assert a class-action grievance.

And, just as Dan's business life was hitting bottom, Martha threw him out of the house, allegedly to protect their daughters from what had developed into a continued exchange of daily insults. Subsequently, life in River City hit an all time low. Mr. Cat resented Dan's failure to run the business and make his daughter happy and lost no opportunity to turn up the voltage on his cattle prod. From Mr. Cat's perspective, Dan had trashed his business, broken Martha's heart and made his lovely wife a miserable nag.

From Dan's perspective, Mr. Cat was an over-controlling, overbearing, insensitive micro manager who held the unholy dollar in higher priority than his family, his employees or his reputation. However, much to my surprise and Mr. Cat's disappointment, Dan sucked up his pride and committed himself to enduring the abuse and regaining his family.

The previously arrogant and defiant Dan grew impressively humble and recognized that the only door back into his home was through marital counseling. Unfortunately, at the outset of this process, his attitude went further into the tank as Martha took every counseling session as a bully pulpit to download a long-term buildup of frustration and anxiety.

However, over a period of about a year, Dan defined his value and character. Martha evidently ran out of insults and recognized that he really did want his family back. They reconciled their relationship and regained unity. It was interesting that they achieved unity, not only on marital issues, but also on how business would fit into their lives. In short, they concluded that more money was not going to bring more happiness. They also agreed that Mr. Cat's insecure micro-management style and brutal communication tactics, which he had taken to an art form, were incompatible with their future plans.

Dan simply came into work one morning, went directly into Mr. Cat's office and resigned. "I do not love this business more than my wife. She has faith in me and if you don't, I need to find work elsewhere."

Martha was wound very tight and she had lots of emotional energy. Now that she and Dan were back in harmony, she refocused her emotions toward her dad. Wisely concluding that she was too volatile for a one-on-one discussion, she wrote him a letter, expressing how much she loved him. She continued to say that, because she loved her Dad, she needed to tell him that he was inconsiderate of his family and managers and well on his way to creating another walkout that would destroy the business. She further stated that she and Dan had no interest in the business unless he retired.

The bomb was this: If Dad did not retire, she, Dan and their children were moving to pursue a career elsewhere.

Mr. Cat faxed me a copy of the letter followed immediately with a pouting, woe-is-me phone call soliciting my support. Needless to say, I did not gain any points when I agreed with Martha. In response to Mr. Cat's defensive whining, I contended that she was showing a lot of love by expressing her feelings. I further pointed out that Dan, by enduring the adversity of this unfortunate experience, had made impressive gains in three critical components of a Succession Bridge - character, confidence, and commitment. He was defining his values and assuming responsibility. Moreover, I generally agreed with her points that he was a micro-manager and, in attempting to rescue his daughter, he had gone too far in his indictment of Dan.

I also contended that Martha was illustrating that she was growing up by getting her priorities right. She was making an admirable attempt to bring the family back together and acting as a wife, not a spoiled brat. I concluded by asking, "Is not the happiness of your daughter and grandchildren a higher priority than the profitability of this business or any personality conflicts you may have with Dan?"

After an extended silence from a man who always had something to say, he offered a very simple response, "You know, you are right. I think my little girl is growing up. And although I never thought I would say it, Dan has got far more grit (character and commitment) than I ever expected. Martha and I can dish it out and this guy was not about to cut and run. He looks like the perfect husband for my feisty little girl."

Thereafter, life around the heavy equipment business began to improve. Not only did Dan illustrate his quantum growth in character, he matured in his community consciousness. Dan's new found humility enhanced his listening skills, which in turn enabled him to earn acceptance by the other employees. When his employees understood that they were not just pawns in his advancement game, his department started doing much better. There were occasional exciting growth experiences that always accompany the combination of family and business, but Mr. Cat and Dan ultimately worked out their issues.

Hopefully, you recognize that this story illustrates that the halo around a management phenomenon can be so bright that we cannot see obvious cracks in the foundation. Furthermore, there is no substitute for relying upon fundamentals ("The Five C's) to identify potential weaknesses and affirm strengths.

I cannot over-emphasize that succession success is dependent upon recruitment, motivation, and retention of competent managers. The point of this book is that some uniquely qualified managers can be utilized to fill a gap in family successor manager resources. The question is, how do we identify which managers can be utilized in the development of a Succession Bridge? The answer will be discussed in our next chapter.

3 Key Manager Classification

"How's Business?"

"It's killing me. My problem is, there just is not enough of me to go around. I just run out of hours."

That is common dialogue in the realm of a growing business. But on the other hand, for those of us who are faced with payroll, that dialogue sure beats, "I've got nothing but time on my hands because we don't have any customers." The reality of developing a business is that, as we grow, the ability to personally address the expanding work is stretched. It is always difficult to justify an over abundance of costly and complicated employees. When the workload becomes unbearable, we hire help and change our focus from direct productivity to overseeing the methods, practices, and attitudes of our help. Then we realize that some words and some activities motivate and some discourage. As we grow accustomed to this new role we recognize the skill or even the art of management and the impact we can have upon productivity.

The next cycle of growth stretches the ability of the owner to supervise the increasing number of motivated employees. Consequently, a star employee is usually elevated to a manager. With the good fortune of more growth, the employee base expands and more managers are needed. As the management group grows, it becomes apparent that some managers distinguish themselves as executive vice presidents, operations managers, chief financial officers and general managers.

Managers generally represent the epitome of a love-hate relationship: hard to live with 'em, impossible to live without 'em. They are either lacking the confidence to reach their capability or they are confident beyond their capability. Having discussed assessment of managers through the "Five C" concept in the previous chapter, our next endeavor is to gain a better understanding of the attitudes and goals of your mangers. This information will then allow us to categorize the managers into progressive classifications that will enable us to effectively construct a Succession Bridge. Due to the profound impact mangers have upon business operations as we consider the development of a Succession Bridge, we must understand with whom you are dealing, and how they think, so we can determine how best to motivate and retain them.

As you reflect on the ranks of managers you have encountered, you will quickly recognize that each manager has a different impact upon a business. The reality is that no two managers are created equal. The attitudes, motivations, and expectations have varying pact upon business operations. Based upon my experience, I have recognized that these attitudes create key manager classifications that are very helpful to the design of the succession bridge structure. Attitudes, motivations, and expectations of each class of managers significantly impacts the career motivation and retention mechanism utilized to set the foundation for the Succession Bridge.

A Succession Bridge structure must impact both motivation and retention. Although commitment and motivation are inherent in the definition of a key manager, this is not something we can take for granted. This would be especially true in the absence of the owner due to retirement, death, or disability. Therefore the "bonding agent" of a Succession Bridge should be a strong financial and/ or career advancement opportunity. As the/a leader of your organization, a Succession Bridge manager should have a vested interest in the continued profitability and growth of the business. Furthermore, recognizing the value managers can bring to the business, a Succession Bridge mechanism should also encourage a long-term career commitment.

Back in high school, as I was failing miserably at bedazzling a pretty young lady from a well-to-do family, my father offered me this advice: "It is difficult to woo a princess with a soda pop." This concept also applies to motivating and retaining key managers.

You cannot expect to motivate a prince of a manager to assume more responsibility and make a long-term commitment with the same benefits available to all common employees.

Furthermore, unless you have been standing too close to the exhaust pipe, you cannot realistically expect to motivate and retain distinctly different classes of key managers with the same form of benefit.

For purposes of our discussion, we will segregate managers into four classifications based on their value to the business and the unique perspective they have about their job. These classifications are:

- Manager
- Key manager
- Special key manager
- Very special key manager

A Manager is an important employee who has been delegated supervisory responsibility over other employees. The loss of a manager is an inconvenience because, for the short term, others will have to carry more responsibility and put in a few more hours to keep control of the business operation. There are no presumptions that a manager is loyal. To the contrary, most managers are very ambitious and are searching for opportunities. In most circumstances, equally ambitious assistant managers are prepared to step in to an opening. Managers must be regularly supervised, given direction, and held accountable.

A manager has the attention of ownership but has not fully developed all aspects of the "Five C's." Notably a manager has not gained the trust of ownership to be relied upon during times of adversity and therefore is not a current candidate for positioning in a Succession Bridge.

Progressing in impact, a key manager is very important to the daily operations of the business. The loss of a key manager would cause an intermediate term disruption in the delivery of the goods and services under his or her supervision. They are frequently peculiar, even excessive-compulsive achievers. Key managers have unique talents or they are over achievers with a phenomenal work ethic and a never-say-die attitude. They may gripe and moan about an assignment, but they usually arrive early, typically stay late and always get the job done. They have no problem applying accountability or being held accountable. Although often not pretty, classy, or trendy, they characteristically have an intense commitment to do things right. By nature, key managers lead reasonably simple and conservative lives. Key managers are generally conservative. They are concerned about financial security and are careful not to over step their management responsibilities. Predominantly, they anticipate putting in their time and retiring to their hobbies. They do not particularly like change and generally have a limited spectrum in which they can excel as managers.

Conservative by nature, they would be adverse to high risk or overly complicated incentive packages.

They have no problem staying on track but can be so focused that they lose perspective of the big picture. They are capable of operating independently with a well-developed business plan. However, key managers need regular refinement and reassurance. Whatever they do, they do well. Without ongoing monitoring a key manager can even do the wrong thing very well. These are very loyal, highly trusted managers.

Key managers constitute the most populous group of Succession Bridge candidates and, by every means, are the backbone of the business. However, a key manager would have difficulty assuming a critical Succession Bridge leadership role. They are the implementors, not the innovators or negotiators. In the event of the loss of a key manager, the business would incur significant operational challenges. Key managers are receptive to making a career commitment as considerations for enhanced financial security.

A special key manager provides a higher level of management services that are very important to the achievement of the strategic goals of the business. The loss of a special key manger would cause an intermediate term significant reduction in profitability. Special key managers do not appear to work as hard as key managers, because they better understand the concepts of delegation and empowerment. They have positive "coach" attitudes and usually are not threatened by talented subordinates. They are more secure, have higher self-esteem and therefore are willing to take the risk of trusting subordinates to fulfill delegated responsibilities. These are the primary champions of teamwork. Special key managers are accustomed to change and generally look forward to new challenges as an opportunity to prove their value. They are capable of developing and implementing business plans. They operate most comfortably and effectively without close supervision. They have no problem applying accountability, but, because of their high self-esteem, would predictably argue or even challenge criticism.

These are the guys and gals who have always had the confidence they would become a senior manager. They are well paid because they know how to take optimum advantages of an incentive bonus. More aggressive by nature, they would be receptive to more complicated incentives with moderate risk. They are entrepreneurial, and therefore would be receptive to incentives providing opportunities for advancement and an element of control over their career.

Special key managers would only be receptive to making a career commitment if incentives included both increases in financial security and career growth opportunity.

They are confident and frequently have an unrealistic assessment of their ability to own and operate their own business. They are opportunist and therefore less loyal than key managers. In the event of the loss of a special key manager, the business would incur operational challenges that would result in significant financial loss until an individual of equal talent could be installed as a replacement. The owners may have to modify their intermediate-term personal plans.

A very special key manager is an individual who provides services that are critical to the business profitability. They are movers and shakers who; but for timing, bad luck, or something beyond their control, would own their own business. They have the attitude of an entrepreneur but have not put together the resources to become an independent business owner. In their minds, being a business owner is an issue of only timing or choice.

In addition to being able to leap tall buildings in a single bound, very special key managers are trusted without reservation. Due to this trust, they generally are very loyal. However, there is no blind assumption of loyalty, because these management phenomena are in high demand. Consequently it is only prudent to assume that, in the absence of an appropriate golden handcuff, they would reluctantly go for another opportunity if the right one came along. They generally do not think in terms of money, but in terms of power, potential, and prestige. Therefore, do not try to tie down a very special Key manager with security based retirement benefit that would motivate a Key Manager.

Not only are Very Special Key Managers accustomed to change; they are constantly creating change as they pursue higher levels of productivity and efficiency through innovation and borrowed ideas. They are calculated risk takers, but their sound judgment gives the business owner no concerns about their ability. They have no problem applying accountability but they have difficulty receiving accountability because they consider themselves at least a peer to the business owner. Fortunately, they rarely need to be held accountable. They demand the trust of an owner and will not work for a control freak.

Very Special Key Managers are rare managers who have profound impact upon the profitability and even viability of a business. In the event of the loss of a very special key manger, the business is in for trouble. They cannot be allowed to go without a fight. Whatever it takes; money, stock, or promises to back them in a business, you have to give deep consideration to keeping them on board. In the words of Hank Sames, a cherished client who has an art for attracting good managers, "I'm going to keep this guy, even if I have to adopt him." In the event of a loss, owners would have to modify their intermediate-term personal plans and the business would incur operational challenges that could result in financial losses, which could threaten the viability of the business.

A very special key manager would only be receptive to making a career commitment if incentive included increases in financial security and an <u>opportunity to be a stockholder.</u>

It is also important to understand that there is a reasonable chance that a very special key manager will be unwilling to limit his options by making a long-term career commitment, regardless of the incentive offered. With this in mind, prepare yourself not to be offended. These are just unique individuals.

As we reflect upon three classifications of the key managers who are Succession Bridge Candidates, you could easily identify an important manager who does not fit clearly into one of these classes. Not to worry, because commonly a key manager exhibits characteristics of more than one class. The manager may be reflecting high versatility or he may be in a state of transition, up or down the scale. Management classifications are dynamic subject to slow movement up or down based upon innumerable criteria including experience, education, maturity, health, family issues, etc. When a classification is not clear, be conservative and go with the classification reflective of the manager's movement. For example, if you feel the manager is advancing in capability you would generally make a liberal interpretation. If the manager is retreating in capability due to age, health or personal issues, make a conservative interpretation. Regardless, the issue is not the nomenclature of the classes. The issue is designing a career retention and performance motivation mechanism that is appropriate for the psyche of the Succession Bridge candidate. An appropriate golden handcuff design can only be achieved by effectively understanding the feelings, values and goals of managers who could play a critically important role in the succession of the business. The classifications are simply methods of associating simple adjectives as reminders of the behavior we should expect from specific managers as we endeavor to build the appropriated Succession Bridge structures. Otherwise, we may find ourselves trying to pound square pegs into round holes.

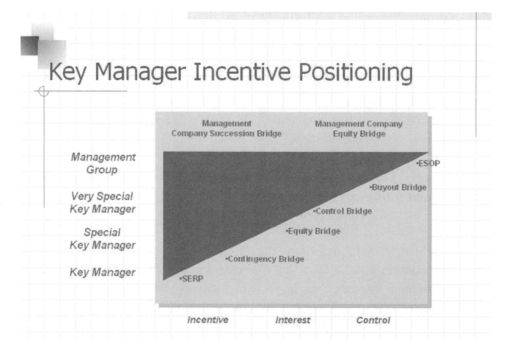

34

To illustrate the different attitudes and motivations of these various classes of key managers, here's a story about a fabulously successful business owner who had but one glaring flaw, he was terminally cheap. Actually, he was so tight, he could not bend at the waist. His idea of a charitable contribution was giving his wife enough money to make a mortgage payment.

Case History: The "Tired" King

This client, TW, asked that I drive over to talk with him about locking down one of his general managers in a very successful chain of tire stores. I had been encouraging him to consider a golden handcuff for Wilson for several years. Wilson's store was the leader of the 13-store chain in almost every competitive category. Furthermore, he also supervised 5 of the stores that were in his part of the state. These stores also excelled. In every respect, Wilson was a special key manager who clearly had the potential of becoming very special.

"I think it's time to do something for Wilson," TW expressed with confidence. "You're right; I'd be in a real pickle if I lost this guy. I'd like you to set up a retirement account for him and I'm going to fund it with maybe as much as $7,500 a year. I would have a very difficult time replacing this young man. He does a great job in his store and I even think there is a good chance he could come into the home office in the near future to assume more supervisory responsibility. Everyone seems to like him. Even my wife likes him and she is suspicious of everyone."

TW continued to sing the praises of Wilson. He was a lot freer with words than he was with his money. After what seemed like an eternity, he took a breath and asked, "Loyd, what's wrong with you? Why are you smiling?"

Being a bit embarrassed by his question, I fidgeted with my papers and notepad and after a few moments responded "TW, I cannot help but be amused by what you are saying. You have just described a very important part of your operation. This is an individual you want to keep around. This is an individual you want to impress by communicating that you really appreciate the contribution he makes to the business. This is an individual you pay approximately $300,000 per year. Now you are going to try to lock him into your organization with a golden handcuff of $7,500 per year. Do you see anything strange about this picture?"

When it came to money, TW was a bulldog. In defiance, he responded "No, I don't see anything strange. What I see is that I am going to set aside $7,500.00 of my money in an expression of gratitude to this guy. This will be new money to him. He should be very excited and appreciative."

"TW, if you are going to give Wilson an additional $7,500 per year of deferred bonus, I have no doubt he would be appreciative. However, I think I know you better than that. What are you expecting for this $7,500.00 deferred bonus?"

A little sheepish now, he took a few moments to think and then responded, "Well Loyd, just what you said. I think he should sign a non-compete covenant and I don't think he should have access to this money until he retires."

I could no longer hold back my amusement. With my most reserved chuckle, I asked, "TW, do you understand what you're asking? I know Wilson pretty well and

I can give you assurance that he is gifting more than $7,500 per year to the Boy Scout Council. You know his son was an Eagle Scout, didn't you? My point is that, with an income of over $300,000 per year, Wilson is not going to be motivated by your $7,500 golden handcuff. I think you're setting yourself up to be embarrassed."

"The hell you say!" TW responded in anger. "Wilson, above any of my employees, appreciates a dollar. You can bet your sweet butt, I don't want him talking to you, because I can see what you would do. You would coach him into pushing me for more money, just so you could sell a bigger life insurance policy."

"No, TW that is not the case. Increasing the contribution to a single SERP account is the last thing on my mind."

Unfortunately he had made up is mind. "I don't want to hear any more about it." TW was now in his back-up style, not willing to listen to any of my explanations. "If you want to discuss any other issues, go ahead otherwise I'll just take care of this matter myself and let you know what happens."

Thus passed another frustrating afternoon in the life of a succession planner. With no apparent hope of being heard, I gathered my papers and left his office with my tail between my legs.

About a week later, I received a phone call from TW. "Did you call Wilson! Did you talk to him and tell him that I should invest more money on his behalf?"

"No, what makes you think that? I haven't spoken to Wilson in 2 or 3 months. What happened?"

"The stupid ingrate quit! I cannot believe he can be so brainless."

I had an inkling of what had transpired because I knew Wilson was a very out-spoken, passionate person with an enlarged ego. I had seen him and TW go round and round. Wilson had a lot of pride and had no problem telling TW how he felt on any issue. He wouldn't think of backing down if he thought he was right. So, sus-pecting that TW had insulted Wilson, I continued, "Just what transpired?"

"You wouldn't believe it. I told him how much I appreciated him and explained that I was going to put $7,500 in a supplemental retirement plan and he would have access to that money when he retired. We continued to have a nice conversation. He was joking around and even saying what a generous man I was. We were on the phone for about 10 minutes and everything went well up until the end, when I felt I needed to tell him that there would be a non-compete covenant and a 15-year vesting schedule. At that point, he went ballistic and told me I could take the $7,500 and his job and stick it where the sun doesn't shine."

I knew exactly what had transpired, just exactly what I had hoped to avoid. I pondered for a few moments the various ways that I could explain to TW what had happened and then concluded that the best way to deal with this headstrong gen-tleman was to be direct. "TW, he wasn't laughing with you, he was laughing at you. You have insulted him. He views your $7,500 offer as your appraisal of his contri-bution to the organization. He has a standing offer to assume a management position at Tire World and he may have just had all he can handle from you."

"You don't really think he would leave, do you?"

"TW, I don't believe Wilson knows how to lie. If he told you to take the job and shove it, I believe that is exactly what he meant." Speaking frantically, almost faster *than I could comprehend, TW continued, "I can't afford to lose him. I don't have anyone to replace him. The only real money we make in this organization is the profits from his division. What do you think I should do Loyd?"*

Again, I thought about what I should say to him and how I should say it so that I could keep him from blowing his stack. TW and Wilson were just alike, prone to go ballistic if you stepped on their pride. "How important is it for you to keep Wilson?"

Without hesitation, TW responded, "If I lose him I'm going to sell the place because it's just not worth the fight without his profitability. Having said that, I suppose I'll do whatever it takes. How much money do you think we would have to put into a golden handcuff to keep him?"

"Unfortunately TW, you may have blown your chance to impress Wilson with money. Based upon what you've just described to me, he is a very special key manager. Consequently, I would be reluctant to propose any form of restricted retirement plan."

"What do you mean? What else could I do? Are you suggesting that I make him a stockholder?"

Recognizing that I was again in the midst of a minefield, I thought about how to lead him through deductive reasoning without getting a leg blown off. As delicately as possible, I asked, "Didn't you just tell me that if he leaves, you're going to sell the business?"

Sheepishly, he answered, "Well, yes. But eh --------------"

Cutting him off, I asserted, "Wilson is either critical to your long term operation or he his not. Which is it?"

"Well," responded TW taking a pause to think. "There's no doubt, I cannot continue this business without him. I see where you're going, Loyd. I would rather have him as a stockholder and frankly, I would rather have him as my successor than sell out to Tire World. What do you think we should do?"

Feeling less vulnerable to the emotional landmines, I responded, "I think you're only option is to apologize and offer him an opportunity to be your partner. Don't attempt to make any excuses for what you've already done because he knows you're a tight wad and he's not going to change his mind about what transpired. However, I'm 100% sure, he will accept your apology."

"Oh Loyd, you are giving me a stomach ache. Can you help me here? How can we make this simple?"

"TW, I know you're having trouble with the concept of an apology. Unfortunately, I cannot help you there. The reason Wilson is such a valuable, even critical member of your business is because he is just like you; strong willed, highly passionate, and highly principled. Your $7,500 golden handcuff retirement plan has deeply offended him and it wouldn't matter if you were going to sign over the business to him, he will not hear anything you have to say until you apologize. After you apologize, I can take care of all the other details."

I could hear the thumping of TW's heart through the phone. What I was recommending that he do was against every fiber of his psyche. It was silent for a few moments, then he continued, "Loyd, you're killing me. I have to go." He then hung up the phone.

I didn't hear anything for almost a week. During this time, I wondered if TW had made another ill-advised attempt to buy Wilson's favor or if he had swallowed his pride and apologized. When I was almost at the point of giving up hope, I received a phone call.

"Loyd, this is Wilson, how are you doing? Have you got a minute, I want to talk to you about how I'm going to become a stockholder."

"Hi, Wilson, good to hear from you. What do you mean? What's going on with this stock?" I asked innocently.

"You won't believe this Loyd, but TW and I have been going round and round over the last 2 or 3 weeks. I even quit about 1½ weeks ago. But you know something, the most amazing thing has happened. Can you believe that Daddy War Bucks wants me to be his partner and maybe successor?

"You don't say? Tell me about it." Wilson explained his side of the entire story which, from his very expressive point of view, was very amusing.

The net result -- Wilson did become a 10% stockholder with an option to purchase an additional 15% of the stock over the next five years. We ultimately structured a buyout agreement wherein Wilson was able to develop the confidence that he would be TW's successor. Even though there were moments in which I questioned whether this relationship, or even the business would continue, all worked out for the best. However, had TW recognized from the outset that Wilson was a very special key manager, all of this trauma and humiliation could have been avoided. Hopefully, this shows there is truly a different perspective between key managers, special key managers, and very special key managers. When addressing incentives that are designed to retain these maestros of productivity, you'd better have your wits about you.

Moving forward, we will look at the various mechanisms through which we can establish incentives for these various classes of key managers.

Golden Handcuff Structures

Having learned how to identify a good manager and confirm who are your key managers, our next goal is to learn about the various tools utilized to retain these gems.

Quite a few years ago, I suggested that a client consider a golden handcuff to facilitate his succession plan. Before I could elaborate, he responded, "Consider a golden handcuff? I've been trying to shed of the darn thing for fifteen years! What have you been smoking Loyd? The reason you are here is because all my gold is in this business and consequently I am handcuffed to this cussed chair to make sure no one runs off with my security. I'm still waiting on you to show me how to hand this albatross over to my lazy son and hold on to the gold."

This client had a very vivid, but, just the same, incorrect perception of a golden handcuff. Fortunately, I was able to clarify my meaning and lead him in the development of a key-man Succession Bridge incentive program that allowed him to retire. Unfortunately, I was not able to liberate him completely from the business or light a fire under his lazy son. Eight years later, he is working half days and he has substantial cash in the bank. A key manager now owns 49% of the business and is positioned to buy the balance if Sonny does not get the lead out of his butt.

In the previous chapter we discussed the various classes of managers and their respective hot points. Now we are going to turn our attention to the supplemental executive benefits that can be utilized to motivate a manager to make a career commitment and become a Succession Bridge. Bear with me, because this is going to be on the technical side.

Although I would rather be sharing my experience, we have to have trust in a foundation in order to build a strong bridge.

And so we'll talk more about golden handcuffs.

As the term implies, a Golden Handcuff describes an executive incentive benefit designed to retain (handcuff) and motivate (gold) a manager to bring exceptional value to a business.

Golden Handcuff Succession Bridge

- ◆ Funded by a non-qualified SERP
- ◆ The Gold:
  - ▪ Cash
  - ▪ Cash equivalent
  - ▪ Ownership interest
- ◆ The Handcuff
  - ▪ Service requirements
  - ▪ Performance requirements
  - ▪ Non-compete covenants
  - ▪ Confidentiality covenants

The gold is a financial benefit in the form of cash or business ownership. The handcuff refers to an assortment of employment contingencies that the key employee must satisfy in order to receive the gold. These contingencies always include a minimum length of service and frequently include performance requirements. The theory is, if there is sufficient gold in the benefit, the key employee will feel handcuffed to the business and think very seriously before leaving.

A golden handcuff is a discriminatory deferred benefit for one or a relatively small group of key managers. If the employee benefit program discriminates in favor of the more highly compensated managers, the benefit must be what is technically referred to as a "non-qualified benefit." Although I want to avoid getting too deep in the technical weeds, it is important that you understand the concept. "Non-qualified" means that the plan is not subject to the cumbersome controls and reporting of ERISA, the Employee Retirement Income Security Act. It also means that this plan is what the IRS refers to as a "Top Hat" plan that is being made available to only a select group of highly compensated key employees whom the IRS deems sufficiently knowledgeable and sophisticated to represent their own interests.

Non-qualified plans can discriminate in favor of this select group of presumably more sophisticated employees as long as they represent the higher-paid executive group. Furthermore, vesting can be according to any timetable deemed appropriate. As long as the funding reserve remains subject to the claims and creditors of the employer, the plan is exempt from the fiduciary implications of ERISA, other than a simple one-time, one-page disclosure filed with the Department of Labor.

Being exempt carries several very important ramifications. Specifically qualified plans must comply with burdensome and ultimately expensive reporting and accounting provisions of ERISA. On a positive point, qualified plan contributions are tax-deductible. The qualified contributions are deposited into a trust account that is protected from creditors and claims of both the business and the employee. The funds must be invested according to strict guidelines and accounted for on an annual basis. A designated administrator as a fiduciary must also comply with a regimen of periodic reports to the employee, the IRS and the Department of Labor. There are relatively harsh financial penalties for noncompliance with asset management, reporting and administration requirements.

Although the tax deductibility of contributions is very attractive, qualified plan benefits must be made available to all full-time employees with at least one year of service. Vesting must be within seven years of the initial plan participation. Therefore, there is very little opportunity to discriminate in favor of one or more key managers who substantially impact profitability.

In contrast, a non-qualified Supplemental Executive Retirement Plan (SERP) is much more flexible and versatile. These plans come in many forms ranging from simple retirement benefits to deferred compensation, stock options and restricted stocks. All of these dynamic programs can be exempt from the cumbersome compliance of ERISA as long as a few simple rules are followed. Notably, only the highly compensated more sophisticated employees can participate. And the funding reserve cannot be protected from corporate creditors and a simple one-page notice of ERISA exemption must be submitted to the Labor Department.

Utilizing a non-qualified structure, the business owner can design -- with respect to structure eligibility, vesting and funding -- a plan to address the specific needs and motivations of his key manager group.

The requirement that non-qualified plans be subject to corporate creditors is a positive design feature that keeps key managers focused on corporate welfare.

Also it is noteworthy that non-qualified plans do not have to be funded with anything other than a promise to pay benefits from future resources. Why is this important? Because contributions to a non-qualified plan are non-tax deductible. The unavailability of a tax deduction for non-qualified plan funding is a very important. Far too many business owners overlook or forget the tax treatment until their accountant informs them that their tax deposit has increased. In a 40% tax bracket, non tax-deductible means that $1.66 of profit will be required to set aside $1 in funding for a non-qualified plan. However, this is not all bad news. Taxation of non-qualified plans is timing issue because a tax deduction is available when benefits are paid. Furthermore there is a potential bonus because, during the deferral period, the invested reserves should grow. Assuming growth, the tax deduction should substantially exceed the initial non-deductible allocation to the funding reserve when benefits are paid.

Qualified and Non-Qualified Benefit Plans

	Qualified	Non-Qualified
Funding	Legally set aside in trust	Not set aside, no funding required
Tax to Business	• Deductible when contributed	• Deductible when paid put to employee
Tax to Employee	• Not taxable until received	• Not taxable until received -- unless funds set aside
Rules, Requirements	• ERISA	• Generally none
Vesting	• 7 year, or 5 year cliff	• Any
Contribution limits	• Subject to ERISA	• None
Investments	• Regulated	• Unregulated
Exposure to creditors	• Immune	• Exposed -- assets part of corporate assets

Funding for a golden handcuff can range from a very simple promise by the corporation to pay benefits to a program that sets aside liquid reserves to meet the liability of future cash payments.

The funding of non-qualified supplemental benefit programs is a subject near and dear to the business owner because of the impact on cash flow and taxation. The first legitimate thought is "why fund the plan if we don't have to?" The answer is that a key manager is not a chump. They know the differences between funny money and real money. They also know the differences between a cheap promise and a sincere commitment. The structure that has the most positive impact upon naturally skeptical managers establishes a funding reserve, which will realistically satisfy future payout obligations. Just be realistic. Although a contractual promise has personal significance to a business owner, if you want to get a manager's decision, put up some cash.

As a non-qualified plan, the investment structure of the funding reserve can also follow any style acceptable to the business owner and the executives. The reserve can be invested in CD's, stocks, bonds, mutual funds, annuities, life insurance and even be loaned to the business in lieu of borrowing from a bank. As a rule, I always recommend that business owners consider the investment preferences of the manager, but take a conservative approach. The reason for conservatism is that, until the manager vests, the business owner still owns the reserves. If the executive does not vest, the business owner wants to be sure he recovers real money. Also, if downturns in the investment market reduce the reserves, the strength of the handcuff will be reduced.

In deference to the general disdain, life insurance is far and away the most popular funding vehicle. No doubt, there are carrying costs associated with any form of life insurance. However, life insurance has several features that are conducive to golden handcuff funding. Life insurance, as the name implies, carries a death benefit that provides funds to relieve salary continuation concerns following the trauma of a manager's death, irrespective of the equity buildup. The business is also indemnified for the loss of a key manager through the recovery of income tax associated with the payout of the life insurance proceeds as a survivors' benefit.

To explain, let's assume that the life insurance contract carries a death benefit of $1 million. In the event of the manager's death, the business, as owner and beneficiary of the policy, would receive the death benefit essentially tax-free. Subsequently, when the business pays the $1 million to the manager's family as salary continuation, the business will receive an income tax deduction for the payment.

Assuming the company is in a 40% tax bracket, the company should receive a $400,000 tax refund to help reconcile the trauma of losing a <u>key manager.</u>

Another popular feature is that, with the exception of equity investment options of variable insurance, life insurance is generally acknowledged as a conservative investment. If you pick a quality company, it is hard to lose your money. It is also worthy of mentioning that, due to the popularity of insurance in a golden handcuff, the life insurance industry has the most refined support services. One of the most attractive features of life insurance is that policy accumulations are tax deferred. Unlike all other classic investment options, the sponsoring corporation will not have to report annual dividends as taxable income. Most life insurance policies can also include a disability benefit that can enhance the operation of the plan.

And finally, for all of you who have been frantically avoiding talking to any agents, life insurance has evolved into a very versatile financial tool. Contrary to the inflexible whole life policies of the past, we now have universal life and variable life, which offer premium funding flexibility. This premium funding flexibility is essential when funding varies, as would be the case when based upon a percentage of compensation. Variable life insurance also provides classic mutual fund investment options mirroring the capability of a contemporary 401(k) plan.

Far too often, the provisions of a golden handcuff are only formalized by a handshake. Formal documents are strongly advised, because, if either the employer or the employee slips, jumps, or defaults to an inappropriate assumption, the ensuing excitement is always painful and costly.

And, as we'll see in subsequent chapters, covenants between owners and managers can become the glue that allows them to move forward with a <u>genuine understanding of where they're headed.</u>

Golden Handcuff documents are generally in the form of contracts for each manager that describe the details of the golden benefits to be received and the operational handcuff responsibilities of the employee. The handcuff commitments within the manager's contract generally cover vesting, covenants not to compete, covenants not to recruit managers and privacy covenants.

The focal point of a Succession Bridge is to customize versatile non-qualified supplemental benefits to meet the performance motivation and career retention needs of the various classes of key managers. As we have just discussed, there is a great deal of latitude in the design. However, there are several categories of golden handcuffs, which, depending upon circumstance, are commonly utilized or considered in Succession Bridge construction. The following is a brief description of each category.

Deferred compensation: "As one of my key managers, allow me please to distribute earned income to you, but to defer it until a time when you will be in a lower tax bracket." As the name describes, deferred compensation is the calculated deferral of a manager's taxable income. According to the terms of the agreement between the manager and the employer, the manager is allowed to defer receipt of a predetermined amount of compensation and postpone the income tax until a later date when the compensation is requested. Because the deferred income rightfully belongs to the manager, vesting is typically triggered upon employment termination for any reason. The expectation is that the deferred income will grow during the deferral through prudent investment. Another motivator is the anticipation that, upon receipt, the manager's income tax bracket will be lower. The risks of deferred compensation is that the cash is subject to traumatic creditor claims. As an example, consider a massive fire with no insurance or the discovery of a major EPA infraction.

Many deferred compensation programs offer a match from the employer that is subject to the traditional vesting of an employer funded program. Due to the immediate vesting, pure deferred compensation plans have limited impact on Succession Bridge design.

Supplemental executive retirement plan (SERP): "If you make a long term commitment to this business, I will fund supplemental retirement benefits that will substantially enhance your security." A SERP, as the name describes, is an additional benefit provided to a key manager to encourage enhanced productivity and a long-term commitment to the business. According to the terms of a SERP agreement, the employer provides additional benefits to the key manager.

The terms of the agreement stipulate how the benefits are determined, vesting requirements and the terms of payout, including non compete covenants.

Access to funding is typically subject to a 10 to 20-year vesting. To give more potential bite to the non-compete covenants, upon vesting the SERP benefits are usually paid out over five to 10 years. The payout of SERP benefits are tax deductible to the employee subject to all applicable payroll taxes. SERP funding formulas are very versatile. In that most management pay plans are performance driven, SERP funding is normally based upon a percentage of annual compensation. Funding is also frequently contingent upon achieving reasonable benchmarks including, but not limited to minimum profitability, customer satisfaction and gross profit margin. Matching deferred compensation can be optional or it can be required. During the deferral, funding is invested in anticipation of growth. The most powerful plans are interactive, allowing the managers to take part in investment decisions, similar to a 401(k). A SERP can also be convertible, which means that, under the appropriate circumstances accumulations could be utilized to exercise stock options. A life insurance leveraged survivor's benefit is generally well received and even anticipated by managers. Due to long term vesting capability, a SERP is a fundamental aspect of a Succession Bridge.

Phantom stock: "If you make a long term commitment to this business, I will enhance your security with a lucrative benefit that is indexed to the growth and productivity of the business." Phantom stock is a complex non-qualified benefit that focuses a manager's attention on the value of the business and the net profitability of the business. It is really just a funky form of SERP. The financial reference for benefits is stock in the business.

Through contractually documented awards appropriate for the circumstances, hypothetical stock, hence the name phantom stock, is contractually accrued for a specific manager.

The objective of phantom stock, in lieu of a plain vanilla SERP, is to provide the special key manager a vested interest in the value of the company and annual profitability without actually owning stock.

This concept is supported by the question: What is minority stock in a family owned business worth anyway? If a manager can enjoy all the financial awards otherwise, why go through the trouble of issuing stock?

Phantom stock can be awarded through a variety of techniques including direct award and conversion of deferred compensation. Direct awards are supplemented benefits that are subject to long-term vesting. However, deferred compensation that is converted to phantom stock would have immediate vesting. Documentation clearly defines the valuation of a phantom stock unit under all contingencies considered feasible. Although admittedly funky, there are several benefits to phantom stock. The conversion of a manager's bonus into phantom stock is almost twice as efficient as the purchase of stock because phantom stock is usually accrued for the manager before tax.

As the owner of phantom stock, a manager usually receives a proportionate share of annual dividends, which can be utilized to earn more phantom stock units. Greater accruals of stock units create even greater payout of dividends. Upon retirement, death or satisfaction of other specific vesting requirements, the manager is paid the value of the phantom stock according to a specified formula. And last, phantom stock does not usually dictate a funding reserve and the benefits are not subject to market risk.

The disadvantages of phantom stock are that there is no actual stock ownership and there is no opportunity for capital gain. All benefits are ordinary income. Phantom stock is a powerful tool that is frequently utilized in the development of a Succession Bridge. Key managers would consider phantom stock too complex and very special key managers may find phantom stock a poor substitute for actual stock ownership.

Stock Appreciation Rights, SAR: "If you make a long term commitment to this business, I will enhance your security by funding supplemental benefits that are indexed to the appreciation of the business stock." Similar to phantom stock, a SAR is a more complex contractual benefit utilized to focus a manager's attention on growth in the value of the business. A SAR allows the owner to provide a manager an opportunity to share in the growth of the business without being required to transfer more complicated and much more expensive stock. SARs are generally utilized in regular corporations that do not pay dividends, with an impressive prospect for growth. The accrual of benefits is indexed to the growth in the value of a stipulated number of the employer's shares according to an expressed valuation formula.

Clearly defining the method of setting the stock value is a critical aspect of the documentation, because most family owned businesses are not publicly traded. In the absence of a very clear, easily computed, previously agreed upon formula, an SAR is just a prequel to a nasty argument that will do more harm than good. Similar to phantom stock, the accrual of an SAR is much more efficient than the purchase of growth stock because there is no cash outlay and the benefits are accrued before tax. Also there is no vulnerability to stock market volatility. In operation, a SAR program is relatively simple. Upon retirement, death and/or satisfaction of other specific vesting events, the manager is paid the growth in value of his SARs over the number of years specified in the agreement.

An SAR program does not dictate an interactive funding reserve and, therefore, less cash is needed to establish a reasonable reserve. Capital gain is not available. All SAR benefits are ordinary income. An SAR is a viable funding medium for a special key manager Succession Bridge. Key managers may find this form of golden handcuff too intangible and very special key managers may find a SAR program a poor substitute for actual stock ownership.

Management Company Succession Bridge, MCSB: "Although I cannot make you a stockholder, I want to acknowledge you as a special key manager by providing you with an opportunity to be my partner and I want to empower you to share in the growth you create." This is an actual management company formed to give special key managers and very special key managers an ownership interest without actually owning stock in the family business. The MCSB is usually most appropriate when there are several key managers who have an impact on a family enterprise, which is composed of several businesses. Dispersing minority stock in multiple businesses to multiple managers is either impossible, impractical or incompatible. The special key managers become owners of the MCSB, which achieves genuine value through the implementation of management contracts for the various businesses. The management contracts define management responsibilities and the performance requirements for management fees, which could include profit thresholds, customer satisfaction, accounts receivable or cash on hand. Generally, a stipulated amount of MCSB revenue is pledged to fund a golden handcuff SERP on behalf of special key managers. Revenue above the threshold is distributed to the managers in proportion to their ownership.

The management company also enables the management to build "good will" value, which is usually pegged at one times the average revenue. The advantage of this Succession Bridge structure to key managers is that they are now owners and partners with a vested interest in all aspects of the business.

An advantage of this structure to the employer is that he has potentially locked in a group of special and very special key managers without giving up any stock.

Furthermore, an MCSB reduces a business owner's dependence on a single very special key manager. An MCSB is an outstanding method of acknowledging, motivating, and retaining a group of special and very special key mangers. Key managers will not appreciate this structure.

Restricted stock (Section 83): "I want to acknowledge you as a very special key manager by awarding you with stock. However, you are going to have to meet a few reasonable, well-documented contingencies before this stock becomes your property. The good news is that this stock bonus will not be taxable to you until after you have fulfilled the service and/or performance contingencies." Restricted stock is a funky form of deferred stock bonus. The stock is actually issued to the very special key manager with a bold legend stating that ownership is subject to restrictions. Depending upon the circumstances, these restrictions could include years of service, profit thresholds or customer satisfaction. If the contingencies are not satisfied, the stock certificates are canceled.

In light of the fact that a transfer of stock actually occurs, risks of forfeiture must be well documented to assure deferral of taxation. As the recorded owner of the stock, the very special key manager receives any dividends declared and can exercise voting rights. Formal documentation must describe the process for valuing the stock because it is taxable income, in addition to the substantial risks of forfeiture. Otherwise, the IRS could easily take exception to the amount of tax or the timing of the tax generated by a Section 83 stock bonus. This is a viable, often very effective Succession Bridge tool for very special key managers. This benefit is always accompanied by a comprehensive stockholders agreement that restricts the transfers of stock.

Stock options: "I want to acknowledge you as a very special key manager by giving you an opportunity to purchase stock in this company after you have fulfilled reasonable performance and/or service requirements." Stock options are documented in a contract that specifies when stock can be purchased, how much stock can be purchased, what contingencies have to be satisfied, the price and the terms. The options can vest in lump sum or over a period of time. Contingencies for vesting can be years of service and or various performance thresholds. The option price is usually fair market value but can be a bargain. As you may have guessed, bargain options are subject to some unique income tax considerations. The terms for the purchase of stock are always dependent upon the resources of the managers. Rarely do managers have plentiful resources to pay cash for the stock. The more valuable the managers, the more flexible and lucrative the terms of purchase. A stock option program is always accompanied by a stock transfer restriction agreement that prevents inappropriate stock transfers. When very special key managers are involved, stock options are very common features of a Succession Bridge.

I hope these explanations aren't too technical. Trust me; I do not wear a pocket protector. I work hard to keep these discussions practical but the foundation of any form of bridge does require a bit of know how.

Let us move on to lighter subjects. Our discussion will now move to an explanation of the various forms of Succession Bridges. I want to show you how to use these tools. We will begin with relatively simple management-support structures and progress to more complex contingency structures, and then to more exotic structures that can accommodate a group of superstars who can actually run the business for the family.

Recognize that different packages are needed to suit the key employees/managers who have a higher value to the business. As we look at Succession Bridge options, keep in mind several very important points. First, this won't be a complete list. Rather, it's a summary of the significant categories. Within each of them, there are an infinite number of variations, limited only by the owner's needs and creativity. Second, the suggested structure and the examples should represent a starting point to help you develop the appropriate structure for your specific circumstances. Third, you are going to need help designing the appropriate structure for your situation and then building it. And, hopefully it is already obvious your technical advisors must be both competent and experienced.

5 Important Bridge Considerations

The tremendous advantage derived from linking together beams and pillars to build a pathway over an otherwise terminating break in the landscape is a metaphor for the management structures needed to support and facilitate succession of family-owned businesses that have no viable successors. As you have seen in your travels the structure of a bridge must vary with the landscape and the size and nature of the area being traversed. To build a bridge across any ravine, there are fundamental engineering principles that must be addressed, such as the length of the bridge, the strength of materials needed, the stability of the foundation and the potential impact of the environment. Building a bridge upon which others will rely, even risk their lives, is a major responsibility. The process requires a formidable commitment of resources including time, money and technology. And during the process of construction there must be constant accountability to assure that the weight-bearing expectations are being fulfilled.

Similarly, there are critical engineering and construction process for a family business Succession Bridge. Much will be at risk, including financial security, social standing and a family legacy. A major commitment of resources will be required to achieve the ambitious goal of business succession through key managers. As reflected by the wrinkles in my forehead, achieving business succession without qualified successors is not a simple black and white issue. Owners cannot just stop, make a decision, call in an order for a specific category of Succession Bridge and continue on the way toward the fulfillment of a business continuity dream.

In our consideration of the potential of a Succession Bridge, we are in a position of transition. We began building our Succession Bridge foundation with an explanation of the Succession Bridge theory. We followed with a review of the various categories of managers and a process for assessing each manager's potential value to your organization. And subsequently, we reviewed the role of golden handcuffs in the Succession Bridge and provided a brief but probably over-complicated description of the most commonly utilized structures.

We are now ready to begin discussing real life Succession Bridge applications. You are going to recognize that a succession planner must be more than a bean counter or a legal beagle.

As a succession planner, I represent a complex mixture of financier, tactician, psychologist, sociologist, paralegal, estate planner and entrepreneur.

More important than labels, my role or my purpose is driven by my passion to facilitate the perpetuation of family business legacies through the next generation. As a practitioner, not an academic, I am delighted to move on from the laborious detail involved in building a foundation to the second aspect of this book, which describes proven Succession Bridge structures with real life examples of how these structures have impacted family business legacies. Hopefully, you will find these upcoming discussions motivating and thought provoking.

However, as we transition into the exciting development and construction of a Succession Bridge to meet your specific needs, let's step back from the technical and focus on the practical. Allow me to impart a few hard earned pearls of wisdom that will impact your consideration of the upcoming structures as you take the precarious position of simultaneously dealing with attorneys, accountants, family partners, money, dreams and, of course, finicky key managers. If your thermometer reads above room temperature, you know that this combination will create some excitement, so a little practical forethought could save you many headaches.

First, try these supporting thoughts on for size:

1 As a foundation, you'll need a high level of what we call "Succession Success." We are not talking about just profitability. Succession Success is outstanding business performance/positioning across a broad spectrum of business criteria as described in Seeking Succession. A business candidate for a Succession Bridge must be a real winner or have the unquestionable potential to rise to that level. Unfortunately, tunnel vision about profitability can handicap the opportunity for achieving Succession Success. Objectivity and honest self-evaluation of Succession Success positioning are essential, because the fall from a succession bridge is brutally long and hard.

2 The implementation of a Succession Bridge depends upon a commitment by a business owner and/or family to continue the business. Pride in the unique accomplishment of building a successful business is critical. The family understands that a successful business represents more than money. It is a culture that has an impact far beyond immediate family. Irrespective of the absence of capable, motivated family members to assume the leadership of the business, there must be a genuine love for the business culture and all it includes: colleagues, industry acquaintances, employees, conventions, associations and vendors. There must be a desire to perpetuate the unique and personal nature of their business, if

only to give hard working, deserving and caring managers (including motivated family members) that invaluable boost to an ownership position.

3 Succession planning is not a project; it is a journey. Make a long-term commitment or do not even begin. Sure, there is room to change your mind or even change the structure, but bridges are not built overnight. Substantial foresight and preparation are needed to establish the dependable foundation for the construction. Sufficient lead- time must be allowed to "cure" the management pillars to determine if succession expectations can be achieved. There should also be reasonable expectations that some management pillars will have to be replaced if performance is not maintained or anticipated growth is not achieved. Immediately upon implementation, business succession prospects are enhanced because at least there is infrastructure to deal with contingencies, such as the death of the current leader. However, it takes time to achieve confidence that the supporting pillar(s) have the goods to deliver succession.

4 Follow the advice of Ricci M. Victorio, MA, Vice President of The Family Business Resource Center, "Get independent help evaluating family members and key managers who will or could participate in the Succession Bridge." Developing a realistic assessment of family members and managers is difficult because of the subjective perspective of every owner. Attitudes are profoundly impacted by past events. Bias is the norm. The natural instinct of a parent, partner or supervisor is to look either favorably or negatively upon the aptitude, motivation and attitude of their children and key managers.

In most cases, thinking the best, hoping for the best and expecting the best provides favorable direction to children and facilitates a more successful career.

However, where the family jewels and the welfare of many employees and vendors are at risk, you cannot afford to wing it.

A business owner who is Seeking Succession against the odds must achieve a realistic assessment of the core competencies, team potential and leadership ability of their family members and managers.

This uncompromising, realistic approach to succession is the bedrock upon which the decision is made to sell the business, pass it to family members or establish a Succession Bridge.

5 Heed the advice of Russell Phillips, MBA, LMHC, LMFT, Relationship Specialist for The Family Business Resource Center, and "don't build a Succession Bridge unless you are willing and capable of letting go." There is no reason to burn the brain cells, time and money to identify and build management plans, performance incentives and non-compete covenants for a successor leader if

you are just going to frustrate him. Control Freaks should only consider the Contingency Succession Bridge, which will provide crisis management when Mr. Everything becomes nothing.

6 Owners pursuing a Succession Bridge must also have an innovative, adventurous attitude. Innovation often leads to consideration of unconventional methods. Unfortunately, it's often difficult to bring this sort of creativity to the family business succession realm. Typically, individuals and families adventurously combine daring innovation and hard work to build an outstanding business. They apply the theory that the best defense against failure is a relentless offense. Being offensively minded admittedly increases vulnerability, but also increases rewards. Combined with the belief that failure is a temporary condition, they are continually striving for ways to achieve their business dreams.

However, after achieving their dreams, some business owners fall under the malaise of a sphincter mentality. Concern and fear about losing what they have achieved tightens down the parameters for innovation, adaptation and growth for the next generation of managers. This protective default reaction often translates into a perception that there is no perfect family successor and the business should be sold.

7 Understand the concept of guarded trust. These key personnel are indeed the metaphorical pillars of the Succession Bridge. They have been running the business as managers and are willing to assume responsibility for its continued success and welfare. Accordingly, these special managers assume responsibility for the ownership family, the employee family and others in the community who derive their welfare from the ongoing viability of the business. If you have been a control freak, do not waste your time looking within your ranks for these jewels. They are working for your competitor.

If you have trusted key managers on board, stop reading this book and
thank God for His wisdom and blessings.

Then, immediately go thank these special managers and tell them you are about to brew up a concoction that they are going to like.

8 Remember the planning theorem of Daniel J. Thill, CFP, Chief Operations Officer of The Rawls Company: "A Succession Bridge will require a substantial incentive to motivate a key manager to assume a successor role". Key managers are not naïve, nor are they chumps. Although they may have a very close relationship with one, several or all members of the family, very little time will pass from the introduction of the Succession Bridge concept to their recognition of the significant responsibility they will be assuming and the unique circumstances in which they will be asked to perform their services. For a brief passing moment, they

may be content with the honor of having been selected as the anointed one(s). Not to worry, they will recognize soon enough the implications of the position they have assumed. To quote a client, a leading pillar in Succession Bridge automotive history, "Dan, I had no idea what I had undertaken." When reality sets in, reasonable gold will be required to handcuff these special managers to the business and motivate them to achieve the family's succession goal.

9 Trust the experience of Donald J. Doudna, PhD, President of The Family Business Resource Center: "A Succession Bridge will require a management performance monitoring and accountability program." Just keeping your finger on the pulse and dressing down managers as the need arises is not sufficient for a Succession Bridge environment. Earlier, we talked about guarded trust of managers. This concept describes the highest level of trust in business.

The fact is that no level of trust overrides your responsibility to establish reasonable safeguards and accountability for those who are or will be <u>empowered to run the business.</u>

Only a certifiable bonehead would turn his business over to a manager and give away unbridled control over their family's most precious asset. A Succession Bridge dictates that key managers have unrestricted capability to carry out their responsibilities, including managing day-to-day operations. However, prudence, stewardship and good sense dictates that family owners fulfill their responsibility to hold managers accountable for protecting the business asset and achieving reasonable performance benchmarks. The guarded aspect of guarded trust does not represent any lack of respect for the character or the ability of a key manager(s). It reflects a common sense vigilance regarding the welfare of the family's asset.

10 Keep your Succession Bridge consideration as simple as possible. It matters not how sexy a program may look from a distance. If everyone involved cannot fully understand how the program works and how it will benefit them personally, it is worthless. Avoid excessive, unproductive complications that will consume time and money and frustrate everyone involved.

11 Good, bad or ugly, the only safe policy is honesty. When dealing with key managers, remember a point made in Chapter 2: "It's the character stupid." However, in this instance it is the owner's character. To paraphrase a statement of Dr. James Dobson, of Focus on the Family, "values are not bought, they are taught." No amount of gold will handcuff a quality manager to an owner the manager does not respect. Managers hear everything an owner says. A sophisticated manager sees everything that the owner would prefer to keep under wraps and a good manager always understands the real agenda. Be honest and straightforward in

all communication. These guys know you like a book. They know your family and other managers as well, if not better, than you do. To not tell them all of the truth is a brutal lie. Any questions about the character of the active owner, regardless of foundation, can be disastrous. Any questions about the character of future owners, such as children, will surely be disastrous.

12 Remember, key managers are a peculiar breed. They have a lot of pride, so never convey that you are doing them a big favor. They think they have been doing you a favor by hanging around. They fully believe that they do not need a job in your business because they believe they are in demand and can find another job in short order. If your golden incentives have value, they will figure it out in a nanosecond. Regardless of how reasonable, they will always feel that your handcuffs are unfair. You should not sell the program. If you do sell, they will think something is wrong. Your planning facilitators should do the selling.

13 Money is not the critical component of attracting and retaining key managers. Key managers want first to be associated with people they respect. Equally important, they want to be respected by those they respect. Key managers need affirmation and recognition for serving beyond expectations. All of you pinheads who are too large and in charge to look a manager in the eye, shake his hand and say thank you can stop reading and give this book to one of your humble friends who can really use it. The heart and soul that your managers give you (and your family) will only be the reflection of the heart and soul you give them. If it is just about money on either side of the equation, Succession Success is just a dream.

14 Do not overreact to a manager's emotions, especially his response to a golden handcuff proposal. He has a right to feelings. Give them both the opportunity and the time to react, reflect and recover. When you mention gold, handcuffs, family members, leadership, and competitors, you are going to open a spigot of feelings. When you make a proposal, you are soliciting a response. The manager may tell you what you want to hear, what they have been dying to tell you or what you have been afraid of hearing. Whatever the response, take a deep breathe and say, "We can work through this."

15 Do not pencil pay plans so that you can afford to fund a golden handcuff. Key managers are not brainless. They will pick up immediately any attempt to take their money to fund your program. Current compensation must not be an issue if you are going to effectively showcase the value of additional gold and the reasonableness of associated handcuffs. Skeptical by nature, a manager will always be looking for hidden agendas. Manipulating compensation would equate to shooting a hole in the bottom of your boat.

16 Tread lightly when discussing the non-compete covenants. This is a very sensitive issue to a manager. Notably, it is more sensitive to some than to others. The reality is that non-compete covenants are not a major handicap to a key manager because they generally are only enforceable for a radius of about 25 miles and they are usually limited to two years. With the mobility of our society, 25 miles is nothing. However, some managers cannot see the forest for the trees. They have more difficulty with the concept than with the actual impact. Just because a manager is having difficulty with a non-compete covenant, do not automatically think that he has been thinking about leaving.

The real handcuff is you -- your values, your integrity, your appreciation for them and the gold you are willing to provide if they make a career commitment.

Give them generous time they need to reconcile the covenants. Require your managers to consult with an independent attorney. Otherwise, the covenants could be deemed worthless. Be firm and resolute, but do not appear insensitive to their concerns and feelings.

17 From the experience of Ken Rosenfield, CPA, understand the total cost of the plan before you announce it. Total costs include legal fees, variable upside incentives and the income taxes on the funding reserve and any match. Don't nickel and dime the managers. Be prepared to totally underwrite implementation. You have more important and more productive issues to address than who will pay the legal fees. Also, prepare yourself for the managers exceeding your highest expectations. The shortcut to trashing a life-time of hard earned respect is for you to proclaim that the deal that you approved several years earlier is now is too good for the managers.

18 Have high expectations of managers. Of course you must be realistic. However, within aggressive but realistic boundaries of what you feel and what the individual or group can achieve, expect that they will achieve their full potential, make lots of money, enjoy a wonderful lifestyle, become financially secure and even possibly become a stockholder. Communicate and reaffirm these expectations regularly, expressing enthusiasm for the inevitability that exciting goals will be attained. Express these expectations to others, especially their spouses and colleagues. Express that you are depending upon them to reach their full capability.

Stepping out with an outward expression of faith in what a manager will accomplish is a profound blessing. Remember, most of us who have advanced through the ranks began with an attitude of fake it until you make it. Our greatest fear was that someone would figure out that we really did not know what the hell we were doing. Remember how you felt when someone made any form of expressing that you were actually making it. Now, as you are embarking on one of the most formidable undertakings of your career, those are the exact feelings that you want to convey to a manager(s). Do not assume that a manager(s) has unwavering confidence that they can fulfill your expectations of them as a Succession Bridge.

If you want to make an assumption, you could even bet the farm that a public and frequent expression of confidence in a manager(s) will position you as a coach not a critic, reinforce the confidence they have and help them build additional confidence that they are going to need.

Greater confidence will be the fuel for greater achievement. They will respect you more and become more loyal. They will predictably put out a greater effort not to disappoint someone they respect, who, through public expression of confidence, has taken on an element of responsibility for their success.

19 Establish a conservative first year funding threshold for incentive golden handcuffs. Be prepared to lower the threshold in the second year. Key managers feel part of their job description is to be optimistic. However, this optimism is a curse if the threshold is not achieved. If managers go two years or more before they see any gold hit their incentive program, they predictably lose appreciation for the program and resent the handcuffs, resent the business owner and, based upon vivid experiences of the author, resent the Succession Bridge facilitator. Avoid this frustration by making sure the plan gets funded the first year.

20 When you announce the names of the managers you have selected to participate, lock, load and be prepared to defend your decisions with the managers you did not select. They will confront you and you must be prepared to coach or counsel. If they are not ready for prime time, but are showing expected progress, be prepared to coach them with affirmation and encouragement to remain diligent. Give them assurance that if they continue to work hard, their time will come. On the other hand, if they are bull-headed numbskulls who have never performed to their potential, counsel them that the train of opportunity is leaving the station. If they do not get their attitude right, they are going to be left behind.

21 Regardless of how simple or how complex, continually review the Succession Bridge structure with the managers. The provisions of the plan should be explained at least annually. Having previously emphasized that they are not dumb, I now must confuse the issue by stating that they frequently act that way. Maybe absent-mindedness or ridiculous confusion is just a game they play. Regardless, whether you are protecting them or protecting yourself, you must regularly

reinforce the gold and the handcuff because they are vulnerable to forgetting both. Even worse, they are highly prone to playing the "oh, you did not tell me that," game.

22 All of the time and money expended to develop and implement a Succession Bridge will ultimately become dependent upon the owner's conviction and consistency. Any long term strategy that involves money, family, dreams and managers will be subject to questions, challenges, resistance and even rebellion. Everyone has a vested interest. Everyone has an opinion and most of those who express their opinions are self-proclaimed experts. There are a constant series of questions that give discontented souls -- who are not on board with the design or even the concept -- opportunities to peck away at what is being developed. Conviction to stay the course is imperative.

The best technique I have utilized to discourage constant change is to reduce the plan to writing and require the agreement of the planning team before changes are formalized.

Furthermore, in the words of Don Ray, one of the brightest CPA's and consultants in the automobile business, "consistent enforcement of policies that impact both family and managers is critical to implementing any aggressive and ambitious management project in a family owned business. Otherwise we can find simpler ways of making our lives miserable."

Ok, enough of these pearls (more like war medals) of wisdom. It is now time to step out and examine the specific forms of Succession Bridge that can impact your business, family and/or your career. We are going to discuss when and where these various structures could be used and how to build them. We will also have some fun reviewing real life examples of structures I've used over my 30-year career. These illustrations are intended not only to help you understand the application of the specific Succession Bridge category, but to also give you assurance that others have successfully traveled this path ahead of you. You may feel a specific Succession Bridge category does not apply to you, and, in fact, it may not. However, I would encourage you to read each example, because the culture of the Succession Bridge is reinforced, and the culture is more important than the design details of any specific structure. We are going to start with the simple and move toward the more complex. Remember, these are categorical examples based upon my experience. By no means is this list intended to express any design limitations on the plan that would be appropriate for your unique circumstance. Given sufficient time and commitment, we can work out a Succession Bridge for any situation.

The SERP Succession Bridge

As discussed in my previous book, Seeking Succession, the continuity of management is a critical component of business succession. It is not realistic to expect the next generation owner operators to immediately recruit and install a new management team. To the contrary, it is very important that the managers who have achieved "succession success" continue to work with the new owner managers. The presence and support of seasoned management enables successors to learn, grow and understand what it takes to sustain "succession success." Furthermore, the fruit of the next generation often falls far from the trunk. The personalities, interests and core competencies of successors are very different from their parents. Some kids postpone maturity as long as they can and some just never get it. Therefore, in many succession circumstances, proactive incentive is needed to motivate old-line, seasoned managers to remain patient, diligent, and supportive of the next generation. This common need brings forth our proposed solution, the SERP Succession Bridge.

SERP is an acronym for a cash-based supplemental executive retirement plan, which is a golden handcuff program specifically designed to motivate a key manager to stay with the company to provide management support to family successors.

A SERP Succession Bridge is a management continuity strategy that utilizes the discriminating benefits of a SERP to encourage strategically critical key managers to make a career commitment to the business that will assure their talent and experience will be a resource for the next <u>generation owner operators.</u>

A SERP Succession Bridge sponsor assumes that, if key managers stay on board to support current and next generation management, they are worth every penny of the SERP investment. On the flip side, if a manager suffers brain outage and quits, with cliff vesting, the investment will be recovered.

A cash-based SERP means that the plan ultimately distributes a cash retirement benefit that presumably will supplement other retirement resources, such as qualified pension, profit sharing and 401(k) plans, social security and personal savings.

Theoretically, this supplement will substantially impact the manager's financial security. Remember, if the gold is not substantial, it will be unrealistic to expect to substantially impact the attitudes and actions of key managers.

Basic SERP Example

◆ **Additional perk to existing retirement plan as reward given by employer to Key Manager**
◆ **Performance benchmark required**

Given Assumptions for sample illustration:
- Key Executive is 40 years old
- Compensation is $300,000 per year with 5% annual increases
- Corporate tax rate of 40%
- SERP contribution is 10% of compensation

SERPs come in all shapes and sizes, limited only by the planning, goals, preferences of executives and the creativity of all involved. As mentioned under the definition of golden handcuffs, a SERP is a non-qualified retirement plan. This means we can adopt the plan to meet unique circumstances of the family, business and executives without being impacted (frustrated and depressed) by IRS and Department of Labor regulations.

The design of a SERP has several important steps that should address the goal of providing appropriate support for family-management succession, while also addressing the issues of the business and the key managers. The first step is to develop an understanding of how a SERP is created, how it operates and what impact this structure can have upon the business and the key manager. A SERP is a serious initiative and a plan sponsor should understand the operation and impact of a plan before the cat is let out of the bag. Of course, it would be wise to determine if cash is to be allocated to a funding reserve or if the business will simply promise to pay benefits at the time of vesting. Either method works, but depending upon the nature of the business, the impacts are significantly different.

A promise to pay future benefits from future cash flow will not push the hot buttons unless the managers have unwavering confidence that the promise will be fulfilled. If key managers do not have access to financial reports, confidence in the business and confidence in the owner, do not bet that a promise will lock them down. Further, if managers do not trust the next generation owners and decision makers who will be responsible for writing their retirement checks, don't expect them to be impressed with a promise to pay significant benefits in the distant future.

My recommendation, unless your business is a bank, insurance company, utility or equivalent, fund a payout reserve with cash and do everything possible to illustrate to the managers that their future benefits are out of <u>harm's way.</u>

Assuming your business can afford a SERP and your managers would be motivated by this exceptional benefit, your next move would be to record the specific goals of a prospective plan. Why are you going through the cost and headache of developing a SERP Succession Bridge? If good reasons do not immediately jump into your lap, forget about it. A SERP is not about benevolence. There has to be a need to put forth the cash to lock in key managers, support Junior's weak suits and survive the various challenges associated with ownership and management transition. Otherwise, you should take the money and buy yourself a boat or condo.

Assuming you have confirmed that a golden handcuff is needed to support the continuity of critical management, the next step is to determine who should be included in the plan. This is a very important step because, as mentioned earlier, the owner will have to defend his logic. Inevitably, when a SERP Succession Bridge is announced, one or more managers who were not included will boldly ask, "Why?" And, predictably, a famously arrogant manager will take exception to specific colleagues who are included.

When determining who will be in the plan, remember a few fundamental concepts. Above all, go with managers you trust. Pick managers who can work with the next generation. Put up sufficient gold to represent a handcuff. If the SERP funding is spread too thin, the goal of retaining key managers may not be achieved. Regardless of who may be offended, owners should put their money on the people who can carry the business into the next generation.

The next step is to define the funding formula and methodologies. There are several viable general funding concepts. As we discussed in chapter four, the most popular structure is the traditional cash-funded SERP. There are also phantom stock and stock appreciation rights plans. Deciding which technique would be best for your circumstances can be challenging. At this point, a succession planning facilitator who understands the various funding alternatives and the hot buttons of the managers can be of great assistance. This is a very important step, because the funding formula will determine both management focus and the cost of the plan.

The design of a traditional cash funded SERP establishes a formula which defines annual contributions to a funding account for each executive. The owner must determine an effective formula for motivating the executive to serve as a Succession Bridge and clearly understand the impact the resulting cash-out will have on cash flow. Formulas vary according to the unique circumstances of both the business and the executive. Far and away, percentages of compensation formulas are most versatile.

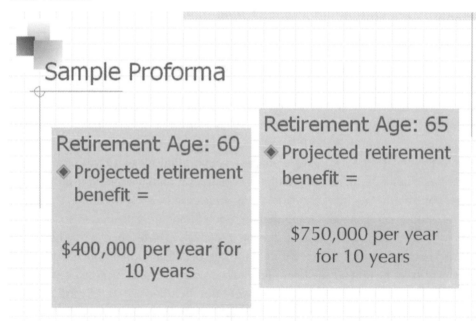

Sample Proforma

Retirement Age: 60
◆ Projected retirement benefit =

$400,000 per year for 10 years

Retirement Age: 65
◆ Projected retirement benefit =

$750,000 per year for 10 years

Upon retirement, assuming satisfaction of service and/or performance vesting prerequisites, the executive is paid whatever the formula has accumulated in his reserve account. This concept is popular with both owners and managers because the manager controls the level of deposits into the SERP account through annual compensation, departmental profit and years of service. Most key executives have incentive-based pay plans. As the profitability of the company or the department increases, the manager's compensation also increases. The more the manager earns, the bigger the contribution to his or her SERP account. This can lock in the key manager and motivate him to achieve higher levels of efficiency and/or productivity.

In businesses where management compensation is not driven by individual performance, it is important to keep the key manager involved in the bottom line.

Bottom line attention can be achieved by a funding formula that, to an appropriate degree, is based upon a percentage of profitability. This could be a percentage of first-dollar profitability or, more commonly, a percentage of profitability after achieving a minimum profit threshold that the business owner feels is necessary to meet a variety of higher priority needs, such as maintaining lifestyle, supporting debt service, keeping the lights on, maintaining working capital and providing a reasonable return on invested equity.

When a plan has funding factors based on both a percentage of compensation and a percentage of profitability, the plan should facilitate the management collaboration and teamwork to increase profitability.

Incentive SERP Example

◆ Based totally upon performance benchmarks
- Not based on compensation
- Benchmark is whatever is agreed upon and can vary with each manager and each store

Given Assumptions for sample illustration:
- Key Executive is 40 years old
- Achieves $50,000 annual contribution
- Benefits paid out over 10 year period

Larger and/or diverse businesses do not want their executives to focus on annual profitability. Some businesses, such as banking and real estate development, are also oriented toward the development of business value or net worth. The traditional index for measuring business value or net worth is stock. However, for the most part, family businesses do not want key managers owning a piece of the family jewels. Furthermore, as we discussed earlier, key managers (as compared to very special key managers) do not have sufficient impact upon business success to merit owning stock. Only when the owner is faced with weighing the loss of a very special key manager versus the achievement of succession is stock a viable golden handcuff option.

Sample Proforma

Gross Return	6%	8%	10%
Account value at Age 60	$ 2,466,000	$ 3,028,000	$ 3,728,000
10-year Projected Retirement Benefit	$ 236,000	$ 316,000	$ 448,000
10-year Guaranteed Survivors Benefit	$ 236,000	$ 316,000	$ 448,000
Account value at Age 65	$ 3,339,000	$ 4,346,000	$ 5,540,000
10-year Projected Retirement Benefit	$ 301,000	$ 458,000	$ 656,000
10-year Guaranteed Survivors Benefit	$ 301,000	$ 458,000	$ 656,000

When growth in business value is the benchmark for business success, phantom stock is a viable method of establishing funding for a SERP Succession Bridge. As discussed earlier, phantom stock is a method of funding a SERP through hypothetically crediting a key manager with shares in the business. The plan document would state how the business is to be valued, the number of phantom shares authorized and the customary service requirements for vesting. When the key manager satisfies vesting prerequisites and retires, the value of the awarded phantom stock is computed based upon the formula and paid to the manager as the SERP retirement benefit. In operation, these are reasonably simple and efficient plans. However, real money, as opposed to phantom stock, is needed to pay out the benefits of a phantom stock SERP. Depending upon the stability and retained resources of the business, it may be prudent to establish a funding reserve to meet these future commitments. In a pass through entity, such as a Sub-S corporation, a LLC or a partnership, the design of a phantom stock plan can also provide that a manager holding vested phantom stock units would receive his proportionate share of annual dividend distributions.

Other businesses are driven, not by net worth, but by business value. However, as expressed earlier, it is generally inappropriate to distribute stock options to key managers in a closely held family business. A popular method of funding a SERP Succession Bridge in a growth business, such as a bank, is through awarding stock appreciation rights (SAR.) Subsequently, management efforts will be focused upon the growth of the company.

> *Granting a SAR creates a golden handcuff by effectively crediting one or more key managers with the appreciation above a stipulated value, on a specific number of shares.*

When the key manager satisfies service prerequisites and retires, the appreciation on the shares is computed and paid out over a period of time as the manager's SERP benefit. Here again, real cash is needed to fund these benefits.

Having established a funding reference payout and formula that works for both the business and the key manager, the next step is to determine the prerequisites that the manager must satisfy in order to receive benefits. Lest we overlook the obvious, the fundamental prerequisite is that the manager is a very valuable commodity. A SERP involves extra time, extra effort and extra money, so be sure this commitment is merited.

Otherwise, at the top of this list would be vesting. The role of a SERP Succession Bridge is to assure that the key manager(s) stays on board during a transition of control and management to the next generation. As we have discussed, vesting of a non-qualified plan can occur over any period of service or at any attained age that the owner feels is appropriate. However, remember that the plan is designed to be a motivator and an incentive. Therefore, an effectively designed SERP must not only reflect what an owner feels is appropriate, but what the manager(s) believes is fair. A SERP is worthless as a golden handcuff if the manager is not excited at the prospect of receiving the benefits. Usually 10 to 15 years of service or attainment of age 62, whichever is later, is considered reasonable. Normally, the manager is not vested until all service requirements are met. Depending upon the owner's generosity, a graduated schedule may also work. However, as more liberal vesting schedules are considered, do not forget the objective of locking in the key manager.

Trust is a prerequisite to considering a manager as a Succession Bridge. However, being trusting does not mean you are stupid. Circumstances change and so do managers. Therefore, to any form of Succession Bridge the adoption of reasonable covenants not to compete, not to recruit employees and not to divulge private business information are very important. The understanding, agreement and ultimate adoption of covenants take time. The key concept in the development process is reasonableness. It is both justifiable and prudent for an owner to request (you cannot demand) reasonable performance covenants as consideration for generous contributions made to a supplemental retirement benefit. Likewise, it is reasonable and prudent for a manager to resist restricting his freedom. Non-compete covenants and performance thresholds are extremely sensitive to key managers. There is nothing to be gained but turmoil and long-standing resentment if the owner's or the manager's expectations are perceived to be unreasonable.

The covenant development process is the by-product of good faith negotiations, assuming both parties have adequate information and neither party is compelled to agree to anything deemed unreasonable. The process should begin with the owner determining the minimum protection that must be achieved to protect the Succession Bridge strategy and justify the SERP investment. This decision needs the input of an experienced attorney because the courts of each state have unique perspectives on the legality of non-compete covenants. The key managers also need the consultation of an independent attorney to minimize emotional reactions and give them the assurance that the non-compete expectations are not unreasonable. The give and take of good faith discussions and negotiations will predictively confirm reasonable non-compete covenant goals.

Another common prerequisite is a reasonable profitability threshold. As an example, it is not unreasonable to require that the contributions to the SERP come only from profits. Depending on the nature of the business, it is also reasonable to require the continuation of profits at a level that has become a historical norm. The theory is that the owner simply will continue to expect from the Succession Bridge the level of performance that initially showcased the individual as a key manager. Other thresholds may include any index unique to the business that is reflective of outstanding performance. These thresholds may relate to customer satisfaction, industry or franchise performance awards, product volume or whatever may be applicable.

However, do not go overboard. If the key manager perceives the SERP to be unrealistic, your TEAM (Time-Energy-And-Money) <u>investment will be in jeopardy.</u>

Another reasonable prerequisite is that the managers participate in a team initiative to enhance "succession success." The forum for this team initiative would be what I refer to as Management Advisory Board (MAB.) This is an official organization within the corporation, acknowledged by a resolution of the Board for the development and implementation of winning policies and procedures. The MAB Charter, which expresses the specific purpose and governance of this organization, is recorded in the corporate minutes. The official and formal nature of this organization offers an attractive element of prestige to the participating members.

In operation, the SERP participants periodically meet as a MAB under the procedures stipulated in the Charter and the leadership of a facilitator and an initially appointed, but ultimately elected hierarchy of a chairman, vice chairman and coordinator. The MAB would initially address issues that ownership requests.

The mission of the MAB is to serve as a liaison to rank and file employees, assist with development of policies and procedures and implement a common culture throughout the business.

Structure

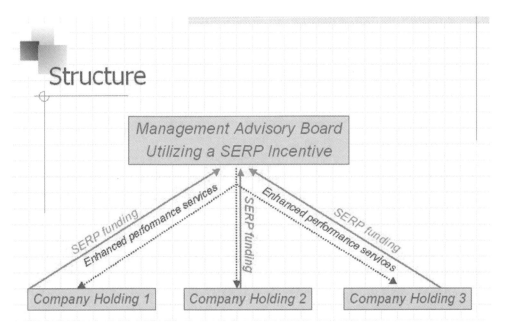

The diversity of perspectives from various parts of the business should bring fresh creativity to addressing problems and issues. However, this is initially an awkward group of strong willed, independent managers who are good leaders but marginal followers. Commonly, they are an outspoken group of know-it-alls, who at first will struggle to maintain order, much less operate like a team.

Fortunately, after a season or so, MAB members realize that meetings and projects are not a waste of their precious time, but in fact are an opportunity for them to significantly influence business management and profitability. They begin to recognize that their joint efforts can move the profit needle, increase earnings, increase bonuses and increase SERP funding. The neatest aspect of the MAB is that the organization is self-disciplined. From a business succession perspective, a mature (two to three years), stable, proactive MAB becomes a very valuable stabilizing factor to successor management. Members of the MAB are generally given the right to jettison any member who is not carrying his weight. And trust me, key managers will cut the wheat from the chaff! They have no tolerance for colleagues who waste their time and don't satisfy their standards.

With a reasonable grasp of the prerequisites to establishing a SERP Succession Bridge, it would now be appropriate to determine if SERP participants will be required or given the option to make contributions to the plan.

Generally, I discourage requiring contributions in a golden handcuff SERP because the personal and business cash flow complications of a required match can easily override the Succession Bridge purpose. Remember, in order for a benefit to be construed as a handcuff, the employer must generate the gold. The requirement that managers also invest in the golden handcuff is frequently viewed on the same level as a root canal.

However, manager contributions can be attractive on an optional basis. Notably, if a manager asks if he can defer some of his hard earned income, this is a good sign that he is buying into the long term Succession Bridge mission. Selling the concept of a Succession Bridge should be downhill from here. If they are willing to put up some of their own money, it's clear that they understand the concept of the golden-handcuff, they are comfortable with their long term role and have no immediate intent to look around.

The next step is to refine benefits and payout terms. In addition to a retirement benefit, most plans also provide a survivor's benefit, which provides enhanced financial security to a participant's survivors. Assuming the plan provides vesting upon a participant's death, the survivor's benefits would minimally be equal to the deceased participant's accumulated account balance, just like a 401(k). When life insurance is utilized as the funding vehicle, the survivor's benefit can be leveraged.

However, the potential costs of leveraged survivor's benefits are hot items of interest to both key managers and the owner. The key manager is usually impressed with the opportunity to provide more family security, but also sensitive to the life insurance mortality charges that are debited against the retirement account. Therefore, if life insurance is utilized, the amount of insurance must be reasonable or the key manager will revolt. And, the owner will be or should be sensitive to the amount of insurance utilized because the contract surrender charges could be debited against forfeited account balances if the manager terminates employment (before vesting) in the first few years of participation. Therefore, the Succession Bridge sponsor will be interested in the surrender charges of the specific life insurance contract being utilized.

Irrespective of benefits versus cost, some people just hate life insurance for any number of rational and irrational reasons. However, managers commonly like life insurance in their SERP because this no cost benefit is perceived to relieve them of the necessity of paying for personal insurance. Many employers also like life insurance funded survivors' benefits because the enhanced survivors' benefit is simple and secure. They would rather run the risk of the surrender charges than run the risk of the stock market. Furthermore, employers also are pleased that a life-insurance leveraged survivors' benefit relieves them of the moral pressure to provide for the dependents of a deceased key manager. A portion of the life insurance and the tax refund generated by a tax-deductible leveraged survivors' benefit can also be attractive as a cost recovery mechanism.

Similarly, disability benefits are also popular aspect of a SERP because of the personal financial trauma created by a disabled key manager who has to be dropped from the payroll. Again, insurance is available to leverage the disability payout of the SERP. However, in most cases, disability insurance is not purchased in the SERP because of the availability and economy of a group disability policy. Most SERP plans simply state that, in the event of disability, the manager is fully vested of all funds deposited or accrued in his account.

Payout terms for a SERP are generally stipulated to be in five to 10 annual installments, with 10 being the most popular.

The reason for the extended payout is to provide enforceability to the covenants not to compete. Technically, the payout of vested benefit and the enforceability of a non-compete covenant are separate issues. However, the covenants have much more perceived enforceability if the retired manager believes that he has something to lose if the rules are broken. Therefore, the benefit payout period should be determined in part by how long the employer wants to maintain hooks after the manager terminates employment.

Presenting the SERP Succession Bridge Concept

After developing confidence in a preliminary design, the next step is the presentation of the plan to the key managers. It is strongly suggested that a Succession Bridge facilitator, attorney and/or accountant assist with this presentation. Explanation of the general Succession Bridge concept, the golden handcuff structures and the MAB operation is a major undertaking. There is only going to be one chance to make a first impression. Unfortunately, many managers fall into the category of "once confused, always confused." So, bring the varsity and let the professionals present how the moving parts fit together. The purpose of the meeting is to introduce the SERP Succession Bridge concept, not to make the participants experts.

The goal is to make a good impression and learn what managers think about serving as a Succession Bridge. They should be told that they will be provided more details later and should prepare to have an attorney help them with review of pro-formas and documents.

Before presenting the program to managers, owners should prepare for a learning experience. Owners can bank on learning something new about managers from their response to the plan. The combination of gold, management voice and handcuff will remove any inhibitions that may have prevented prior straight-up communication. Within a couple of days after this meeting, owners should also be prepared to be confronted by one or more managers who will want to know why they were not included. This will be a very important time to coach the manager on where they must grow in order to be "succession reliable." Traditionally, if the owner is prepared, much can be gained from this coaching. Omission from the plan probably represents solid accountability for numerous past performance reviews. Owners should also be prepared for a severance disagreement with one of those classic managers who just don't get it and are terminally offended that they were not chosen.

Ideally, the business owner should not even attend the next meeting with the prospective SERP Succession Bridge participant(s). This is when the details relating to non-compete covenants and performance thresholds are discussed. If the business owner attends this meeting, he will give up a negotiating edge. This is where a succession planner can serve as a mediator to prevent emotional issues on either side from undermining the plan.

Within the parameters of flexibility expressed by the owner, the succession planner can negotiate a win/win final design. This process can be wonderfully simple or unbelievably protracted. When considering career restraint, mentoring successors, participating in a MAB and supplemental benefits, discussions can get exciting. I have examined the underside of the bus on many occasions when ruthless managers and owners attempted to sacrifice me (instead of the beautiful maiden) to achieve their personal goals. Owners should keep cool and just let the process work, which could include a decision that a SERP Succession Bridge is not appropriate. Likewise, managers should consider the significance of the supplemental benefits received as compared to the restrictions incurred. A SERP Succession Bridge is a significant endeavor that requires the agreement of both parties. Sometimes it just takes a little time to achieve that agreement.

After owners and key managers agree on the major provisions of the program, the process begins to move faster. Financial proformas and document drafts are needed for this phase of discussions. Fortunately, attorneys and succession planners are adept at these steps. The succession planner would first review the draft pro-formas and documents with the business owner to ensure that they have fulfilled expectations. Several drafts may be required before there is sufficient comfort to present the product to the managers. Owners should be totally satisfied with the documents before they are passed on to managers. Otherwise this process can become a disaster.

After approval by the owner, the draft documents would be presented to the manager(s) for review and refinement. The manager(s) would also be given extra copies to give to his accountant and attorney for review. Assuming a survivor's benefit is being provided, the manager would also begin insurance underwriting. Usually within 60 to 90 days, depending upon the size of the plan and the personalities involved, the documents, funding proformas and life insurance can be approved and ready for execution.

The next step is to have a party! This is a significant event.

The business owner should not forego an opportunity to make a public relations score by scheduling a formal signing event with photos recording the handshakes, followed by dinner and any other festivities deemed appropriate for the occasion. This is the first and best opportunity for the business owner to openly express his appreciation to the key manager for succession. A little bit of glitz here can go a long way toward drawing a Succession Bridge manager into the family business. Trust me, they will remember it and it will have meaning.

The final step is maintenance and refinement. Each year at a recurring time, the succession planner should meet with the manager(s) to review the provisions of the plan.

It is prudent to take a proactive approach in assuring that managers do not forget the gold or the handcuff. Reinforcing the benefits, the vesting and the covenants can preclude both natural and purposeful forgetfulness. Reviewing performance may mean "Congratulations, job well done," or it may mean, "We've got to meet with the MAB and find a way to do the job better." Regardless, if annual reviews are routine, they can be used as coaching and counseling opportunities. And, of course, annual meetings would review the account accumulations to indirectly reemphasize to the key manager(s) what he would be forfeiting in the event he were to move to another job.

So, having said all this design mumbo jumbo, how does a SERP Succession Bridge actually work? Here's a case history that illustrates the benefits of a SERP arrangement, as well as the ability to customize a plan to suit any need.

Case History: Mr. and Ms. Rancher

This is a story of a SERP Succession Bridge we installed at a South Texas ranch. My clients, Mr. & Mrs. Rancher, owned a 20,000-acre farm and ranch. Most of the property was native pasture on which they maintained about 5,000 head of cattle. This operation was only marginally profitable because of their skimpy grazing land and the historically poor beef prices. Ten years before I met the Rancher family, one of their cattle hands had convinced Mr. Rancher to convert their best grazing land, about 4,000 acres, to farmland. About half of the available farmland acreage was put into citrus. The balance went to fresh vegetables. The conversion of the grazing land almost sparked a revolt from the three classic "coy boy" children who would have rivaled Santa Anna and Sam Houston.

The kids, actually two children and a son-in-law, were cattle folks to the core. They felt that only "wusses" worked in the dirt. However, the family's fortune was dwindling fast as a cattle ranch, so the weary 62-year old cowboy patriarch went contrary to family feelings and followed the advice of a relatively new foreman who had farming experience.

Although some primo Texas pride took a beating, the humbling move proved very wise. After a couple of marginal years working with various vegetables, they finally settled on melons. Then the cash started coming to daddy. Just a couple of years before I arrived, the maturing citrus also had come on line to make good even better. By the time I arrived on the scene, Mr. Rancher was ordained a visionary and the key manager was considered a genius. On the other hand, the kids were still punching cows and going to rodeos.

Mr. Rancher was very straightforward. "The future of this third generation legacy depends upon prudent and opportunistic diversification. Although my kids have started respecting Ramon, I have lost respect for them and I believe that, in my absence, they would meddle with his authority and second-guess his decisions. I want you to establish a program that will require my kids to respect him and prevent him from getting recruited by one of our envious competitors."

I subsequently evaluated the business records and interviewed the family members, Ramon and several other key managers. The business was kicking out a couple million dollars per year cash flow after Mr. Rancher took a salary of $450,000 and paid the children $250,000 each. Ramon, on the other hand, was being paid a salary of $60,000, plus a discretionary bonus that brought his compensation up to approximately $85,000 per year.

Notably, the oldest daughter, Susan, who was divorced and trying to raise a couple of teenagers, worked about 25 hours per week as office manager. The middle child, Cathy, did not work in the business at all, but her husband, Art, was a cattle foreman. The youngest, Ricky Jr., was a reincarnated Jim Bowie, knife and all. His job was to oversee the nine hunting leases that brought in about $175,000 per year in net income. As a 23-year old, dedicated outdoors-man, Junior was just married and appropriately matched with a booted, blue jean baby who could stare down a mountain lion and tell a mortal man where to go in a New York second.

After my interviews, I appreciated Mr. Rancher's concern. For openers, it was a very difficult problem to schedule a couple of days when I could meet with all three heirs because of their preoccupation with rodeos, teenagers and deer hunting. No one would sit down with me. Instead, they took me with them as they pursued their various interests.

The obvious conclusion was that these kids were all into what the business was doing for them. Their Mom and Dad had never held them accountable and they had no grasp of what it really took to keep that ranch going. Ramon, on the other hand, was a 47-year old, self-educated, natural leader who had the respect of everyone but the kids. He was strong, proud and a profoundly independent person who was very appreciative of the opportunity Mr. Rancher had given him. He was the commodity that had brought the Rancher family to the promised land.

My counsel to Mr. & Mrs. Rancher was that business continuity would be no major stretch, but their goal of business succession without Ramon would be extremely difficult. The two major obstacles to succession would be finding a leader among their children and keeping Ramon. Notably, I told Mr. Rancher that he had been very fortunate that Ramon was so loyal, because, if he were of a mind, he could duplicate his job and make twice the money elsewhere.

I also suggested to Mr. Rancher that he was the major cause of his children's apparent lack of commitment. They were grossly overpaid and grossly under-managed.

This precarious combination of money and freedom had enabled them to have unrealistic opinions of their ability and most importantly, of Ramon's ability. There were other issues as well, such as a lack of a stock-transfer restriction agreement, inadequate job descriptions and a terribly outdated estate plan.

Surprisingly, Mr. & Mrs. Rancher offered no challenge to my observations. They both agreed that they had over-played the desire for their children to be successful. Without any prompting, they admitted that they had been protecting their children from failure because they did not want the children to relive the hardships they had experienced. Although they had never discussed it openly, they both acknowledged that protecting the children from hardship had been a disservice.

My recommendations included a long list of very important and laboriously technical corporate and estate planning refinements. However, the focal point of my recommendations was a family management company and a SERP Succession Bridge for Ramon and several other key managers. The purpose of this structure was to free up the kids to pursue the career of their dreams, initiate accountability and lock in Ramon to manage the business.

The four Rancher family members would own the management company. Mr. Rancher would hold operating control of a limited-liability corporation. Rancher Management would draw revenue from the various operations in the form of management fees. These management fees would be passed through to the various families. With this cash conduit in place, Mr. and Mrs. Rancher could relieve all of their children from the need or requirement to work in the business and not have to worry about their standard of living.

In more succinct terms, they could terminate their kids' bogus careers, get them out of Ramon's way, and invite them to reapply if they were of a mind to work. If they were unable to make a commitment to become role models for work ethic, they could pursue the hobby or career of their choice. In other words, security is assured, so lead, follow or get out of the way.

I suggested simultaneously that he promote Ramon to General Manager of the entire enterprise and give him an incentive-based pay plan that would enable him to double his income. His job description would include not only supervising business operations, but also leading a Management Advisory Board consisting of seven other managers who would collaborate as a management team. Ramon would also be responsible for training family members who expressed a genuine desire to be a role model employee. The other members of the MAB would assist Ramon in his mission as consideration for MAB participation and these managers would participate in the SERP based upon a simple 15% of compensation. Ramon would have a right to add or terminate participants on the MAB.

The job description emphasized that Ramon had no obligation to train any family member who was not willing to be a role model employee in whatever position they were assigned.

As motivation and incentive for Ramon, I also suggested that his SERP would have non-contingent funding of fifteen percent of his income, or a minimum of $15,000 per year. Supplementing this base, I suggested funding of an additional 10% of his income if he achieved annually agreed upon performance benchmarks. Vesting would be upon 15 years service, death, disability or involuntary termination. In addition to the above, I suggested a 25% bonus to the accumulated SERP funding upon Ramon's retirement in 15 years if he were able to turn over the general manager job to a family member acceptable to his parents and siblings.

As would be expected, Mr. & Mrs. Rancher were initially very confused by these concepts. The free-wheeling Mrs. Rancher had difficulty getting beyond the immense joy and satisfaction she was going to feel when she fired her son-in-law. Much to my surprise, they had no problem with telling their kids to apply for a job with Ramon. The fact that the management company would provide them adequate income to maintain a comfortable lifestyle relieved their concern about hurting someone's feelings.

On the other hand, it took them some time to understand the structure of the SERP Succession Bridge and that their only real risk would be $15,000 per year guaranteed contribution to Ramon's SERP. They were so fond of Ramon that they wanted to guarantee him a $50,000 per year contribution to make sure that he would not become frustrated with their children and quit. They ultimately realized that it was smarter to enhance his pay plan than over-pack the SERP. Fortunately, the attorney and accountant, both of whom had long-standing relationships with the family, were very supportive of my contention that Ramon would be equally motivated by an opportunity to educate his children and elevate his lifestyle.

The real excitement began when we started our implementation process. I did my best to prepare Mr. & Mrs. Rancher for the fireworks, but fell short. For openers, three old time employees who were not included in the SERP quit. Mr. Rancher, in spite of my warning, was caught totally unprepared. He was devastated by the emotional confrontations and called an emergency meeting to demand that these guys be included. Fortunately, Ramon, who was the key figure in the design of the SERP and MAB charter, showed his mettle. He shocked Mr. Rancher when he said that these old timers believed their tenure and the relationship with Mr. Rancher should generate privileges and concessions. And that was causing discord among the other employees. "Assuming you were going to give me authority to run this place, I was going to give them a shape up or ship out ultimatum. The fact that they quit in hissy fit has just saved me time and money. Although shocked again to hear this bold message from Ramon, Mr. Rancher calmed down and trusted Ramon's judgment. His trust was validated quickly as two of the three who had quit humbly asked for their jobs back within 30 days.

On the heels of the three offended old timers, the kids came over to their parents' home in the evening and expressed as a group that they were profoundly offended at being fired from their jobs and given management fees. They felt that it was ridiculous and embarrassing for them to report to Ramon. They appealed to Mr. Rancher to forget the garbage I had been feeding him and rely upon them to run the company. In turn, both of the employed children and the son-in-law said that they were capable of taking over as general manager whenever Mr. Rancher retired.

Mr. Rancher confided in me later that this was the toughest meeting of all time. One side of him wanted to enable his kids and one side wanted to kick their butts up around their ears. Fortunately, he did neither. He acknowledged the only thing he had been unable to give his children was what they needed most -- accountability. He later said, "my children will never develop as managers until they understand the dynamics of being a good employee." So, with regrets but conviction, Mr. Rancher sent them packing, referring them to Ramon to see about a job.

Then all three of the children and the son-in-law as a group arranged a surprise meeting with Mrs. Rancher and pleaded with her to talk some sense into Dad. When Mr. Rancher heard about this meeting, he suspended all four of them for 90 days with these parting words: "If you want to work in this company, you will have to come in through Ramon."

As if this weren't enough excitement, Ramon got squirrelly. When I presented the concept of the SERP to him, he was appreciative, but unusually quiet. Later, after reviewing it, he called me and said he did not want the SERP. Although he appreciated the potential $15,000 to $50,000 contribution to his retirement security, he just felt uncomfortable about the arrangement.

The pay plan enhancement was generous, plenty for his circumstances. The SERP was perfect for the supporting managers, but he would rather not participate. Needless to say, after having told Mr. Rancher how much Ramon was going to appreciate this tremendous benefit, I felt like a buffoon.

Mr. Rancher, the other advisors and I spoke with Ramon, attempting to determine what was on his mind. Was it the non-compete covenant? No, he had the utmost respect for Mr. Rancher and had no intention of leaving the job. Was it the responsibility of supervising the kids? No, he was raised in a large family and, as the oldest child, had dealt with these issues many times before. He liked the kids, but really put no great stock in whether they liked him. I concluded that Ramon was scared of the control that substantial money inside a SERP could have upon him. He was a unique, highly focused, hard working and independent young man who felt he would be compromised if someone "owned" him.

At that point I struggled to explain to Mr. Rancher that he should not expect Ramon to bail out on him simply because he did not want the SERP. After several explanations, he understood that Ramon wanted the financial security but did not want to feel controlled. I explained that Ramon's reaction was an affirmation of the power of a golden handcuff. When he accepted my theory, I recommended that we proceed with the full scope of our plan. We would appoint him general manager and institute the exciting new pay plan.

Furthermore, initially unbeknownst to Ramon, we would develop the SERP documents and begin setting aside the funding generated by his pay plan. At the end of the first year, we would advise Ramon that a unilateral plan was in place, and -- if at a later date he chose to endorse the documents and if he met the service terms -- he would be paid the retirement benefits. We would further advise him that, if and when he elected to endorse the plan, he would be eligible for the 25% successor bonus and survivor's benefit for his family in the event of his death.

Ramon assumed the general manager role as though it was made for him. He and Mr. Rancher had a great relationship and it became immediately apparent that they were going to work well together. Ramon designed an effective management structure and, with the help of a friend who had experience as a human resources director, developed job descriptions and innovative pay plans for each position. Then, within the existing ranks, he slowly and deliberately began filling positions. To his credit, he realized that Mr. Rancher's children might be returning and it would be popular if he had jobs for them.

We also began having monthly family management company meetings. When I called each of the kids and invited them, none of them planned to attend because "they did not want to cause their parents any problems." I was surprised to see them at the first meeting. Later I learned that Mr. Rancher had informed them they did not have to attend meetings, but if they didn't, there would be no distributions. His brash Texas logic was "being lazy was one thing, being a childish dumb-ass was something else altogether."

In the meantime, I had been prepared to distribute a Family Business Employ-ment Policy and a list of Family Member Employment Expectations. In the unexpected presence of the children, I stammered and diverted to issues on corpo-rate structuring and estate planning. Having completed those, the now bolder and more confrontational Mr. Rancher called for discussion and ultimately approved both policies in the form of corporate resolutions. Without a word of chastisement, he scuttled the good ship "Enabler."

Although spoiled, the kids were no dummies and they got the message. There were no more attempts to subvert Mr. Rancher's succession plan. Over the next 12 months, by virtue of sitting in management company meetings, they came to under-stand that their Daddy was going to run the ranch like a business, give them an opportunity for succession, and in the absence of successors, sell the business when Ramon retired.

As soon as the 90 days were up, Junior came in and asked Ramon for a job. To Ramon's credit, he sent Junior to an outlying operation. Mr. Rancher did not know he had gone back to work for another 60 days. Art was next, and interestingly enough, he did not like the job Ramon offered him. So, much to Mrs. Rancher's delight, he found a job to his liking with a trucking company in town. Susan, with the blessing of her parents, recognized that her highest calling was to her teenagers, so she became a full-time mother.

Five years down the road, this once frustrating, volatile and unproductive situation was back on track. Susan's teenagers graduated from high school and she began working as an accounts payable clerk and going to night school to get a degree in accounting. She enjoyed her job but realized that, based upon the growth created by Ramon, she might not ever want the responsibility of office manager. Ricky had been working part-time and pursuing a degree in business administration. He had become a disciple of Ramon with an expressed goal of following in his footsteps. Ramon was impressed with his attitude and said only time would determine the level of his commitment. Art, to his credit, became the vice-president of the trucking company. He accepted an opportunity to purchase stock and there is a reasonable chance that one day he and Cathy will own that baby.

Ramon, to no one's surprise, continued kicking butt and taking names. As this book went to press, the cattle operation had been further reduced and the profitability of the ranch had tripled.

And when he learned that we had already put the SERP in place, he again objected. I met with him several times to give him assurances that this benefit was provided totally at the discretion of Mr. Rancher and that he should not feel pressured by these circumstances.

Mr. Rancher astutely said, "You just keep doing your job and don't pay any attention to what I do with my money." A year later, Ramon casually asked how much was in the funding reserve account and was surprised to learn it held more than $100,000.

If he signed the plan and then died, would his wife and children receive that money, he asked?

I said no. If he died, they would receive the proceeds of a key-man life insurance policy worth $1.1 million. He hardly said another word through lunch. About two weeks later, Mr. Rancher sent me a copy of the SERP agreement that Ramon had endorsed with a note quoting something I had expressed to him many times: "The difficult we do right away. The impossible takes a little time."

Today, this organization has challenging moments, but no one is confused as to specific roles and no one misunderstands who is leading. Ramon is happy and secure. Mr. and Mrs. Rancher feel fortunate to have him as a permanent member of their organization. The kids have learned how to be employees and are on their way to understanding that, as a member of the ownership family, they were given prominence, but in business they must earn significance.

7 The Contingency Succession Bridge

The next variation of Succession Bridge is what we call the Key Manager Contingency Bridge. This is a SERP with extra bells and whistles to protect the family's business from the possible death or disability of the only family member who is currently capable of operating the business. Classically, the Contingency Bridge is a succession structure utilized to address business continuity concerns of a relatively young business owner, 30 to 50 years old, with young, late arriving, or unrefined children who are not ready to assume a management leadership role.

The key predicate to the Succession Bridge is that the owner hopes and even anticipates that the son or daughter will be ready and able to fill a succession leadership role, or would at least give serious consideration to doing so. Faced with the possibility that if the owner were unable to perform, his family would lose a very lucrative business, the business owner rejects the default reaction, "just sell the business."

Why address this remote contingency? Hopefully because you have so much passion for business succession that you could not bear the thought that your kids or partners would not have a chance to carry on what you have started.

With hope that a child will be motivated to come in the business and faith that the child will have the core competencies to serve as a leader, a <u>contingency plan is deemed prudent.</u>

However, more specific answers could be any one of several, including too much investment in the business, too many operational liabilities, too much pride in the family legacy or too much concern for the welfare of all those associated with the business. My personal justification for a Contingency Bridge is stewardship responsibility.

If you have developed a successful business, you did not do it alone. Family members, including spouses and children, provided encouragement and support while you were obsessing over making your mark on the business world. Partners and employees gave you all they had to help you convert your dream into reality. Banks, manufacturers and vendors gambled that your passion would pay off. And, from my perspective, regardless of your circumstances, your age, or wavering goals, you owe these loved ones and business associates a contingency plan that will not leave them high and dry in the event of your death or disability.

The Contingency Bridge becomes viable when the owner believes that, in the event of his death or disability, a key manager with a vested interest could serve as a management bridge to the next generation.

The ultimate goal of the Key Manager Contingency Bridge is to maintain the power and cultural strength of the business until one or more children have an opportunity to mature, assume the leadership role and <u>qualify as the next generation leader.</u>

The Bridge is established by establishing an agreement with one or more key managers that, in the event of the owner's death or disability, the manager(s) will assume operation responsibility and train the family successors. This key manager(s) has the very special character, personality and skills to operate the business, and deal effectively with the surviving spouse and the prospective successor children.

At this point, it bears mentioning that you cannot spontaneously convert a key manager into a very special key manager. You either have one, have one in development, are on the market in search of one, or you had best consider other options. It also bears mentioning that this very special key manager must meet three simple criteria: you like them, you trust them and you are impressed with their ability.

The motivating incentive for this unique manager is a very lucrative SERP and the possibility of ownership. The SERP provides significant financial incentives that specifically vest at a time when it is reasonable to assume that the children will have had an opportunity to mature and/or acquire the needed experience and skills. As with the "Mr. Rancher" illustration in the previous chapter, other key managers may also be included in the SERP to assure that the management support team stays in place.

A Contingency Bridge is only appropriate for fully mature managers because, after adoption, the manager could be called upon to assume the helm at any time. This program offers win/ win opportunities. If, as expected, the owner lives, the SERP will provide the special key manager exciting financial benefits. Upon retirement the SERP will represent a substantial enhancement of financial security. In the event the manager quits before retirement, the business would suffer, but the owner would recover the forfeited SERP reserve to offset the loss. In the event the owner dies, the key manager's continuity becomes critical to the survival of the business. In this event, the Contingency Succession Bridge provides the resources for the key manager to become a minority stockholder.

The most probable course of events is that the owner will live a full life. Therefore, the SERP must stand alone as a golden handcuff. The retirement benefit would be a byproduct of an affordable and compatible funding formula as described in the preceding chapters. When considering Contingency Bridge funding, do not be penny wise and succession stupid. Remember that if this management and leadership gap is not filled, your business will be road kill.

Also, as discussed earlier, the formula could vary from a very simple fixed retirement/termination benefit payable for a specific number of years to a variable benefit based upon percentage-of-compensation funding and the investment return of the reserve. Phantom stock could also be utilized. However, with the family legacy on the line, the only reliable plan is to make the funding both simple and significant.

The second defining aspect of a Contingency Succession Bridge is a stock purchase "put." The business owner and the manager enter into a formal stock-purchase contract that states that, in the event of the owner's death prior to a specified date, the manager will vest on the accumulated SERP funding and a life insurance policy on the owner's life. Subsequently the net after-tax distribution from the SERP, plus the life insurance proceeds, would be pledged to the purchase of a predetermined amount of the business, perhaps 25%, at a predetermined price.

The fundamental assumption of a Contingency Bridge is that a more attractive, golden handcuff is required to convince a special key manager to assume the responsibility for both business continuity and training/mentoring family members to become successors. A better than average SERP (remember Ramon), plus the possibility of stock ownership, are assumed to be appropriate benefit kickers that will motivate the manager to hang in there in the midst of calamity, when most managers would be rushing for the door.

The process of implementation follows that of the SERP, discussed in the previous chapters, plus the additional time and effort required to address and document the contingency stock purchase arrangement. Notably, time is needed for the key manager, the business owner and the owner's spouse or children to consider the prospective implications of a minority stockholder arrangement. It is very important that the spouse and adult children are involved in these discussions because they are the ones who may have to deal with a new, minority partner.

There is nothing to gain and much to lose if a shallow, hasty implementation process attempts to create a partnership between a widow/child and a manager who do not express mutual respect.

A traumatic death or disability creates enough problems.

Life insurance on the owner is critical to providing the contingent cash to fund the purchase of stock from the deceased owner's estate. It is presumed that the SERP accumulations would be insufficient in the early years to pay for the stock. The insurance can be reduced as the SERP reserve grows. Disability buyout insurance is also available. The key manager would own insurance within an irrevocable trust administered by a third party, typically the business owner's attorney or accountant. The trust documents would state that, in the event of the owner's death or disability, the trustee of both the stock purchase agreement and the irrevocable trust would utilize the manager's accumulated SERP reserves and the insurance proceeds to purchase stock. Premiums on the insurance are paid by the manager through an insurance premium bonus.

This business equity would be intended to lock in the special key manager and give him the incentive to generate profits in the business on behalf of the business owner's widow and children who, in the meantime, are hopefully developing the skills and experience to one day assume management control. The widow would also receive attractive liquidity that would reduce the family's vulnerability to a downturn in the value of the business in exchange for the stock. In the event the widow just wants to get out of the business, the new partner may have sufficient equity to obtain financing for a buyout. On the other hand, if a buyout were not feasible, the manager's equity ownership would provide sufficient vested interest to lead a sales process that pursued top dollar in the market. The stock owned by the key manager would also satisfy the equity ownership requirements for the successor addendum of franchise agreements. This is specifically important in the automobile and beverage wholesaling business.

No doubt, the greatest concern regarding a plan to potentially sell stock to a key manager is getting the stock back. This legitimate and prudent concern is addressed in the plan documentation. The stock that the key manager would receive would be controlled by the previously mentioned Stockholders' Agreement between the owner, the manager, the corporation and the trustee. This agreement would document the desired controls, restrictions and parameters of stock ownership and inevitable stock disposition. The provisions would include, as expressed above, the specific number of shares that the key manager can purchase, the criteria for valuing the stock and the requirement that the accumulated SERP equity or life insurance proceeds be used to purchase the specified stock.

The agreement would further state that the family and/or the corporation would repurchase the key manager's stock upon employment termination for any reason. Notably, the agreement would stipulate specific buy-back stock valuation procedures. Generally I suggest that the stockholder's agreement state that, in the event the key manager quits prior to retirement or a minimum number of years of service, or if the key manager is terminated for cause, the stock will be repurchased for purchase price or discounted fair market value as determined by a qualified appraiser, whichever is less.

In the event the manager dies, is terminated without cause or retires after the stipulated number of "bridge" years, the stock would be repurchased for the original purchase price or appraised fair market value, whichever is greater. Terms of payment for the stock would also be more favorable in the event of the key manager's death or retirement.

In theory, this agreement should provide that, if the key manager is working for family members who are less informed, less confident and more dependent, the importance of this contractual agreement is greatly elevated. And when the new minority stockholder hangs in there and successfully performs the Succession Bridge mission, the sale of the stock would provide a very handsome reward.

The final facet of the Key Manager Contingency Bridge is an employment contract for the key manager. Any time money is set aside as an incentive for employment, owners should go to the effort to document the specific services expected from the manager, the parameters of acceptable behavior and the method of measuring both.

The fundamental benefit of this process is to set the stage for deliberate explanation and negotiations that facilitate a clear understanding of expectations between the owner and key manager. In the event of the owner's death, these expectations establish the foundation for performance accountability. The importance of this documentation can best be appreciated when one considers that a strong willed, highly confident and well informed manager may be working for a widow and/or children who are less informed, less confident and, more specifically, both dependent and vulnerable. In the absence of this stabilizing documentation, there is a much higher probability of an ambitious initiative by the manager who instinctively takes advantage of situational leverage. The fact that the key manager could become a stockholder only adds greater emphasis to the need for a documented agreement.

One of the most important provisions of the employment contract is the expression of the manager's responsibility to train the successors whom the owner anticipates will enter the business.

After all, supporting and training these successors is the motivating purpose of the Key Manager Contingency Succession Bridge. Of course, the employment agreement would also include traditional covenants prohibiting competing in the local market or divulging proprietary information and the grounds for termination for cause.

The current pay plan and any enhancements in the event of the owner's death would be expressed as an attachment. Do not require the surviving widow or her representative to negotiate a pay plan with a new stockholder. A special key manager is no dummy. He would recognize his leverage and more than likely use it.

I've had the opportunity to implement a Contingency Succession Bridge on many occasions. Fortunately, in most instances, the owner did not die or become disabled and the golden handcuff SERP became the operative incentive for the key manager. However, the norm of succession planning is the bizarre of life.

Here's a case history that illustrates the benefits of thinking through the full menu of contingency:

Case History: Jack, The Beer Wholesaler

A 43-year-old beer wholesaler needed a Contingency Bridge to protect a business succession opportunity for his two sons, who were still in high school. My client, Jack, implemented the program with his general manager, Bill, who had been hired by his father right out of high school. Bill was about the same age as Jack but, due to a different socioeconomic background, had less refinement and less formal education.

Although Bill was a blue-collar guy, he had done very well for himself through long hours, hard work and dedication. He was, by any measure, a natural for the beer business and had worked his way up through the ranks. Bill had developed into a complete management package with the total support of Jack and, even more impressively, the franchiser brewery.

Actually, the brewery had thought so much of Bill that, to Jack's dismay, they had offered to finance him in the purchase of a separate franchise in an under-performing market.

Jack and his wife, Jill, were the benefactors of excellent planning on the part of Jack's parents. Appreciative of prior efforts, they were also attentive to estate planning details and the possibility that the succession (the good life) of their distributorship to the third generation could be tanked in the event of Jack's death or disability within the next 10 or 15 years.

Historically, the breweries, such as Anheuser Busch, Miller and Coors, are not very tolerant of passive caretaker owners of their distributorships. Astutely, Jill realized that, if Jack were to predecease her, she would probably have difficulty holding onto the franchise because she had never worked in management. Jack was also not too pleased with the prospect of losing Bill. At best, that would mean that he would have to go through the hassle of finding Bill's replacement. At worst, he would have to go back to work. Perish that thought, as he had accumulated a vast array of expensive boats, airplanes and homes to occupy the time.

Jack was not fond of the long days and demanding schedule required to operate a beer distributorship. He had served as general manager under his hub-and-spoke taskmaster father.

However, upon his father's death, he immediately promoted Bill from sales manager to general manager and took an empowerment approach to leadership that enabled him to spend more time with his family and hobbies. With this history supporting his thinking, and with me reminding him of his risks, we preempted Bill's departure to purchase his own franchise with a Key Manager Contingency Bridge.

Fortunately, Bill had a strong attachment to his community and was impressed with the lucrative retirement package. Specifically, if Bill continued to meet reasonable business growth expectations, he would continue to receive his salary for 10 years after age 62.

The approximate value of the total retirement package would be based upon a stock appreciation right. Bill would receive 25% of the growth in the value of the business at the time of his retirement, with the value of the business at that time pegged at $3.00 for every case of beer sold. The business was currently selling three million cases per year. In 20 years, when he could retire, we figured the business should be doing about eight million cases per year.

At this reasonable growth assumption, the growth in business value would be worth $15 million. Twenty five percent would be worth $3.75 million to Bill. Those growth assumptions would subsequently fund a retirement income for Jack of $375,000 per year for 10 years. If Bill died, the SERP guaranteed his designated beneficiary that same amount. On the other hand, if Jack, who was a poster boy for middle age fitness, were to die prior to Bill's retirement, Bill would be provided funding to purchase 25% of the business through a life insurance policy on Jack's life.

This aspect of the plan got little attention, as Mr. Jack appeared to be the picture of health and fitness. He was an avid outdoorsman, enjoying jogging, boating and skiing. Jill also was a fitness buff. Bill's reliability gave them the freedom to lead the good life.

Bill's response to this proposal was classic. "Hey, I can deal with these alternatives: A: I win, B: I win and C: I win.

"Why should I move away from my kids to own a second-class distributorship (he was divorced), disrupt the outstanding team I have put together, put my meager net worth at risk and take on the challenge of rebuilding a whole new business? With this package, I am building financial security without the risk of being a new business owner and I can continue to build on what I have started. For me, this is a no-brainer."

Fortunately, implementation of the Succession Bridge proceeded as planned. There were no hitches in the design, adoption and funding of the plan. Their relationships were terrific, so they were able to talk through most issues without help. Other than the annual servicing reviews that confirmed business value and accrued retirement benefits, little attention was paid to existence of a Contingency Bridge. Bill was content with the security he was building and Jack and Jill felt secure pursuing their many hobbies.

Six years later circumstances changed. While on a ski trip with a group of friends, Jack developed an upset stomach and a fever. Both he and his friends concluded that he had either contracted the flu or was reacting to some bad wine. He stayed in the condo while the others skied and progressively got worse. That evening he went to the local walk-in clinic, where they also supported the contention that he had the flu.

The next day, with no abatement in his fever, he returned to the doctor, who admitted him to the hospital, where he was found to have acute appendicitis. During an appendectomy, surgeons discovered that the appendix had ruptured. Three days later, Jack, the symbol of fitness and long life expectancy, died of complications.

To say that his family, friends and employees were shocked would be a profound understatement. The funeral was a large dramatic event supported by eulogies from friends, politicians, fellow beer distributors and the dependably eloquent brewery management.

Despite his untimely death, the business didn't miss a beat because of Jack's planning. The brewery, which traditionally takes a very active role in franchise succession, did not offer a single word of concern. They had signed off on this program six years earlier and had approved Bill as the Successor Wholesaler. Bill remained vigilant as the general manager and assumed the duties of chief operating officer. With the triggering of the Contingency Bridge approximately 60 days after Jack's death, Bill also became a 25% owner, which escalated his highly conservative business net worth to approximately $3 million. Of course, this stock was locked down through a stockholder's agreement executed six years earlier when the bridge had been initiated. The agreement restricted Bill from selling the stock to anyone outside of Jack's family and it substantially discounted the purchase price of Bill's stock if he were to quit work before 62.

Regardless of the restrictions, Bill was a humble, appreciative, unassuming and professional. In fact, he felt very awkward for realizing an advantage from Jack's death. He told Jill that she didn't have to sell him stock because he wasn't going anywhere. He was pleased with how he was being treated. However, Jill insisted on following through with her husband's plan, partly at the insistence of the predictably pushy suits from the brewery.

As the selling party, Jill had an additional $3 million in cash from the proceeds of the sale. Nevertheless, Jill was not exactly pleased with the unexpected reality that she now had a partner with whom she would have to take an equitable approach to corporate benefits. She also would be relinquishing 25% of the subchapter-S dividends.

She also astutely recognized that, according to the stockholders' agreement, she or her two sons would be obliged to buy back Bill's newly acquired stock upon his retirement, death or disability. This was a natural point of concern and she was greatly relieved when I explained to her that the down payment needed to buy back Bill's stock was already in place in the form of Bill's golden handcuff salary continuation reserve. It had also come to her in exchange for Bill's stock.

Jill's two sons, aged 22 and 24, were naturally grieved at the loss of their father, but also relieved to have Bill as their continuing mentor. Bill clearly understood that his job now included training the young men. The boys looked favorably at the opportunity for training, as well as the security of continuing to work under Bill's supervision and guidance. The Key Man Contingency Bridge was working according to our highest expectations.

Although Bill and Jill had started out awkwardly, Bill was very accommodating. After a year or so, they had worked out the details of corporate boats, airplanes and vacation homes. Fortunately, we had specified in the stockholder's agreement how profits would be distributed. After a couple of years, Bill and Jill developed a very good working relationship. Actually this Contingency Bridge would have been a fabulously boring success but for how well Jill and Bill worked together.

As circumstances unfolded, the situation was reasonably well described three years after Jack's death by the questions of Jill's oldest son, who was not gifted with the ability to recognize the obvious. "Why am I always seeing Mom in Bill's office? I can hardly get enough one-on-one time with him to discuss our marketing plans or route adjustments. Why do they both also insist on going to those brewery and association meetings in Vegas? Since when did the brewery start having monthly meetings in Vegas?"

You guessed it. Jill and Bill had developed a very close working relationship. Evidently "Einstein" (the oldest son) whined so much about not getting enough time with Bill that Jill finally came clean. Jill said that the common love she and Bill had for the business ultimately had evolved into love for each other. She apologized for her secretive behavior, but made no apology for not liking the solitary life. Bill was smart. He did not say much of anything because he was embarrassed with the appearance that he might have been gold digging. All he did was deflect questions regarding their relationship with; "You ought to talk to Jill about that."

As was reasonably predictable, the boys created quite a fuss. They were both angry and confused. They had never thought of Bill as a stepfather. He was the hired help. They enjoyed working with him, respected him as a supervisor. Bill's promotion to step-dad was not even on their map. However, they felt access to their Mom was not a reasonable fringe benefit for being general manager, chief operating officer and partner. They felt betrayed by Bill.

Jack's surviving mother was also taken back by these developments. She and her grandsons called a meeting, with the bank serving as a fiduciary of the trust that held the distributorship stock. The boys and Granny were so outraged that they did not realize that they would need Jill's approval, as the other co-trustee, to terminate Bill.

To emphasize their disappointment with the circumstances, both of the boys quit the business and moved out of town. This widow and key man hookup became quite the gossip gem. Four years after Jack's death, Jill and Bill married. Neither the sons nor Granny attended the ceremony. Much to the shock of Jill's two sons, all of the family's friends attended the festivities. Furthermore, none of the other managers quit and the distributorship did not fall on hard times.

Actually, to the contrary, the business thrived. Rumors started that the place was doing better without the owners' sons involved. The brewery's only interest was in selling beer and Bill was showing that he could hustle the suds.

Getting a bit nervous about their seats on the bus, the boys ultimately confronted their Mom. She wanted me at the meeting to act as a control rod. Jill listened to them whine for about 10 minutes about losing their mother to the hired help.

Then, after having her fill of their self-pity, she cleared the air with, "You boys have got it all wrong. Bill did not pursue me; I pursued him. Actually, he held me off out of his concern for how our relationship might appear to you. It was no easy task to convince him that both of you were mature enough to handle this because you would put my feelings as the higher priority. Obviously, I was wrong."

Essentially she told them they were welcome to a job when they stopped the pity party, grew up and regained a positive team attitude. Otherwise, they could pursue independent careers or, in other words, work for a living. Most succinctly, she expressed that she was a big girl and she could take care of herself.

On the secondary subject of the business, I pointed out to the boys that they really had little to be concerned about. Their father's stock was in a trust that, upon their mother's retirement or death, would be distributed to them (not Bill). Furthermore, I had personally supervised the adoption of an ante-nuptial agreement that protected their mother's assets, including her stock, from the vagaries of a divorce court's property partition. And, as they were aware, Bill's minority stock was subject to buy-back upon his retirement or employment termination.

In fact, the biggest hazard to succession would occur if neither one of them returned to the business to qualify as the successor wholesaler when Bill retired. Fortunately, the reality of life shared by their mother and humbling experiences in the real world helped soften their attitudes toward their mother. Evidently, they experienced a few of the educational realities of being a true employee. Aside from the family friction, it actually had done the two boys a world of good to experience life as a pauper versus a prince.

I cannot guarantee such far-reaching benefits in all Contingency Succession Bridges, but clearly they can be dynamic succession vehicles. Actually most Contingency Bridges never are fully deployed because Dad does not die prematurely. The SERP becomes the operative Succession Bridge structure. However, the cost of the SERP was considered reasonable if the Contingency Bridge candidate stayed in place and rendered exceptional service until retirement. He would be worth every dollar that was set aside as a Bridge for the family legacy. If tragedy occurred, the contingency was covered through the minority equity position.

Unfortunately, there are potential weaknesses to the planning technique. Notably, as with all business relationships, the strength of this structure is dependent upon the character of the players. However, with quality players, this structure gives hope and peace of mind regarding contingencies that otherwise only yield precarious uncertainty.

The Key Manager Equity Bridge

We have all heard, usually when it is the last thing we want to hear, that money isn't everything. In the realm of securing a Succession Bridge, we must be prepared to deal with managers who take this cliché to heart. The fact is, there are circumstances when a Key Manager SERP Succession Bridge just will not get the job done. All reasonable forms of financial incentives involving creative structures such as a SERP, phantom stock or stock appreciation rights fail to motivate a very special key manager to enter into a Succession Bridge arrangement. Usually, his response to these purely financial incentives is: "I am not impressed with the money and I am not going to restrict my career options by signing a non-compete agreement."

Something more is needed to seal the deal, a piece of the proverbial rock. When faced with this equity obsession, by really hot managers in their 30's and 40's, owners are very likely wasting breath talking about financial incentives. If his lack of responsiveness to a significant financial golden handcuff gives the owner a sense of panic, it is time to recognize he is not your ordinary key manager.

The owner must then reconcile just how disastrous it would be if this manager moved on to a new job or worked for a competitor.

What is the likelihood of losing this manager? What are the consequences of losing this manager? How risky would it be for this manager to become a stockholder partner? Depending upon succession priorities and circumstances, this may be a risk that the owner is willing to take or, frankly, one that has to be taken.

Subsequently, there are only three viable courses of action: up the ante on the SERP in hope that you can get the manager's attention, forget the whole Succession Bridge concept and not worry about the prospects of the manager leaving or make a proposal for an Equity Bridge.

If you think you can afford to increase the contribution to the SERP, why not make an offer to sweeten the pot? If the manager is still not interested in signing the covenants, step back and consider the circumstances. Put your thinking cap on. This manager is telling you something. He is saying he's in the process of looking for a new job, he's only interested in owning stock or he's just a certified weirdo. If you are having trouble figuring this out, get some help from a succession planner.

Also, give some serious thought about how important this manager is to your operation and the succession of the operation in your absence. The manager has given you some very important information and it is now time to read the tea leaves. If you think there is interest in a new job, you just might want to pick up the pace of your thinking before circumstances are out of your control. If you think you are dealing with a weirdo, keep on pushing and the answer will become self-evident in short order. The best way to deal with a weirdo is acknowledge their preference and get back to business. Don't waste your time trying to rationalize why they should be a Succession Bridge because it has now become clear that they do not qualify.

If you suspect that the only incentive that will motivate the manager is owning stock, you must assess how valuable this manager is. Can you afford to lose this hot shot? If you can, call the bluff and stay with a SERP Succession Bridge proposal. If you cannot afford this risk, we are dealing with a very special key manager and it is time to present a Key Manager Equity Succession Bridge.

The issues or perceived risks surrounding the acceptance of a very special key manager as a partner are what I classify as "eco/emo" -- a dicey combination of economic and emotional issues. The gamut of questions includes:

- Will a partner impact my control?
- Will my very special manager and partner become an ego monster?
- Could my new partner become even more demanding after he holds me up for stock?
- Could this stock get passed on from my partner to his heirs, ex-wife or creditor?

The hardcore reality is that, yes, any of these circumstances, and even worse, could occur. Therefore, an owner had better believe that this manager holds the keys to the vault and is able to leap buildings with a single bound. Indeed, this must be a very special manager, bordering on the irreplaceable, before they ought to be made a stockholder. If that must happen, however, don't panic. In the real world of comprehensive, sophisticated succession planning, measures can be taken to preempt these risks. We will discuss these later in more depth.

The Key Manager Equity Succession Bridge is the first of two programs that provide immediate opportunities for providing golden handcuff equity ownership for very special key managers who feel they cannot achieve career gratification without stock ownership. The utilization of business equity as the bonding tool is a natural advancement in the Succession Bridge concept. However, this structure is simpler than the Contingency Bridge, because there is no alternative funding structure. There is no Supplemental Executive Retirement Plan to design, document and fund that provides for the non-equity purchasing contingency.

The bedrock of this concept is an opportunity for the key manager to own stock in the business, immediately, or at some designated time. Owners shouldn't suffer heart palpitations. The stock isn't just handed over. Generally, the very special key manager is provided an opportunity to confirm his worthiness to be a stockholder and to earn or purchase equity in the business. This isn't a stock giveaway.

Regardless of how outstanding their skills may be or how valuable they are to the business, making a gift of stock to a key manager is contradictory to building a vested interest and achieving a <u>proprietary attitude.</u>

As expressed in my previous book, regardless of family or key manager, less respect is given to business equity that did not cost money, time and special effort.

Stock can be transferred to a key manager in two ways, sale or bonus. An Equity Succession Bridge generally has two distinct steps. The Equity Bridge is usually initiated with the sale of stock to the very special key manager. As we will discuss later, the transfer could be through a stock bonus, but this will have less meaning for the manager. This initial stock acquisition is designed to seal the deal by requiring a financial commitment by the key manager. Most of the time they do not have much money. That is OK.

However, whatever they have, we want it paid down on this initial transaction. A second mortgage on the home or a loan against a 401(k) plan will be just fine. An Equity Succession Bridge merits a financial commitment, otherwise you might be embarrassed to find that this manager was the weirdo we mentioned earlier. No doubt, if he really wants to be a stockholder, he will come up with some cash from home, retirement plan, Mama or friends. Remember, without some cash investment, regardless of how modest, an Equity Succession Bridge is a risky transaction.

The second step is the issuance of stock purchase options. Actually, this is a simultaneous transaction. In order to get the options, the manager has to make an initial investment. As you might expect from prior design discussions, the exercise of these options will be predicated upon meeting criteria, generally centered on continued service and achieving or maintaining benchmark performance. The stockholder's agreement specifies the other terms of the option, including striking price.

The initial purchase of stock and the awarding of stock options is a memorable undertaking that provides the very special key manager with both the prestigious recognition of an equity partner and a poignant understanding of the hazards and handicaps of being a stockholder. Life as a business owner takes on a whole new perspective when eager beaver hot shots draw down savings, take a home mortgage or some other measure to write a check and put their assets as risk.

The documentation package of the Equity Bridge further formalizes the key manager's ability to purchase any additional stock beyond the initial purchase. The stock purchase provisions clearly stipulate the amount of additional stock that can be purchased and the terms. Notably, the terms of purchase usually limit the source of funds to incentive bonuses and dividends on the initial stock purchase to motivate the very special manager to higher levels of performance. This stipulation, if utilized, also protracts the buy-in period. The manager is relieved of the need to come up with more cash and the owner is given an opportunity to examine how the new partner behaves.

In order to allay fears, the stock obtained by the key manager is subject to ironclad stock transfer restrictions and stock repurchase provisions in the Stockholder's Agreement. Specifically, if the manager terminates employment for any reason, the owner gets the stock back via a repurchase agreement. The stockholder's agreement documents the arrangement to ensure the owner's peace of mind and the handcuff aspect of the Equity Bridge.

It would be reasonable to ask why a manager would want to spend his hard earned money to purchase this stock. After all, they would have to sell it back to the owner if they terminated employment for any reason. If the business were to go down the tubes, the manager could actually lose money.

To answer this question, one must understand the nature of the person involved. The very special key manager wants this stock for several reasons, foremost because he simply is driven to be an owner. Maybe this was something that was branded on his brain as a youth. Regardless, having a piece of the rock means more to them than any reasonable monetary award. Risk is no big deal. This unique breed of manager believes that, if they are not provided with an opportunity to own stock in the business, it is just a matter of time before they go out and find this opportunity.

Further, there are perceived financial incentives to owning stock, including dividends, retained earnings and appreciation in value.

A manager's willingness to accept the market risks and the borrowing risks of becoming a stockholder is a good indication of the commitment they are going to make to maintain and grow the profitability of the company.

Voila! That is what a Succession Bridge is all about!

Therefore, I believe that an Equity Succession Bridge requiring an out-of-pocket investment by a key manager provides more than a SERP.

The Stockholders Agreement of the Succession Bridge typically provides the opportunity for the purchase of 10% - 30% of stock. The most common key man ownership level is at 20%. Ownership in excess of 30% generally presumes other considerations, such as a buyout. By and large, the amount of equity a manager receives is contingent upon existing stock ownership circumstances, the manager's service history and how much the business and the family depend upon his services.

The longer a manager has been a key player in the business, and the greater the contribution to business success, the greater the stock award. The greater the value of the business, the lower the percentage of stock the key manager can afford to purchase. Further, the earnings and financial resources of the key manager impact the amount of the stock that can be purchased or how much income tax he can afford to pay on stock bonuses. These factors dominate the determination of what would be a feasible equity position for the manager.

A Succession Bridge provides an opportunity for the key manager to convert sweat equity into real equity. This sweat equity conversion is predicated upon a long-term service commitment, a bargain sale and reasonable stock purchase terms. The long-term commitment is the essence of a Succession Bridge endeavor. Remember: We are only offering stock to lock in this exceptional manager so that he will continue to diligently lead the business and serve as mentor and guide to family successors. The stock purchase and sale terms convert sweat to stock ownership over 10 to 20 years. The most common time frame is 15 years.

As generous as these packages can be, there still are times when the manager needs a wake-up call. In a recent negotiation with the non-family president (the key manager) of a family-owned bank, the young president was offered stock options that would vest over 20 years. He appreciated the opportunity to purchase stock in the future, but said the program did not adequately recognize his prior 22 years of service. He wanted us to bonus him stock immediately, so he would have something to show for his previous contributions.

My reaction was that any immediate vesting of stock ownership was counter-productive to the intent of the Golden Handcuff. I cut short his otherwise very reasonable argument by explaining that the invitation for him to participate in the program, along with the bargain option price, was the recognition he sought for past service. I invited him to look around the bank and the banking community to determine if anyone was being offered any better opportunities. I emphasized that his acquisition of stock would be dependent upon his continued performance.

Before we go much further in our discussion of stock purchase documentation, I want to emphasize that an Equity Succession Bridge is also expected to adopt an employment contract that records the customary non-compete, privacy and non-recruitment covenants. These are fundamental with all Succession Bridge structures. Just because a manager is becoming a stockholder does not make him immune from doing potentially stupid, harmful or resentful things. We have spent much time describing and justifying these covenants. Suffice it to say that covenants are also fundamental documentation of the Equity Bridge.

We'll also talk later about covenants to formalize the understanding of the values and philosophy of the business. It's especially important with key managers, who often have strong relationship with the owner, but not with his children. Now let's look at some techniques to customize the program to your circumstances.

The price designated for the transfer of equity (via bonus, sale or other technique) can be an emotional subject because stock represents cash value, income and creativity.

Case History: Building Equity

John, an automotive client, is a good example. Jeff had two sons who were likely to enter the business at some point. However, they had no management experience, so he felt compelled to lock in an exceptional key manager who had previously been a dealer with an Equity Succession Bridge. I explained to John the concept of converting sweat equity. Nonetheless, as a self-confessed master of frugality, he had difficulty with the term "bargain" when referring to the automobile dealership that he had spent 15 years developing into a highly respected and very profitable business.

Regardless of my repeated attempts to explain why it was appropriate to offer stock at a bargain price, John continued to have difficulty accepting that the bargain was not simply a gift. No one had given him anything while he was struggling to survive. Although he really needed to lock a key manager into his business, he was not going to give anything away. He was so focused on the generosity of the package that he was unable to recognize the built-in protections inherent with the concept.

I tried to explain that the stockholders agreement stipulated that the purchase price for the initial block of stock, along with subsequent optioned additions, would be at the appraised value, taking into consideration minority and lack of control discounts. I also explained that a third-party appraisal would avoid a negotiation with his key manager and any subsequent feelings by the key manager that he had been the victim of a "cram down" on the valuation.

I also described this discounted pricing as a conditional benefit. Yes, the stock option provisions stated that his manager could purchase stock at this favorable price, but the subsequent sale of stock was controlled by very strong conditions. If the manager quit within 10 years or was terminated for cause, as defined in his employment contract, his stock would be repurchased for the appraised value, using the same discounts or purchase price, whichever was less. In other words, if the manager was not on board for a career commitment, he would have no upside potential. This long-term stock appreciation benefit threshold would discourage anyone from pursuing stock who was not genuinely interested in a long-term succession bridge relationship.

However, I continued to explain that the most profound incentive would be that the repurchase of the manager's stock would be for appraisal value, without any discounts. The lucrative non discounted value would be provided in the event of the manager's death, or disability or upon the sale of the dealership. These inflated values would immediately apply to these contingencies or after 15 years service, which should be enough time to address the anticipated growth and experience of his sons. This going concern valuation would amount to at least a 35% bump in value when the manager achieved the target service qualification threshold.

I was not sure if John was impressed with my forethought on this issue or if he was finally accepting the notion that he was not making a gift to his manager. Regardless, he had calmed down enough to listen. I explained that we would only allow his manager to exercise future stock options to the extent of his proportionate share of the annual subchapter-S earnings on the stock he purchased. Therefore, we would have a timed buy-in that would be predicated on the manager's impact on the profitability of the company. Up to the prescribed option limit, the more money the company made, the more stock he could purchase. The buy-in timetable would be affected by compounding values.

In this case, it would take about five years for the manager to exercise his option for 25% of stock. Subsequently, he would share in the cash flow on a proportionate basis. This Equity Succession Bridge represented a mutual good faith commitment to achieve succession appropriately. The payoff was the handcuff of a very special manager who could give Jeff peace of mind that he could retire, die or become disabled and still attain succession.

John smirked, "I still think it's a gift." I let out a frustrated sigh and started in again with my argument. As I was pushing hard again with a new point of debate, I noticed a twinkle in his eyes and the corner of his mouth break into a restrained smile. "You're working me, aren't you?" Evidently I had made my point.

Fortunately, my persistence paid off. John had grasped the big picture of a long-term, low risk Succession Bridge conversion of sweat into equity.

The contractual right to purchase stock provides a very effective method of establishing a golden handcuff incentive that will promote a career service commitment and the continuation of a high level of performance.

The owner can have the peace of mind that he is not giving away the farm because the manager can be required to pay the bargain value debt exclusively from corporate profits. The understanding of "no profits, no stock" can give greater peace of mind on the sell side. On the buy side, the manager will not quibble about price when he realizes that as long as the business continues to be profitable, he can keep his money in the bank and the stock will pay for itself in a reasonable period of time.

Career commitment is achieved through a vesting schedule that triggers the options over a period of time, generally ranging from three to 15 years. Performance goals can also be supported by subordinating the stock purchase option triggers to any one or more operating indexes, such as profitability, customer satisfaction or stock price. Depending upon the perspective of either owner or key manager, an advantage or disadvantage is that the bulk of the stock in the Key Man Equity Bridge program does not change hands until options are vested and exercised. Due to the impact of dividend distributions in a subchapter-S corporation or a limited liability corporation, the business owner usually views this as an advantage and the key manager sees it as a disadvantage.

Another way of selling the key manager on the concept is through attractive purchase terms. To some extent, these terms are essential, because most key managers do not have excess cash sitting around. Otherwise they would own their own businesses and not be working for you.

Consequently, spreading payments for the stock over three to five years will create an attractive opportunity for the key manager. However, do not make the stock purchase too easy or there will be no respect for this program. Generally it is good for the key manager to struggle to make payments. He will gain a better respect for the challenge of business ownership if he pays a price in extra effort or concern.

In an outright sale, there is no future option to purchase stock. Therefore, the price of the stock is the defining aspect of this simple transaction. The owner can set the price anywhere, as long as it is deemed a value by the purchasing key manager. Be prepared for the conflicting paradigms. The owner will naturally feel reluctant to give up a piece of the business at any price. However, because the owner is not retaining any long-term service hook, he will naturally lean towards a high value. On the other hand, the key manager will feel that his hard work has created a substantial portion of the current stock value and therefore will lean towards a conservative value. In the absence of a service commitment, owners should not be eager to give away significant value, but should recognize the impact, if any, this exceptional manager has had on the business.

If the manager has been paid well enough to create the cash needed to make this outright purchase, it is also reasonable to assume that a bargain is not warranted. If they haven't been well paid, a bargain may be fair and even essential. This deal is predicated on providing the key manager and his fragile ego with a reasonable value considering relevant circumstances. The last thing the business owner wants to do is initiate an argument. A valuation disagreement is a sure sign of a big mistake, either in the valuation of the stock or in the selection of the Key Manager Succession Bridge.

A long-term installment note, in contrast to an outright sale/purchase, could serve as a long-term service commitment and take the focus of this transaction off of the value of the stock. Satisfaction of this note is generally through annual payments with interest. The ownership of corporate stock, which in family environments is usually subchapter-S stock, should produce dividends that could help pay interest and even principal on the note.

Another method of conveying stock in a Key Man Equity Bridge is through a stock bonus.

Fundamentally, in lieu of being required to generate cash and actually purchase the stock, the key manager takes the value as income in the form of a stock bonus. There are two forms of stock bonus, a direct stock bonus and a deferred Section 83 Restricted Stock bonus.

The income tax impacts of these two forms are significantly different. With both forms the corporation issues treasury stock directly to the manager. This issuance of treasury stock dilutes pre-existing stockholders. Notably, the owner does not receive any cash in this transaction. If the business owner holds 100% of the corporation's issued stock, evidenced by 1,000 shares, and he makes a bonus of 250 treasury shares to a manager, he will subsequently own 80% of the 1,250 issued shares.

When a direct stock bonus is awarded, the fortunate manager (he does not have to pay for it) reports the value of the stock on his W-2 as of the date the stock was issued. The bonus is considered ordinary compensation that is subject to income tax and payroll tax. The effective cost to the manager is the income tax and the employee portion of payroll tax on the value of the stock bonus received.

The corporation must pay its portion of the payroll tax on the value of the bonused stock. However, the corporation receives a benefit of an income tax deduction for the value of the stock bonus and subsequently realizes a tax savings. In order to achieve a golden handcuff and spread out the income tax cost, the bonus is usually the by product of a formal plan recorded in a corporate resolution that describes the awarding of a predetermined amount of stock over a period of time ranging from three to 15 years. Notably, with a direct stock bonus plan, the manager receives no benefit from the stock until it is received as reportable income. Depending upon the circumstances of the key manager and the business, the golden handcuff can stipulate performance triggers (sales or profits) for the stock bonuses. The plan can also establish a graduated scale that allocates more or less stock to the near term or extended future.

The other form of stock bonus is derived from Section 83 of the Internal Revenue Code. Generally, this is a lump sum stock bonus that can be structured any way the owner feels is appropriate. A Section 83 plan provides executives with stock bonuses that are subject to substantial risk of forfeiture. This means that, during a predetermined period, as described in the formal restricted stock bonus agreement, the executive could lose this benefit if he does not meet specified service or performance requirements. The key feature of this plan is that there are no income tax or payroll tax implications until the substantial risks of forfeiture lapse.

The risk of forfeiture can take any reasonable form, but usually includes a service requirement that serves as the handcuff.

The attractive aspect of a Section 83 stock bonus plan is that the business owner can custom design ownership contingencies that meet the specific needs of both the business and the manager.

The manager has the immediate psychological and financial benefits of stock ownership, but does not have to pay income tax on the value of the bonus until the contingencies are satisfied.

When the traditionally graduated performance vesting prerequisites are satisfied, the key manager assumes unrestricted ownership of the stock. In the calendar year these restrictions are removed, the executive receives a W-2 for the value of the liberated stock. Similarly, the business reports an income tax deduction the same year. If the manager terminates employment before satisfying the service or performance incentive, he forfeits the restricted stock. At the discretion of the business owner, the plan can provide exceptions to the forfeiture provisions in the event of death, disability, sale of the business or involuntary termination without cause.

The advantage of either bonus program is that the manager does not have to come up with sizable cash or incur substantial debt. The need to pay only the income tax on the stock value represents a definite bargain.

However, in a 25% to 45% effective personal income tax bracket, the tax cost represents a vested interest that commands respect. The primary disadvantage of a stock bonus is that the business owner has no opportunity to build cash through the stock sale.

On total, considering both methods of establishing key man equity, a stock bonus is considered more favorable to the executive and the installment payments are more favorable to the owner.

As would be expected, when issuing dry W-2's and taking corporate income tax deductions, there must be a very reliable basis for determining the stock value. A professional appraisal is appropriate to preclude challenge by either the IRS or the manager. It should also be noted that there is reasonable flexibility in the determination of value. Either a "going concern" or "bargain discounted minority" value can be utilized. However, having concluded the desired approach to valuation, it is important that the approach be consistent, in the event the IRS and the manager contend that the owner isn't playing fair.

The major difference in the impact of an indirect bonus of restricted stock versus a direct stock bonus is that the recipient of Section 83 restricted stock has the voting and dividend benefits of stock ownership with the deferral of the income tax. This is a very attractive feature to a manager who does not have capital to purchase stock. Additionally, the inherent risk of forfeiture provisions are ideally suited for the golden handcuff. The key manager immediately obtains an owner mentality, but is required to meet long-term service and/or performance criteria. As mentioned earlier, Restricted Stock can be utilized in combination with a direct stock bonus or the sale of stock. I suggest in all programs that the ticket for admission to an Equity Succession Bridge opportunity is that they purchase some stock with their hard earned money to give assurance that they are spiritually buying into the program. The mind and heart will follow the pocketbook.

As you might expect, when any benefit program defers income taxation, there are specific IRS rules and/or guidelines that must be addressed. Fortunately, as a "non-qualified, Top Hat" benefit program for select highly compensated employees, there is a very limited requirement to conform to the reporting and fiduciary requirements of the Employee Retirement Income Security Act (ERISA). Therefore, to make sure the ERISA exemptions are achieved, these plans should be under the supervision of an accountant and drafted by a qualified attorney. This attorney would also be responsible for drafting the Stockholder's Agreement to ensure that the owner has established the indisputable methodology for regaining ownership of the stock if the manager terminates for any reason.

Case History: Design Variations

I was referred to a couple of gentlemen who had at one time owned a large chain of gas stations and convenience stores. They had grown weary of the management frustrations of the convenience stores and the EPA liability of gas stations. So they sold their operations, but kept the real estate with very attractive leases. As developers, they retained their zeal for the deal despite their ages. Brooks was in his late 60's and Frank was in his mid 70's. When I met them, they were effectively reinvested into several new businesses and real estate. With a net worth in excess of $30 million each, they were doing in retirement what they always wanted to do, play business. They were having so much fun that they had converted the resources of a previously simple business into a complex assortment of both passive real estate and active businesses.

They wanted my help in making strategic business decisions and reducing their estate taxes. As 50/50 owners in most of their assets, they had come to grips with the reality that estate taxes would create monumental problems for the surviving partner, spouses and children. Frank had undergone bypass surgery the year before and Brooks sported three balloon catheters in his heart to open occluded veins.

Further, they had a great attorney who was not pulling any punches with his descriptions of their estate taxation circumstances. Each had two daughters and several grandchildren, but no other family members were active in the business.

I initially directed my efforts to formalizing partnership, joint venture and corporate agreements that they had not taken the laborious time to address, as well as individual estate disposition documents. We then embarked on the more complex estate tax reduction activities. The estate tax reduction involved recapitalizing the existing management company with non-voting stock, forming three separate family limited partnerships for each family, as well as the adoption of charitable trusts, management contracts and grantor retained income trusts. As we were completing the details on these projects, I conveyed to them what I perceived to be good news and bad news.

The good news was that there was great probability that we were reducing their estate taxes by 50%. The bad news was that, in the process of reducing their estate tax, we were further complicating their business affairs and estate administration. The structures that reduce estate tax would make their assets less liquid, more restricted and more interdependent than before. As an example, how could either of them or their heirs readily sell or mortgage a limited partnership interest in half of a real estate parcel? In other words, the estate tax reduction structures would restrict their ability to sell or mortgage assets to pay estate taxes or to endow a child who wanted money.

I recommended that they carefully consider the implications. They could stay as they were and have independence, flexibility and high taxes or they could fund the structures and reduce their estate taxes, but in so doing, become interdependent and cash poor. Their attorney and accountant validated my caution and, as a group, we urged them to be sure that exchanging lower taxes for less flexibility was a worthwhile trade.

The accountant, attorney and I privately made a little three-way bet. That was like taking candy from a baby. Both the attorney and accountant believed these two dynamos would choose liquidity, independence and simplicity. As you might expect, I had been down this road many times before and I knew that the primal instincts of an old school, Yankee capitalist would win out over logic. These gentlemen never hesitated in their instructions for us to do whatever it took to lower and if possible, totally avoid estate tax.

They were confident in their goals and united in their commitment to avoid estate taxes. However, they had no response when I asked who was going to run the company when they were gone? The funding of these structures would create a united business venture into perpetuity. With no one from their immediate families to run the business, I subsequently asked if the four daughters could work together as a supervisory organization? Their response was hopefully so, but the daughters had never done anything like that before. They clearly had more experience in income consumption than income production.

It was a rare moment to see two highly successful, cocky, reasonably arrogant businessmen at a loss for words. They had no answer for who was going to run the company or how they were going to manage their company in the next generation.

In our next meeting, they no longer exhibited unwavering confidence. Based upon the dilemma that I had identified, they decided to postpone funding the partnership. They knew the subject of management succession had to be addressed. None of their current employees could run the company and get along with the four daughters, much less lead them. They had been talking with their daughters and none of them had expressed any interest in changing lifestyles, uprooting their families and pursuing a career management position. At their ages, there was also insufficient time for Brooks and Frank to train a family member or anyone who lacked substantial experience in real estate and business management.

They knew they were facing a tough situation. They had run their company very profitably. A significant factor was their low overhead and low management compensation. Their philosophy had been: "Why pay someone else to do something halfway that either of us can fully do ourselves?" They had neither the quality nor the quantity of management support to carry on the company after their retirement. Although very profitable, they had not achieved Succession Success because they did not have a single manager who could support their succession goal. The best manager they'd ever had quit five years ago, after fifteen years tenure, over --- you guessed it -- compensation.

My response -- their succession prospects did not look good. I identified two viable options: postpone estate tax avoidance activities and begin winding down the business with a goal of dividing assets within five to seven years, or contact a headhunter and initiate an executive search to recruit the caliber of talent needed to manage and grow their operation.

Brooks, the younger of the two, who was clearly the more feisty, stood up and began pacing back and forth in the conference room, bantering his displeasure. Waving his arms for emphasis as he looked at the ceiling, he worried that they would be creating a disaster if they tried to liquidate their real estate because of the very low tax basis and inevitable soil contamination issues.

And he expressed little confidence that he and Frank could achieve a fair division of the properties between the two families. They had some appreciating real estate investments that neither of them wanted to relinquish. They had been down this road before and had resolved that partitioning their assets was not a realistic alternative.

Frank, who was more calculated and less impulsive, agreed that unraveling their business would be a very complicated and expensive project. And he thought that the alternative did not appear much better because he did not know where they would find someone to run a business for four female directors. Knowing the four daughters, I concurred, as these ladies were by no means compliant. This would be a challenging talent search.

However, in light of their unwillingness to pay their previous general manager, I cautioned him not to begin the search until they had come to grips with the reality that they were going to have to pay handsomely for this talent. Their concept of "never spending a dime before it is time" was not going to work in this case.

Brooks, still pacing around the room, in frustration blurted out again, "Here we go with another Jack ordeal." I inquired what he meant by "Jack ordeal" and Brooks said that he was referring to the very difficult and ultimately unsuccessful negotiations that had led to the departure of their general manager five years ago. Jack, he said, had been a very good manager, but was just greedy. Over a 15-year tenure with the company, Jack had shown outstanding initiative and had developed into an excellent manager with outstanding real estate instincts. They trusted him implicitly but, five years ago, he had insisted on being given a 50% pay raise. He turned directly to me lifting his hands in exasperation and said, "Can you believe he wanted us to increase his pay from $50,000 a year to $75,000 a year?"

I hadn't been expecting humorous entertainment. First there was just a smile as I shook my head in disbelief. Then I could not contain myself and started to chuckle. Unfortunately neither of my clients found any humor in my reaction and compelled me to express what I was thinking. "Just think about where you are", I told them, "what you need and what you have done.

"You've got a business with assets in excess of $50 million, kicking off about $5 million a year in cash flow. In order to maintain these profits at an acceptable level you desperately need a trusted, competent, experienced manager who can run this business in your retirement and for your daughters after your deaths."

So, with these circumstances, what had they done? They had run off the perfect candidate because they were unwilling to pay him $75,000 a year to manage more than $50 million in assets. A 50% pay raise is irrelevant if the compensation requested is reasonable. If they called a headhunter to find the talent they needed, the search cost would be $150,000 and the starting compensation package no less than $150,000. Further, regardless of references, they would not trust this new manager for many years. With some disbelief, I concluded by stating that the worst part of this situation was that, in all likelihood, they would have to go through a search exercise two or three times before they found the right manager.

As might be expected, a formidable debate followed. These were two tough, old-school businessmen who took very little at face value, especially something so contradictory to their business culture as paying a manager what he was worth. Hardball negotiating was Brook's favorite pastime. He contended that he would rather be called cheap than stupid. I agreed but countered by cautioning him that losing the best and only candidate over $25,000, when a replacement could easily cost another $100,000 could be classified as stupidly cheap.

I told them some relevant war stories and concluded by giving them the names of a couple of headhunters. I told them that there was nothing I could do for them until they made a Disposition Decision and came to grips with the ramifications.

I received a call a couple weeks later requesting a meeting. When I arrived, I was greeted by three gentlemen. The older partner motioned me over to the stranger and said, "Loyd, I would like for you to meet Jack, our new general manager." Wow, was this a shock! My comments had obviously made an impression and they had made the moves to bring their old general manager back. Brooks described the sequence of events. After much more discussion between partners, wives and children, they had concluded that business succession was a profoundly better option than partitioning the properties. They felt that their experience with Jack positioned him as their best successor manager candidate.

So they called Jack and explained to him that the development of circumstances now supported the management position that they had discussed five years earlier. Jack responded to the overture and was here to discuss details of the job. Specifically, they wanted to hear my ideas and suggestions on a compensation package.

Jack immediately took the initiative. As he spoke I quickly realized that he was nobody's fool. He said, "This is not going to be a complicated discussion. I am not signed on yet, but if we can establish a reasonable compensation, I am excited about the opportunity." In order for him to give up his current job, which was very satisfactory, he would need a salary of $100,000 a year and a reasonable bonus opportunity. Before I had a chance to say anything, Brooks responded, "What about the $75,000 salary we discussed previously?" Being nobody's chump, Jack reminded him that the discussion had taken place five years earlier.

He now was making $90,000, plus bonus. For a move to be worth the effort, he would expect an increase in compensation.

In bewilderment, Brooks was mouthing words without sound. Frank just shook his head in disbelief. Before anyone could say something stupid, I convinced them to defer what could otherwise become heated discussions until we had confirmed that the job description was compatible for everyone. I subsequently explained to Jack that we were looking for a long-term career commitment from a capable manager who would serve as a Succession Bridge between these two elderly gentlemen and their four daughters. I pointed out that the job would include managing the existing holdings of the organization, serving as a leader to grow the organization and acting as a liaison for the four daughters and subsequent grandchildren.

Jack was impressed with the forethought of our planning. He was fully aware of the long-term management succession issues, but had not been sure that his two former employers would even let go of the precious cash needed to come to grips with them. He said he thought he was a good candidate for the position. He understood their business and could grow it. He also knew each of the daughters very well and would be comfortable working with them.

He effectively closed our discussions by noting that Brooks and Frank acknowledged that he could handle the job. The only issue was whether these tightwads were going to part with the money to get the job done. With a crack of a smile, he concluded by saying their love/hate relationship would survive, regardless of whether they hired him.

A few days later I met with Brooks and Frank to work on an offer for Jack. It was evident they were not going to bully him into taking the job for less than it was worth. As a result, neither of them was in a good mood. They were not accustomed to being without significant leverage in any negotiation.

Brooks was depressed because he took such pride in winning negotiations. They had been talking about offering a package of $80,000 per year salary, plus car, insurance and a bonus program that would allow him to earn another $10,000 a year. They believed he was bluffing with his salary demand because they had trained him to be a very good negotiator. To their shock I responded that I sincerely hoped he would turn down that offer.

I explained my view, that they needed someone who was worth more than $90,000 a year to administer a $50 million capital resource. I further stated that I was impressed with this 42-year-old and, if they low-balled him, I believed he would be insulted and walk out once again. They had no other viable candidates to choose from and this young man was well aware of his strong bargaining position. I urged them to recognize the significance of what they were endeavoring to do. They were not hiring a manager. They were securing a long-term steward of the assets they had spent a lifetime accumulating.

They did not want someone to take this job just for the money, I contended, because that person could get frustrated and walk away, leaving their daughters high and dry. What they needed was someone who would take a proprietary interest in their business and invest the balance of his career, relying upon the fruits of his entrepreneurial efforts to fulfill dreams of financial security.

In essence, I was presenting a major cultural shift in what they were expecting to pay Jack. They had not accumulated their multi-millions by being generous employers. They were card-carrying members of the "pay as little as you can and hope for the best quality" club. I argued that their econo-management plan worked well with both of them, as they had been around to apply the motivational poker and follow up on any performance issues.

I cited their in-house CPA, whom they were paying $36,000 per year. Sure, he was a CPA, but he did not have the energy or initiative of a slug. I also pointed out they would not be around to personally supervise a Succession Bridge. "Brooks," I asked, "how would you feel about driving across the Golden Gate Bridge if you knew the primary design motive was economy?"

Fortunately I'd struck a nerve. They agreed Jack was their man and asked me to design a compensation plan that I felt would achieve a level of commitment that their families could rely upon. The first thing I did was meet again with Jack. I figured that, in keeping with my traditional style, if I could get him to talk, he would design his compensation program for me and remove the guesswork. Unlike Brooks and Frank, I felt no compunction to create high-tension negotiations.

I also wanted to keep insulating Jack from the two partners so that we could maintain a positive dialogue until we reached a deal. In private discussions I found Jack more relaxed and very enthusiastic about the opportunity to hook up again with his old employers. He enjoyed describing how he understood them. He asserted that, given the opportunity, they would negotiate their own mothers into the ground just for sport. Jack said that he did not need much cash flow to live comfortably, but he knew that they would not respect him if he were not paid well.

The only way he would accept the job would be under reasonable terms cemented with a contract. In order to gain their respect and put up with their pushi-

ness, he would need to make at least $100,000 a year with the opportunity to make more if he did an exceptional job.

Being an equity partner was actually more important to him than the cash flow because he understood how productive this job could be over the long term. He summarized his position by saying, "I know I can get a job and I am not afraid of working. If this is only going to be a job and not an opportunity to be an owner, I would rather work for people who are less demanding."

It was time to present my recommendations to the partners. I was not particularly concerned about Jack. Although he portrayed a cocky, cavalier attitude, it was apparent to me that he was ready to come on board as our Succession Bridge if I could keep Brooks from insulting him and present a reasonable offer. He was in every respect the dream package. Lacking a more creative approach, I again offered my recommendations in the form of good news and bad news. The good news was that Jack was willing to take the job. He was qualified and capable. His salary demands were not unreasonable and they could certainly afford to pay him.

The bad news was that, because he was good, he was under no pressure to take the job for less than he felt it was worth. Therefore, we had to bring him on board and, at the same time, find a way to lock him into the job. The challenge of his compensation package was twofold. First we wanted conservative compensation and second, he wanted entrepreneurial ability to grow the business. The incentive had to be reflective of the extraordinary commitment of time and energy that growth would require.

As though they had been practicing, these two gentlemen looked at me with astonishment and said, "You want to do what?" My tentative groundbreaking had not kept them from quickly comprehending where I was going. "I understand what you are struggling to say and there is no way we are going to allow a non-family member to become an owner," declared Brooks. "I thought you understood that we don't want any more partners. We would not have wasted the money on your fee if we wanted to make him a partner. We both feel that our one partner is bad enough and two would be deplorable. All we want to do is hire this guy. We don't want to marry him or adopt him as one of our children."

I told them that I fully understood their feelings, which explained why I had approached the subject gently. I added that they had hired me to give my honest opinion and not be intimidated by their famous huffery. I wrestled with them for the next hour about the advantages and disadvantages of bringing Jack in as a partner. Reaching the end of my wits, I explained that they needed to face reality and make two important decisions, and then have faith in me and their attorney to put together a package that would work for everybody. The reality was that Jack did not need this job and was not going to take the predictable pressure of it unless he had an opportunity to be a partner. Subsequently, the decisions were simple. After a reasonable trial period during which Jack would prove himself, without a doubt to be the man they needed to achieve succession, could they accept him as a partner in their organization? If he could be a partner, how much could he own?

They were even wearing me down. I was beginning to think they were just terminally cheap. No doubt, they were profoundly hardheaded. It seemed like we had been over this subject ad nausea. Drawing on patience that only a higher power could provide, I reviewed with them again their viable options. They could hire Jack at a reasonable wage and give him the opportunity to work his way into the partner arrangement over the next 20 years. Their second option would be to go into the marketplace and find someone else within the next six to 12 months.

If the replacement were really high caliber, he would want a partner arrangement as well. Their last option would be to do nothing, go with the flow and resolve themselves to deal with management challenges as they arose over the next few years -- unless of course, one of their medical conditions deteriorated, which was certainly a possibility. Options 1 and 2, in my opinion, would certainly cost approximately the same in real dollars.

They could hire Jack for less, but he would want equity. They certainly would not want a new recruit to be a partner, so his pay would have to be higher. Option 3 could have a devastating cost, due to the probable unwinding of their business. The primary impact of the option chosen would be the aggravation and stress they would have to endure in order to achieve their succession objective. This aggravation and stress would only be another contributing factor to their deteriorating health.

The first option was a no-brainer opportunity, a known commodity with proven ability and proven character. The second two options might appear to be cheaper, but represented a frustrating and unending commitment of the owners' mental energies and emotions.

I had hit a nerve again. Brooks remarked with disgust, "Frustrating -- no. This project is, at best, gruesome. This will surely kill me before heart disease." He had always stated that his least favorite subjects were giving up control, paying what was asked, death, estate planning and estate taxes. And now, adding a partner was somewhere near the top of that list. The only reason he tolerated estate planning was that it was an opportunity for him to exercise control beyond the grave. He punctuated his point by stating, "You've got some convincing to do before I am going to agree to bring a non-family member in as a partner."

I challenged him to keep his mind open. By their own admission, their daughters were feisty and a bit overbearing on items of self-interest. It would be difficult for any individual to manage assets for two sisters, much less managing assets for two sets of sisters. Polite and genteel in their fathers' presence, they were sure to be less cooperative and predictably petty in the absence of their fathers. Life would become much more challenging for the general manager when the two partners were no longer around to sooth his frustration. Consequently, I suggested that it would be very wise to have our hooks in this general manager to prevent him from walking out when the fur started to fly.

I then presented the Key Man Equity Bridge program, which would begin with a two-year probation period. Jack would be awarded an option to purchase 20% of the stock in the management company upon successful completion of the two years. The terms of the purchase would be 50% cash and 50% financed by the two partners. The management company did not have much net worth but, just the same, he would have to scramble to come up with $25,000 in cash for a down payment.

I suggested that, even if Jack had to mortgage his house, we wanted at least 50% down so that he had a vested interest in the welfare of this company. Jack's 20% of the cash flow on the Management Company would be pledged to pay off of any mortgage loans or the note involved in the initial acquisition. Of course, Brooks and Frank would hold onto Jack's stock as collateral until all of the debt was satisfied.

At this point, I explained to Brooks and Frank a strategic advantage of Jack owning stock. Jack would relieve the possible, if not inevitable control deadlock between the two families, or any evenly divided factions of the four stockholders. He would serve as a tiebreaker on any strategic control issue.

Frank, who was certainly the more genteel and calculated of the two partners, appeared eager to join the dialogue and offered, "So you think Jack should be a stockholder in the Management Company? Brooks, this isn't so bad. I have to admit that the possibility of a deadlock has been heavy on my mind. He would just be a stockholder in the Management Company that Loyd helped us form two years ago. It's not like we are selling off the family jewels. He would not own any of the underlying real estate that we have been sweating ball bearings over for many years. I think I could live with this."

The irrepressible Brooks was just looking for an opportunity to offer his profundity, but I cut him off. Frank was right, but, in his typical form, he was jumping to conclusions before he had heard the entire story. I asked Brooks to hold tight for a moment while I explained to both of them that, as Frank had described, they could restrict Jack's ownership to just the Management Company.

That would be both clean and simple. But limiting Jack's ownership would not be in their family's best interest. If Jack did not own a portion of the underlying real estate, he would be more inclined to exploit cash flow and not address reinvestment for growth. For the first time, I had the attention of both of them. Seizing this rare moment, I proposed that they not only offer but, indeed, require Jack to purchase 10% of the combined equity of the underlying partnerships. This would be achieved through the continued pledge of the cash flow distributions from the Management Company -- after the payment of indebtedness incurred for the purchase of the stock -- to the incremental purchase of up to 10% of the equity of the underlying partnerships.

Anticipating their next questions, I went on to explain that a Stockholders' Agreement would restrict Jack from gifting, selling, pledging or otherwise transferring any of these stock or partnership assets without first offering them back to the daughters for preemptive repurchase. This comprehensive agreement would require him to tender his interest back to their daughters at discounted appraised value or the price he paid for it, whichever was less, in the event he terminated employment prior to retirement. Upon his retirement or death, Jack and Brooks, or their daughters, would purchase his interest for fair market value.

Brooks, who was no longer able to restrain himself, blurted out, "Jack won't live long enough to buy that. You are talking about $2.5 million to $3 million in value."

At that point I began to feel better. Brooks was no longer tripping over cracks in the sidewalk. He appeared to have accepted the benefits of having Jack as a Management Company stockholder and a partner in the underlying real estate. I had learned from experience that I had to acknowledge his art of exception analysis -- finding fault -- in order to have a prayer that this argumentative dynamo might accept my point of view.

I took this opportunity to pay homage to his keen sense of the obvious. "Yes, you may be right. He will have to generate sufficient profits through the Management Company to repay his stock acquisition loan through his 20% share of the earnings. Having paid off the stock acquisition loan, he will then be required to devote the Management Company profits to the purchase of partnership interest. At the current rate of earnings, he will not be able to purchase the full 10% before his normal retirement date.

He will have to grow the company to fully capitalize on this investment opportunity. I never told you we were going to make it easy for him. Whether he can generate enough Management Company profits to enable him to buy 10% of the partnership is merely speculation, but I sure hope he does. Because that would mean he would have made your daughters, who hold 80% of the Management Company and 90% of the partnership, tons of money.

My estimation was that it would be six or seven years before Jack was in a position to start buying partnership interest. I hoped for everyone's best interest, including Jack's, that he was motivated to partnership interest over the remaining 10 to 15 years of his career.

Brooks just smiled and shook his head while looking over at Frank. He was sold. I did not see that yielding smile very often, but it clearly indicated he had seen the light. He just wanted to make sure that Frank, the irrepressible pessimist, could not shoot down the idea. Frank's gun was already loaded as he looked right up to me and said, "What happens if Jack gets divorced? Will his wife become a stockholder? You know, this is his second wife. She used to be my secretary. She is an aggressive little thing that could push Jack and me right over the edge."

"Not to worry," I responded. "Jack's ownership of both the Management Company and the partnership will be wrapped up very tightly in stockholder and partnership agreements that will restrict him from selling, gifting or otherwise transferring any of these interests to any other party but you or your daughters. The biggest challenge in this deal is going to be keeping Jack motivated, not dealing with unwanted stockholders. Jack's interests will even be held by your attorney, Robert, as the trustee of the stockholder's agreement, so there is no risk of the stock falling into the hands of a hard head who doesn't understand the obligations of a contract."

At that point Frank leaned back in his chair, put his hands up in the air defensively expressing, "Okay, okay, okay. I can't say as I understand every detail, but maybe this dog will hunt. I am willing to give it a try. Let's get Robert and Jack in here and work this out."

Thankfully, this Key Manager Equity Succession Bridge did work out. It took 90 days for everyone to air their questions and develop comfort with the documents involved. As is normally the case, a spirit of good faith prevailed to make the deal. This group continued to press forward as Jack was nearing the completion of his probationary period. He had some rough moments with Brooks and Frank, as well as the four daughters. We all knew this was a minefield and it lived up to expectations.

However, Jack, having an impressive grasp of the obvious, saw a pot of gold at the end of the rainbow and was not going to let a few hassles get him off track. He is indeed a unique individual and I have no doubt that he will fulfill the dreams of Brooks and Frank by successfully serving as a Succession Bridge, as well as reaping the fabulous rewards of being an equity partner.

9 Key Manager Control Equity Succession Bridge

In the previous chapter we discussed the utilization of business ownership equity to lock down a very special key manager into a Succession Bridge role. However, there are circumstances where a very special key manager is receptive to the offer of equity ownership, but no longer interested in playing second fiddle. At that point, an owner must again affirm just how vital the very special key manager is to the success and succession of the business. If the crystal ball says "you gotta keep this guy," then it is time to consider creating what we call a Key Manager Control Equity Succession Bridge.

It means giving up control. And the motivation to pursue this admittedly extreme mechanism involves both extraordinary circumstances and an extraordinary business.

Extraordinary circumstances would include having no qualified successors on board or available within the near future. And the owners would have considered and rejected the outright sale of the business. And the very special key manager would have rejected all prior succession proposals, including the Equity Succession Bridge. The relatively simple option of selling the business has been rejected because, for any number of reasons, it is considered extraordinary.

One could also have concluded that the current value that would be received would be insignificant compared with its growth potential.

Further, the extraordinary nature of the business operation may require a special personality, skill sets or experience that make the recruitment of a new leader on the open market very challenging, risky and expensive. It is the total combination of these extraordinary, and even irrational, circumstances that subsequently justifies relinquishing control of the business in order to remain involved as a minority stockholder with a prospect of regaining control at a later date.

These extraordinary circumstances are often the byproduct of a pressing need to make a Disposition Decision because of a change in health, circumstances or the possible departure of an extremely valuable key manager or minority partner who has been responsible for the success of the business.

The circumstances are further bracketed by the absence of a family member manager who could assume unquestioned, solid leadership. In some circumstances, family members are just burned out and have no more heart for the unique challenges of the business, but are unwilling to totally sell out their interests.

It should be very apparent that, due to the transfer of control, this concept is dependent upon a unique relationship with a key manager or current minority partner. Notably, this is a level of unreserved trust that goes well beyond the contractual peace of mind that could be provided by stockholder's and employment agreements. Frankly, as one considers this Succession Bridge option above the warnings and protests of advisers, family and friends, one should recognize that this trust goes beyond conventional logic.

However, as I have said before, facts are stranger than fiction in the realm of family business succession planning. When extraordinary circumstances are accompanied by an unyielding desire to hold onto a piece of the family jewels, or to achieve business succession, logic may not be the driving force. Unless the owner is certifiably crazy, there should be justification for becoming a vulnerable minority stockholder. The advantage could be that the family can retain a minority interest and continue the benefits and earnings of that interest. At a later date, when the controlling key manager retires or decides to move on to other challenges, the minority partner(s) could plan to assume an active partner role, and/or by preexisting agreement, reestablish control. And there may be children or grandchildren in training.

Perceiving no other viable options, as we move forward with the consideration of a Control Bridge, I cannot overemphasize the obvious, that this program involves transferring control of the business to a very special person. This is a savvy, profoundly productive manager who would ultimately find his way to be the helm of his own ship. He also has unquestioned character and is compatible with the majority, if not all, of the family members currently controlling the business.

This is an aggressive, very strong-willed individual who knows what he wants in life and is willing to pay the price to get it. He has a great deal of respect for the current owners and really enjoys the career environment.

Trust me, there are not too many of these caped crusaders hanging around. There are plenty of outstanding business managers. There are also a few with unwavering character and a few who are compatible with the family's emotional architecture. The combination of the three, however, is very rare. Most of these elite, unique managers own their own business or are on the fast track to the executive floor of a public corporation.

However, they do exist and are actually becoming more common with the increase in the entry cost to private business and the sacrifices of being a soldier in a public company. Most of these unique managers, at least in the franchise realm, are already on board gaining experience in a family business. Others are in the middle management ranks of the public corporations.

Hierarchical executive frustration at Ford, General Motors, Chrysler, Anheuser Busch, Miller Brewing, McDonald's and PepsiCo has created good recruiting opportunities.

It is very common for beer, automotive or fast food family-owned franchisees to recruit proven high-potential managers with the exceptional opportunity of becoming a Key Manager Succession Bridge.

If circumstances evolve, and they pass the test of time with the family, their good faith venture can establish the opportunity of a lifetime as a Key Manager Control Succession Bridge. Still, as expressed earlier, do not lose sight of the fact that an Equity Control Bridge is not just a matter of having an extraordinarily qualified manager. The business and family circumstances also must be extraordinary. The enterprise must be uniquely valuable and/or attractive. That special value must support significant compromises from both the key manager and the family.

Keep in mind that, as an owner, you may have a jaded opinion of the value of your business. An eye-opener can be the manager's response. In the absence of genuine extraordinary value, the key manager may ask: "Why should I fool around with just achieving control of this business, when I could make a power play and get it all by starting my own or buying my own?" When the key manager, who often is already a minority partner, concludes that he could not duplicate the combination of business, community and relationship, it affirms his value.   The initial and most critical step is selection of the Key Manager control candidate. This is the hinge pin of the undertaking. Regardless of motivating circumstances, when considering relinquishing control of the business, proceed with caution. Giving up control carries many risks. Although many of operational risks can be controlled through operating agreements and stockholders agreements, there is no way to avoid all the strategic risks of relinquishing control.

Character and trust must precede any consideration of management or leadership talent. Control transfers are usually contingent upon long-term relationships that have established a comprehensive understanding of the manager's character and have achieved trust. Do not take any short cuts in coming to a decision. Critically evaluate the character and capability of any candidate.

Regardless of how long you have known the individual, do a comprehensive background check, including personal discussions with prior employees, partners and previous employers as well as a credit report.

Give credence to the counsel of others. You cannot rely on instinct, or you would never do such a crazy thing. However, it is worthwhile to listen to what others have to say about this daring move. It would be better to sell the whole package than take the risk of giving up control to someone with dubious character.

The fundamental aspect of a Key Manager Control Equity Bridge involves the transfer of sufficient voting power and equity to give the key manager sufficient operating control to satisfy his ownership goal. Simplistically, this may mean the purchase of 51% of the business equity. Or, depending upon the aggressiveness and ambition of the manager, the transaction may provide the manager substantially more ownership. You will not know this until you get in the midst of the deal and have a gut check with the Succession Bridge candidate.

Making A Commitment

As we venture into the methods of conveying control, do not lose sight of the need for the key manager to have a significant vested interest in the welfare of the business. It would be imprudent and ill advised to transfer control of the business to a manager that did not make a significant investment and long-term financial commitment to the business. There should be no chance that the Succession Bridge candidate will become bored or frustrated and decide to jump ship. The deepest level of vested interest is needed for a Control Equity Succession Bridge. The only way this commitment can be achieved is to require that the key manager make a substantial investment. If they do not have serious money to put into this deal, do not do it. It would be reasonable for the owner to extend some credit because, otherwise, it may be impossible to make this deal. After making a substantial cash investment in the stock, the manager's stock should be pledged against the full payment of the note.

In some instances, the key manager does not have sufficient resources to purchase 51% of the business. Furthermore, in high dividend Subchapter-S and limited liability corporations, there is no incentive to sell stock on an installment note basis. Why give up the income if you do not have to? A popular method of economically conveying voting control is through a non-voting stock recapitalization. A non-voting stock recapitalization focuses voting control on a reduced amount of business equity by diluting the voting stock through the issuance of non-voting stock. For example, in a $10 million company with 100 shares of issued voting stock, each share of voting stock has a $100,000 value. Acquisition of a 51% voting control would require 51 shares with a simplistic value of $5.1 million. Regardless of how much vested interest you wanted the manager to have, this may be a number that is off the planet. However, if nine new shares of non-voting stock were issued as a tax free dividend on each existing voting share, the total number of outstanding shares would be raised from 100 to 1,000.

Simplistically, the value of the voting equity would have been contracted to just 10% of the corporation, or $1 million, and the value of the non-voting equity would represent 90% of the corporation, or $9 million. The net result of this transaction is that the value of each voting share has been reduced from $100,000 per share to $10,000. If the non-voting stock dividend were 99 to 1, the value of the corporation would not have changed, but the value of the voting stock would have been reduced to $1,000 per share, or $100,000 out of a total $10 million value.

Under the assumption of a 9 to 1 non-voting stock dilution, the subsequent transfer of a 51% controlling interest in the corporation would now involve transferring only 5.1% of the corporate equity. The transaction would be for $510,000, as opposed to $5 million. The implications of reorganizing corporate capital in this, or similar, fashion is that purchasing voting control can be made more affordable. Another advantage is that the selling family would be empowered to relinquish control while retaining the bulk of the equity. Keep in mind that, in contrast with my simplistic example, an appraisal would allocate a modestly higher value to the voting stock than the nonvoting stock, known as a "control premium." Furthermore, a single transaction involving a block of controlling stock would dictate a substantial valuation premium.

However, this control premium could be significantly reduced or avoided if the control position was created by several independent transactions of minority blocks of stock.

Before transferring control of a prized family possession, there should be a Stockholder's Agreement.

This agreement would manage and control future transfers, pledges and disposition of stock. The agreements that are formalized within this document serve two major purposes: to provide all stockholders an understanding of the nature (value, liquidity and marketability) of their security interest in the business and to preclude future stockholder disagreements regarding these same issues.

The Stockholder's Agreement for a Control Equity Bridge carries a heavy burden for dealing with contingencies. Therefore, this document should spare no effort to cover every possible contingency regarding the sale, pledging or transfer of stock. Unfortunately, every business circumstance cannot be covered by a formal Stockholder's Agreement. That is why consideration of the character of the key manager is so critical. Each agreement is unique, as it would endeavor to address the particular circumstances of the business, the goals of the family, the goals of the key managers and the relationships between the family and the key managers.

The agreement would include provisions, such as prohibited business transactions and circumstances under which the family may recover control. Depending upon circumstances, the agreement could also provide that, in the event of the death of a family stockholder, other family members would have first option to buy or inherit that stock.

In the event there are no actively employed, career management family members, the key manager may also be given the option to purchase this stock or materially participate in the purchase. There is no standard language for a Control Equity Bridge Stockholder's Agreement because the circumstances are unique for each family, key manager and business environment.

Other important facets of a Key Manager Control Equity Bridge are employment contracts for the key manager and any employed family members. It would not be wise to transfer control and then allow the newly empowered controlling key manager to establish his own job description and pay plan. It would also not be particularly prudent to give the new corporate despot the ability to fire the owner or aspiring family managers without the deterrent of a golden parachute. The employment contract serves several very important functions. First, it clarifies job performance expectations and accountability procedures. Clarifying job performance expectations will relieve concern on the part of both the owner and key manager. The owner needs a clear understanding of the controlling manager's responsibilities. Ambiguity in this area will only create problems.

Further, the controlling manager needs to have a clear (written) understanding of any family member management responsibilities.

In all cases, these job descriptions for family members clarify not only what they do in support of the business, but also what they will not do to complicate matters of the controlling manager.

Clearly specifying operational responsibilities and restrictions in writing is critically important to an Equity Control Succession Bridge. Even after going through the formalities of adopting "operating covenants," which specifically include do's and don'ts, there is a high likelihood that family members will purposefully or inadvertently influence business operations. "Seagull management" (fly in, crap all over everything, and fly out,) comes naturally to an individual who has been at the helm for many years, or someone whose last name is on the building with no cares or worries.

Depending on the method of transferring control (sale of stock, voting trust or gift to family member), the employment contract may be simple or comprehensive. In other words, if the owner has sold the majority of the equity and operational control to a powerhouse key manager, he needn't waste time trying to establish compensation and accountability parameters. The manager will just say, "I'm out of here," and move on to the next career opportunity.

However, in most cases, the key manager is talented and capable, but short of being a complete powerhouse. In these more common circumstances, owners will formalize agreements upon the compensation structure of the controlling manager, as well as performance expectations and the timing and methodology of performance reviews before transferring control.

Equally important, before closing the transfer of control, it is critical to agree on pay plans for the key manager and those family members who continue to work in the business.

If appropriate, employment contracts would also describe the very important subject of training for junior family members. A general, but well thought out Management Development Curriculum should be embodied in the contracts of family members trying to achieve the training necessary to prepare for a future leadership role. This training curriculum is a much easier project to confirm and initiate while the family retains control. Then, when the deal is struck, everyone understands training responsibilities. After control has transferred, there is appropriately an immediate priority shift that may put off or permanently shelve a family member training program. I assure you, in the absence of an agreement for continuing training of family members, there will at least be moments of awkwardness and possibly never-ending controversy. Training kids, brats and heir-do-wells may not be high on the manager's agenda. These are just the kind of headaches that the business does not need when a new leader is trying to, stretch his wings, be large and in charge and begin the long awaited implementation of policies for the achievement of higher performance.

Another versatile structure for conveying control is a voting trust. This vehicle, created by a reasonably simple document, holds a proxy for the voting power of the portion of the business placed within the trust. A voting trust does not constitute a change in ownership and therefore, in and of itself, does not involve a financial transaction.

The provisions in the trust describe the terms under which the vote of the stock in the trust can be utilized by the key manager to exercise various forms of control. These terms would specify control powers, include the number of years the voting authority will be held and the contingencies under which that power may be removed. Removal contingencies could include provisions such as violation of financial covenants, failure to achieve or sustain profitability, termination of employment or conviction for a felony. The trust may also prohibit specific acts or transactions by the controlling key manager, such as sale of the company or pledging of assets without approval of the other owners or board of directors.

A voting trust is a very flexible instrument that circumvents the potential disadvantages or the hardship of actually buying and/or selling sufficient <u>stock to transfer control.</u>

Maybe the stock has too much income or growth potential to sell. Maybe the value of the stock is just off the board, making it totally unrealistic for the manager to purchase. Maybe the key manager is a family member and the sale of more stock to this child would disrupt previous agreements on estate asset division. Or control, not ownership, may be the hot button. The trust can be adapted to the needs of the executive, the family and the business.

I have been involved in numerous succession planning efforts where Mom and Dad wanted to pass their business through their estate equally to two or more children. However, the parents did not want the inactive children to have the ability to gang up on the family manager. Consequently, they provided for the stock that was to be owned by the inactive children to pass into a trust, which gave the active child a voting proxy for all of the stock.

Here's a case history that shows the advantages of giving a high level of control to a key manager. It also illustrates the critical need for an unusually solid relationship between the parties.

Case History: Gary, the attorney

The case involved the construction of a Key Manager Equity Control Succession Bridge in the automobile industry. The circumstances were very interesting. Two stockholders owned three independent dealerships representing six franchises. One of these dealerships was prospering and two were struggling. Gary, the founder of the original dealership and majority partner of all the dealerships, was a 63-year-old attorney who had come into the automobile business in his early 40's as a byproduct of being bored with the practice of law and having had the good fortune to represent a retiring automobile dealer who had no children. A resourceful entrepreneur, Gary offered to buy the dealership rather than have his client put the business on the market. Contrary to expectations, his client accepted his offer. Gary promptly retired from the practice of law and became an automobile dealer.

As with many stations in life, the grass on the other side of the fence was not as green as expected. Gary discovered that there is more to success than mere ownership. Although happy in his new career, he struggled to achieve profits. Fortunately, Gary heard about Rob, a young, very knowledgeable automobile operator who had worked for a competitor.

Rob was 20 years his junior, but was a natural car man and a tireless worker. Gary convinced Rob to come to work for him and, in very short order, Rob helped Gary find that elusive black ink and established Gary's business as a solid, highly respected automobile dealership. Gary's children were very young. Realizing that his good fortune was the product of the previous owner's inability to establish a succession plan, Gary enabled Rob to become a minority partner and they established a very simple buyout agreement in the event of either party's death.

Over the ensuing 20 years, Gary and Rob developed a great personal and business relationship. From a business perspective, their personalities were very compatible and they developed unwavering mutual trust. Rob was a driver and Gary stayed out of his way in operations. Gary was a nitpicky, detail guy, so he directed his attention to administration, banking and franchiser relations. Rob's natural automotive ability enabled him to establish profitable operations.

Equally important, Rob's operational ability enabled them to obtain two other franchises that were the foundation of the outstanding success of the business.

I met Gary and Rob by referral from a very bright and intuitive representative of their major manufacturer who was aware of our firm's unique business succession planning specialty. This executive astutely realized that the smooth, efficient succession of this dealership was in the manufacturer's best interest. He realized that the manufacturer's sales momentum and customer satisfaction were at risk if optimum business succession were not achieved.

I was thrilled that someone on the manufacturing level had agreed with my concept that business succession planning builds and protects value for all those concerned, even the suppliers and vendors. After being introduced, I proceeded with my customary interviews of the owners and managers. Gary's son, Jimmy, had chosen a career in the automobile business and was a significant factor in the planning. He was 35 years old and generally aspired to follow in his father's footsteps as the dealer.

It did not take long to determine that there was something "rotten in Denmark." Gary was out of sorts. He wanted to begin planning his retirement but said that, over the past couple of years, he and Rob had stopped communicating. Even more distressing, Gary said that he perceived growing animosity between Rob and Jimmy. Gary was genuinely concerned about the succession of his business, his relationship with Rob, the future career path of his son and his retirement security.

I remember commenting that he was pretty well overwhelmed with legitimate concerns and pointing out that, unfortunately, their simplistic buy-sell agreement did not address the contingency of disability or retirement.

Rob also expressed concerns. At 49, he was in the prime of his automotive career. His success as general manager had enabled him to build an impressive net worth that would enable him to purchase his own store. He was receiving recognition of his peers and the various manufacturers as a successful, forward- thinking leader in automobile retailing. Without the slightest reservation, Rob said that he had been anticipating Gary's retirement. He had paid his dues and no longer was willing to play second fiddle.

He wanted majority ownership and unquestioned control of any future business venture in which he was involved. He was specifically unwilling to allow Gary to turn his controlling interest in the dealerships to Jimmy. He made it emphatically clear he would not continue to run the dealerships for Jimmy as he had for Gary.

Rob said that he felt Jimmy had questionable drive and commitment, and he resented any assumption that the mutual respect and trust achieved from his 25-year relationship with Gary could simply be transferred to Jimmy. As a reflection of his appreciation and respect for Gary, Rob stated that he realized the difficulty of Gary's family circumstances and therefore would be willing to buy Gary's interest or sell his interest to Gary at values established by an independent appraiser.

Rob had given the situation a great deal of thought and had concluded that there was no way to resolve the three-way dilemma. Consequently, Rob wanted a buyout that would protect his relationship with Gary.

And then there was Jimmy, who had an altogether different paradigm. He was, in one word, frustrated. He felt his father was too preoccupied with planning his retirement to train him. Rob, once a good friend and confidante, was now giving him the cold shoulder. As a byproduct of this rejection, he confessed to having lost confidence in his ability as a manager.

Having no hope or vision for the future, he had lost his zeal for day-to-day operations. After discussing his experience and training background, it also became very apparent to me that Jimmy was in over his head as a manager. As expected, there was friction between Jimmy and other managers in the organization, because he was seen as the privileged offspring. Jimmy confirmed that, irrespective of his lifelong desire to be an automobile dealer, if his dad and Rob were going to continue giving each other the cold shoulder, he and his family would move and he would pursue a career in another community.

Subsequent interviews with three or four managers in the organization confirmed my preliminary assessment of this unfortunate situation. The key managers believed Gary was well beyond his prime and thought it was in the best interest of the organization for him to retire. He meant well, but his dabbling in customer service, business administration and operations always seemed to cause more problems than it solved. He was very well liked and everyone sympathized over his predicament with his partner and his son.

Rob was considered to be the good guy in a bad situation. Each of the managers interviewed, being keenly perceptive, asked "Why should Rob train Jimmy and allow him to ride his coattails into the dealer chair without paying his dues?" From their perspective, Jimmy lacked the enthusiasm, drive and decisiveness to be an effective dealer.

Each of the managers also expressed concern about their own careers. They were researching other employment opportunities because they felt the organization was floundering without a clear direction for succession.

After completing the interviews, reviewing the financial data and examining the relevant documents, I reached a rare conclusion: Everyone involved in this mess was in deep trouble. Gary's retirement was impossible unless Rob stayed on board or sold out to a third party. If Rob did not stay on board or if he sold, Jimmy's career aspirations would be in the tank. If Jimmy quit the business, he would follow his wife's lead and move to a different community, and with them would go Gary's grandchildren.

If Rob forced Gary to sell out his interest to him, there would be hard feelings that would challenge their relationship. Further, Rob would have to endure the significant financial pressure of buying Gary's interest. If Rob sold to Gary, his investment capital would be discounted by capital-gains tax. Consequently, he could only afford a significantly smaller operation, losing both the prestige and economies of scale offered by the existing operation. If he maintained status quo, he would ultimately have to play second fiddle to Jimmy, who, like his dad, was dependent upon him to run the operations.

Poor Jimmy believed that he was the pinball of misfortune. If his father bought out Rob, he would be confronted with running an operation that he admitted he was unprepared to handle. If Rob and his dad maintained status quo, he would continue to be frustrated and disrespected because no one would give him training. If his father sold to Rob, considering Rob's recent insensitive attitude, he expected to be looking for a job shortly after the documents were signed. There was no other job in this relatively small community (which his wife did not like), so he would have to uproot his family.

The auto manufacturer's sales manager, who had referred me, had realized that this historically outstanding dealership was going to suffer under any of these contingencies. He was in a no-win situation because he needed to maintain market share but, according to the franchise agreement, could not force Gary to do anything. By the same token, most of the second-level managers assumed that they were destined to have problems with whatever transpired.

Regardless of whether Gary bought, Rob bought, or they sold out to a third party, the business was going to experience significant change. All agreed that, with change, there would be employment upheaval.

The manufacturer's representative was a very bright, sensitive gentleman who had a strong financial background, including financial-planning experience. I welcomed his input. Amazingly, both of us came up with the same idea, but neither of us had much confidence in how we could pull it off. We agreed that, if there were no intervening acceptable succession plan, everyone was going to be a loser. We felt the way to avoid this loss would be to keep everyone together. The simple question was how to pull it off?

As the planning leader, I felt we should follow my normal Planning Review and Succession Analysis procedure. That includes organizing data, confirming goals, evaluating circumstances in relation to those goals and offering observations, with supporting considerations, regarding problems or opportunities. In private sessions, both Rob and Gary confirmed their objectives. Gary wanted only the best for his good friend Rob, who had never wavered in his loyalty and commitment to his family and his business. He also wanted his son, Jimmy, to follow in his footsteps and eventually take over as dealer. Rob also expressed unwavering respect for Gary. He profoundly appreciated the opportunities he had given him.

However, in private discussion, he acknowledged he was fed up working around both Gary and Jimmy. Although Gary was his partner, he did not help with the operational load. In fact, Gary created work by involving himself in things that he should have avoided. Jimmy meant well, but Rob felt naturally reluctant to train someone who ultimately wanted to be his boss.

Rob wanted to be free of the pressure of his dilemma, but recognized the delicate nature of becoming sole owner while maintaining his relationship with Gary, who had helped him become so successful. As a refreshing change, loyalty was a planning impediment. Rob said he wanted to be "the man." He could no longer stomach being a minority partner. And he could not visualize himself as the operator of an insignificant, single-point operation that could match his capital.

Independently, Jimmy said he felt abandoned. His father, because of his relationship with Rob, was unwilling to assert himself to define and implement a training program that would equip Jimmy to be a manager. On the other hand, Rob, because of his relationship with Jimmy's father, was not willing to address accountability issues, such as job performance and pay plans.

My observations to Gary and Rob were that their individual goals were beset with problems. I told Gary that there was no way he could transfer his relationship with Rob to his son. The only viable relationship Jimmy could have with Rob would be earned through hard work and dedicated performance. Rob was not going to spoon-feed Jimmy anymore.

Jimmy must be allowed to sink or swim. Further, if Gary elected to buy out Rob to "enable" his son's career path, he could forget retiring for at least 10 years. And there was no guarantee Jimmy would ever measure up to the task of being a dealer.

I told Rob that he could probably borrow enough money to buy out Gary, but he would be way out there on a financially leveraged limb in an industry known for its vicious business cycles. In a business environment impacted by public companies with deep pockets, that would be a precarious position. If he sold out to Gary, after paying capital gains tax, he might have enough money to buy a store. However, it would probably be a single franchise operation that could become road kill if the economy dropped.

Although Rob was right to be concerned about whether Jimmy would want to follow his father's path and become an administrative partner, he had to admit that Jimmy was bright, capable and eager to learn the business. If Jimmy could be motivated and trained properly, he could be the perfect successor to allow Rob to take it easy in a few years.

Individually, I presented both of them with a question: Was there any possibility of modifying their goals if we could find a win-win solution?

Their answer gave hope. Both described possible compromise positions. Gary would be comfortable with a plan that provided him financial security, gave his son an opportunity to be a manager, allowed him to retire within a few years and permitted him and his son to continue as stockholders. Rob could be comfortable with a plan that gave him control.

Gary would have to retire, Rob said, because he could not have Gary questioning his daily operating decisions. Rob was willing to train Jimmy, but only if he responded with the energy and commitment of any other manager.

I was beginning to feel more optimistic. The puzzle was not solved, but it appeared the pieces were in hand. Gary and Rob had conflicting priorities because of their improper assumptions, which had been created by misinterpretation and poor communication. However, there was enough common ground and, more importantly, trust and respect to build a Key Manager Equity Control Succession Bridge.

I continued to hold private meetings so that I could encourage commonality and, ideally, enable them to individually identify the solution before I met with them as a group, which would be more difficult to manage. It was important that we avoid open debate until they had sufficient recognition and acceptance of the potential gains of continuing to work together, because their distorted idea of a debate was an ultimatum.

During several discussions on just this point, my persistent question was, "What do you have to lose by pursuing succession?" The respective disadvantages created by any of the other disposition options became vividly clear. Gary's biggest concern about giving up control was the impact this could have on Jimmy's career. My response to Gary was this was a legitimate concern, but Jimmy's career was dependent upon Jimmy.

He was 35 years old and it was time for him to show his commitment and ability. If he were unwilling or unable to perform, it was in Jimmy's best interest to pursue a career less demanding. The chances of Jimmy corralling a willing horse like Rob to ride for his entire career were slim at best. I further emphasized to Gary that he could not depend upon others to look after his son. Jimmy was going to have to make his own way.

Rob's major concern, as expected, was that he would have to continue to deal with both Gary and Jimmy. I said that I could guarantee that Gary would retire, but I could not guarantee that Jimmy would become the perfect employee-manager. I actually was betting Gary would retire, if he thought it was the right thing for Jimmy.

I also told Rob that I could guarantee Jimmy would not meet his full expectations and would probably challenge his patience and leadership ability. But, I asked, what else is new?

To the best of my knowledge, he did not have a perfect manager on staff. In my 30-year career, I told him, I had never met the perfect manager. We both agreed that this phenomenon did not exist. If he sold out and bought another dealership, or if he bought out Gary, he again would have to tolerate less than perfect managers. At least he already knew Jimmy and viewed him as bright and responsible.

Why walk away from a 20-year investment in this dealership to start over, when he could have absolute control of these dealerships?

Jimmy, with both an ownership and a pride interest, could be his greatest asset. Giving Jimmy a fair shake would be his biggest challenge.

Within a short time the jury would be back on Jimmy. He would either be a valuable member of his management team or a bad memory.

Neither Gary nor Rob could be accused of jumping to an impulsive decision. They both realized their biggest challenge would be to give Jimmy a fair shake as a trainee.

Thankfully, over time, sound logic prevailed. After each of them refined the details of their compromise positions, we met jointly and I presented the Key Manager Equity Control Succession Bridge concept.

I proposed that Gary sell to Rob sufficient stock to give him 60% ownership of all the dealerships. Gary would retire within two years. In the transition period until his retirement, Gary would focus his efforts on tying up loose ends of the succession plan, such as gifting stock to Jimmy and community involvement. His employment contract would specify that he would work only as a community liaison and, specifically, that he would not be involved in day-to-day management. After retirement, Gary would be expected to continue in this role and be provided salary continuation benefits in consideration of the services. With the purchase of 60% of all the dealerships, Rob would be in undisputed control of operations.

This was not a "no-brainer" for either Gary or Rob. They had both been frustrated for so long they had almost lost hope. Each of them struggled with a decision, calling me on innumerable occasions. I was at my wit's end, expecting any day to hear that the ball was coming unraveled. When the decision was made, I was shocked at what had taken place. Rob called and said they were ready to move forward.

Jimmy had swung the pendulum. Jimmy had gone to both Gary and Rob to say that they were stupid if they did not give succession a chance.

He told them that they would not have to worry about him. He would do what ever Rob required of him to learn the business and become a solid contributor. Rob admitted that it took a lot of gumption to do that and said he was ready to give Jimmy a chance, promising him he was going to kick his butt up around his ears if he let down his dad.

Subsequently, I met with the group and we agreed that the Board of Directors would consist of Gary, Rob and Jimmy and that they would meet ideally on a monthly basis, but no less frequently than quarterly, to review past performance and consider strategic operational moves. Rob designed a training program for Jimmy that gave him a legitimate opportunity to acquire the management skills needed to be a contributing manager. They also agreed to enroll Jimmy in a formal training program that he should have completed 10 years earlier. Rob realized Jimmy was not a deadbeat. If he could help Jimmy mature as a manager, he would be of value, not only as a manager, but also as another proprietor who would watch the dollars and cents.

Rob also realized, having two daughters who probably would not pursue an automobile career, Jimmy was his natural successor.

We agreed that Gary would sell Rob 20% in each store, giving him a total of 60% ownership. Jimmy realized it was put up or shut up time. In order for him to remain involved in the dealership, ultimately owning at least 40% and potentially buying out Rob, he would have to aggressively pursue acquiring the skills he needed and be a role model to the other managers who would be watching him closely. In the event Jimmy could not make the grade, his father would hold onto 40% of the stock in the near term, so that he could ultimately sell it to Rob. This transaction was to be documented in a Stockholder's Agreement that stated, among other things, all stockholders -- with the exception of Gary --must be actively employed. However, beyond the contractual legalities, it was clearly understood that this complex transaction was in everyone's best interest, but would only work if everyone extended themselves beyond their natural comfort zone to address the needs and concerns of their partners.

This deal had many challenges in its adoption and continues to have many challenges in its operation. I have spent countless hours listening to the fears and concerns of all three parties. Yet this ship has been floating high in the water because all three applied their energies to make it work. Jimmy became a wonderful surprise. Without any assumptions or questions, he has done everything Rob has asked. He has earned Rob's respect. Gary has begun transferring stock to Jimmy with Rob's endorsement and encouragement.

Each of the stockholders realized that, if it did not work, we could pull the plug and precipitate a buyout. More importantly, each stockholder also realized that, if this Control Equity Bridge did work, their lives would be much, much better.

Fortunately, this control Succession Bridge lives on and, ideally, when the time comes, Jimmy will return the favor for Rob.

10 The Key Management Buyout Succession Bridge

In previous chapters we have discussed various methods of providing incentives for a very special key manager to serve as a Succession Bridge. These incentives included providing an opportunity for a manager to buy into the business. The buy-in opportunities included purchasing both a minority interest and a controlling interest. These varied forms of stock acquisition come under the general heading of "Equity Succession Bridge."

However, there are succession circumstances when these buy-in concepts are not compatible. These circumstances usually fall within one of two situations: The key manager(s) is not interested in any stock purchase opportunity that does not ultimately lead to the purchase of all the stock. The nature of the business may reflect that being a minority stockholder is no advantage. And the nature of the very special key manager (VSKM) may be that he is determined to be a business owner and nothing else.

The second very common situation is when the business owner has no family succession ambition. For any number of legitimate reasons, the owner is not interested in taking the stock to the grave or passing the stock to his family. The owner plans to sell the business and the only questions are when and how?

We will call the structures developed to accommodate these circumstances a "Buyout Succession Bridge."

Regardless of the motive, the goal of this structure is to establish a win/win transition of ownership between the current owner and a very special key manager(s) who has a proven history of extraordinary business performance and personal integrity.

Generally, there are unique circumstances inviting the implementation of a Buyout Succession Bridge. Notably, the owner has no current partner who is anticipating a buyout and no succession qualified son or daughter to whom the owner can transfer the business. The handiwork of father time is making the owner, family members and vendors concerned about the ultimate disposition of the business. However, the owner is not yet ready to sell or disengage from the business activity that has become an integral, if not the primary focus of his life. In most cases, regardless of how nervous about death, disability or retirement, the owner is not ready to stop doing what he loves the most, operating the business. In other cases, the owner has just awakened to the reality that if he wanted to retire, but could not, and if he died or was disabled, his business value is in great jeopardy.

Regardless of which circumstance applies, the predictable lead into the Buyout Succession Bridge is that the owner wants to button down the disposition of the business (for family, employees, customers and vendors) as he continues to work and enjoy the salary, profit distributions and perks of business ownership for a reasonable period of time. Further, it is predictable that the owner has a strong motivation to provide an ownership opportunity to a specific child, a special manager, a group of special managers or a combination of everyone and, invariably, this internal sale plays an important role in the owner's retirement income security, equitable estate division and estate.

The architecture of a Buyout Succession Bridge can utilize one or more individuals or a group of managers operating as a management company. The structure of the buyers dictates variations in configurations and mechanics of the transaction. Interchanging a management company for an individual(s) Buyout Succession Bridge requires additional documents that organize, control and establish performance incentives for the management company and the various key managers.

We will use an individual Buyout Succession Bridge structure as an illustration. As with each alternative Succession Bridge structure, a Buyout Succession Bridge is dependent upon the owner making a disposition decision to sell. I have spent what seems like a lifetime trying to convince business owners to either sell or keep a business. I have learned, regrettably slowly, that no one can persuade a business owner to put his business on the market. That decision comes from within, if and when the circumstances are consistent with needs and feelings.

Assuming the business is a profitable and lucrative family establishment, the owner could certainly receive a very attractive sales price. But then there is the capital gains tax. Sometimes this is a valid excuse for tax-a-phobics who just cannot sleep at night knowing they are going to have to pay a portion of the nation's overhead. However, most business owners realize that, if you ride the bus, you must pay your nickel, and capital gains tax is a pretty cheap ride. Therefore, the hissy fit is just a cover up for a sentimental hesitancy to give up their "baby."

Although weariness, burnout and mortality are staring them in the face, they are just not ready to let someone else take control, or perhaps abuse their employees or even soil a pristine reputation. But the frustrating cycle of worry and indecision continues as the owner realizes that if he continues to procrastinate on a decision to sell, as age marches on and circumstances evolve, there is no certainty that a perfect buyer can be found or an acceptable price can be achieved.

This is fertile ground for the Buyout Succession Bridge-- an attractive business, an aging owner who likes the business, no successors and sentimental attachment. A less common, but equally motivating circumstance is good old Yankee ambition. The owner wants to hedge his bets on succession while staying involved to reap more of the financial rewards. The sales price may not match expectations. Financial circumstances confirm the owner could get more out of the business if they continue to be involved.

There is one other critical circumstance and potentially motivating factor for a Buyout Succession Bridge, a very special key manager. We have discussed very special key managers earlier. However, under the context of a Buyout Succession Bridge, we are talking VERY SPECIAL! These unique managers are not easy to find but they are very easy to identify. If one is already on board, they have been the backbone of the business. They are often viewed as a son or daughter by the owner. This is the perfect situation because there will be no need for dating and a short engagement prior to marriage. They are known commodities who have proved their capabilities under a variety of circumstances. Notably, they meet the three critical qualifications of a Succession Bridge: you like'em, you trust 'em and you respect 'em.

On the other hand, if the owner is not so fortunate to have a very special key manager on board, consideration of the Buyout Succession Bridge is more complex. First, the owner has to accept the possibility that one can be found.

The common question asked is "If these guys are out there, why didn't I run into one before I got old and frustrated?" There are lots of possible answers to that question, including the one most owners like, bad luck.

However, the most probable reason is that the owner is such a control freak or is so weird that highly talented and motivated managers would rather be exiled to Iran than work for him.

This being the case, there continues to be a challenge to get these management phenoms to come on board for a Buyout Succession Bridge. The fact is, there are viable Buyout Succession Bridge candidates out there who are looking to fulfill their dream to be a business owner and are willing to run the gauntlet to get there. They do not come like flies to a picnic, but if the owner is reasonable and compatible, they can be found. Every industry has under-recognized, over-ambitious managers who are obsessed with being a business owner.

Unless love-at-first-sight occurs, considerable time could be involved, and this could blow the concept.

By far, the most common Buyout Succession Bridge situation is when a very special key manager is already on board and is already considered a member of the extended family. It is also common to find an owner who wants to recognize the key manager and help him to achieve his goal, or do for them what someone did for the owner at the beginning of his career. Yet, the owner also has several fundamental business motivations, which include continued business involvement, shifting of management pressure to the Buyout Succession Bridge, salary continuation, benefit continuation and profit sharing.

It is the sharing of profits that makes the Buyout Succession Bridge work.

In most circumstances the Buyout Succession Bridge candidate is long on talent and ambition, but short on cash or credit. Therefore, in order to make this program happen, the owner has to provide attractive terms for the buyout. Here is where the "trust 'em and respect 'em" gets the test. The terms include an attractive price, a modest initial "buy" and a contract to purchase the balance over an extended period of time, up to as much as 10 or 15 years. In the realm of "give to get," the financial "get" for the owner is participation in the profits over this extended period of time without having to devote his golden years to the day-to-day grind of daily operations.

The extended buy-in usually takes place in three major steps. The first step is an initial purchase of 5% to 25% with cash and/or notes. The price for this initial stock purchase is generally favorable. If an owner tells me he has to have top dollars on this initial transaction, I tell him he needs to go sell on the open market. "You will get your top dollar price, but you will probably receive less money in the long run and you will definitely miss out on the other benefits." A Buyout Succession Bridge is not about beating one's chest regarding an impressive sales price. It is about getting a very good value and an attractive package of benefits that are presumably very important to the owner and, on total, more valuable than the currently available sales price.

A favorable price establishes a golden handcuff incentive to the manager to justify forgoing personal cash flow from bonuses for up to 10 years that will be utilized to purchase stock. The pressure of establishing an attractively fair value falls upon the owner, who normally is the author of this program. The bargain price can be determined through a "minority" appraisal by a professional (required with a child) or the price can just be determined by the parties or a mutually agreeable index, such as book value or a multiple of earnings. The most popular technique is to establish a fixed, bargain price and terms on the first 49%, and cash for the remaining 51% based upon fair market value without any discounts. The popularity of this approach comes from the manager's enthusiasm for the fixed bargain price for the minority share and the owner's enthusiasm for the floating (hopefully rising) non-discounted appraisal of the remaining majority.

With regard to the initial purchase of stock, think back to our earlier comments on the importance of commitment. Generally, in this first step, the more personal cash the "Buyout Succession Bridge" manager puts toward the purchase of stock, the greater the security the business owner has that the manager is making an all out commitment. The amount of the first step sale is determined by two factors: the manager's resources and the owner's level of trust. Trust is generally dependent upon how long you have known someone. A long standing key manager who is like part of the family could potentially qualify to purchase just a few shares with cash and a second mortgage on his home. On the other hand, in order for an owner to be comfortable with a Succession Bridge recruit, a 25% initial cash investment may be required.

If the Buyout Succession Bridge is a family member, or is treated like one, and must borrow for the initial purchase, the owner can extend a portion of the credit. However, I strongly recommend that the manager be expected to come up with a relatively substantial portion of cash independently.

When borrowing is required, the buyout progression should not proceed beyond this initial purchase until the acquisition note to the owner or to a third party is paid in full.

The Buyout Succession Bridge is a close relative of the Equity and Control Equity Succession Bridges. It uses a stockholder's agreement to control the actions of parties and circumstances under which actions take place. The parties to the agreement are, of course, the owner and the buying manager, but also any other stockholders and any contingent stockholders, such as current or prospective trustees, who will manage the owner's estate in the event of death prior to completion of the buyout. The terms of the agreement primarily reflect the goals and priorities of the selling owner.

One of the more important terms is the timetable that determines when the current owner will be completely taken out of the business. Typically this is an extended period, perhaps five, 10 or even 15 years. During this time, the owner would enjoy the continuation of dividends compensation and the customary perks, such as insurance and automobile, along with special perks, such as participation in associations, conventions and technology sharing groups.

The second stock purchase transaction or, more appropriately, transactions, is the marquee aspect of the Buyout Succession Bridge. In this second step, the key manager, managers, or the management company, incrementally purchase stock with their proportionate share of the annual profits generated by the business. The long-term progressive stock purchase goal is to put the Buyout Succession Bridge on the threshold of achieving voting control. The stockholder's agreement would state that, after all debt involved in the initial stock transaction was satisfied, the manager's portion of the annual profit distributions (as dividend or bonus) are pledged to the purchase of additional stock. In the case of a Sub-S corporation or an LLC, the manager's profits would come from profit distributions. In the case of a regular corporation, the manager's profits would come from a special bonus equivalent to his proportionate share of earnings as described in an employment contract.

Starting Small

The annual incremental purchases of stock, initially builds up slowly because of the initial small stock holding. However, in support of the Proverb, "Forsake not humble beginnings," the buying manager's holdings incrementally increase each year, creating a compounding increase in his portion of the profits. This increased share of earnings is used to purchase an increased portion of stock, and so on and so on. Predictably the initial value appears to be an overwhelming goal. However, the hinge pin of this second step is controlled by the manager's performance. With the Buyout Succession Bridge assuming the role of chief operating officer, it is expected that the Buyout Succession Bridge will seek higher levels of productivity and efficiency. If the manager recognizes this opportunity and takes the business to a new level of profitability, the higher profit distributions will speed up the purchase of stock. This incentive also works to the owner's advantage because, with higher profitability, the owner will also receive higher profit distributions on his remaining stock and the value of the business will be increasing.

Taking The Leap

The third step in the Buyout Succession Bridge comes under the heading of "The Takeout." This describes the final stock-purchase transaction in which the manager, managers or management company purchases the 51% controlling balance of the stock and, with that leap, assumes 100% ownership of the business. Obviously, each Buyout Succession Bridge contains design features that will be unique to the business circumstances and the owner.

An important design decision is when to empower the final takeout and what price to set for the majority share. "Takeout" usually occurs when sufficient time has passed that the owner is ready to get out.

Apart from the sentimental issues, an important question of timing is when the owner's participation in the profit distribution is sufficient to make the deal worthwhile.

That question cannot be answered in advance. As circumstances evolve, both the owner and the business will determine the fairness of the deal at any given time. Every time I hear a manager or an owner celebrating or griping, I always advise them to lay off the espresso, because circumstances are sure to change before the buyout is complete. In anticipation of profit distributions, it is reasonable for the agreement to stipulate that, irrespective of profits, the takeout will not occur until the manager(s) has purchased 49% of the business, or a minimum number of years, or a specific date, whichever is later.

After the manager makes the initial purchase of stock, it is reasonable to allow him an extended period of time to buy the balance of the 49%. In retrospect, if the stipulated time period was not sufficient for the owner to build a formidable nest egg from the proportionate allocation of profits, the price associated with the Buyout Succession Bridge was too low. To prevent regrets over pricing, the agreement usually stipulates that, if the Buyout Succession Bridge manager gets to 49% ownership before the completion of the target time period, such as 10 years, the stock purchased is usually put on hold to allow the owner to fulfill profit participation expectations.

A fundamental assumption of the buyout Succession Bridge is that the manager will be able to borrow or beg enough money to buy the remaining 51% in a lump sum after he has achieved free and clear ownership. The assumption is that 100% of the profits would be sufficient to amortize a loan to purchase the remaining 51%. If this is not the case, the situation becomes significantly more complicated.

Although the sale of stock could be structured in any fashion, I strongly endorse requiring cash for the balance of the stock. Unless an owner is especially comfortable becoming involved in a Control Equity Succession Bridge, I do not recommend giving up control and becoming dependent upon the good faith and character of the manager to satisfy income and security needs through the payment of a note. With my concern about control, I would recommend re-capitalizing the corporation with non-voting stock, and continue the incremental sale of non-voting shares while retaining voting control, if the manager cannot muster the resources to buy the remaining 51 percent of the business.

Even if done incrementally, the third takeout step would be based upon a fair-market appraisal, based on the date of the transaction that includes a control premium. Or it can be based on the minimum amount the owner needs to make the deal work.

The bottom line is that the deal has to work for the owner.

Regardless of how the stock is purchased and the stock valuation methodology, the deal has to create sufficient cash, benefits and security for the owner. It is critically important that there is agreement at the outset on the timing of stock purchase and the valuation basis of all stock purchases. If both parties want to change the terms later, no problem. However, there is no room in a Buyout Succession Bridge for ongoing negotiations. Trust me, there are other more important and more enjoyable activities than renegotiating the terms of a buyout.

For the most part, the mechanics of the Buyout Succession Bridge involves three major agreements: the buyout agreement, the manager's employment agreement and the owner's employment agreement. In franchise or high credit circumstances, documents securing the continuity of the franchise and credit line are also involved. When the business rents real estate from the business owner, contemporary leases or purchase options are also a part of the package. The fundamental document is the stockholder's agreement, which is also the buyout agreement. It establishes a wide range of parameters for the sale of stock. No detail is spared in an effort to address all contingencies. Remember, the best agreement is one that precludes all disagreements. It is only modest consolation to have an agreement that stands up in court. The best document is one that is so well understood that it keeps you out of court.

After the initial legal recitations, the agreement usually stipulates that, after the document is adopted, the manager will have purchased five % or more of the stock. The document also sets the repayment provisions of any debt on the initial purchase and it describes how annual profit distributions would be used to purchase up to 49% of the remaining stock.

The agreement must describe in detail how corporate profits are determined for the Buyout Succession Bridge. These are very important provisions. In order to minimize taxes, each business has unique methods, such as LIFO, write-downs and reserves of computing profits. These unique practices are unimportant. What is important is that the owner and the key manager agree precisely how the profits will be computed. This agreement should also address the distribution of business profits, which, of course, are critical to empowering the manager's stock purchase. How the accountant would apply the net after-tax revenue received by the manager to the purchase of additional shares would also be specified.

The method of valuing the stock must be described in sufficient detail to assure certainty of business value. There are several options for valuing the stock, including fair market valuation by an independent appraiser; a fixed, agreed upon price; or a formula. The preferred method is described in detail to assure clarity and long-term viability.

Authorized transfers and stock transfer restrictions are described. The manager is generally restricted from transferring any existing or future stock to anyone other than the owner. The owner would be authorized, for estate planning reasons, to transfer stock to family members as long as that stock remains bound by the buyout agreement.

Typically, the owner retains the right to sell the entire company, but the manager is given a first right of refusal at the stipulated price within the agreement.

The manager, the manager's estate or the manager's guardian is generally required to sell the stock back to the owner in the event of employment termination for any reason. The owner's transfer restrictions usually have more latitude. In the event of the owner's death, his estate is required to continue the scheduled buyout. Based upon the preferences of the owner, his family and the key managers, life insurance can be utilized to facilitate or complete the buyout. Minimally, I recommend that the key manager own a life insurance policy on the owner, pledged to the purchase of sufficient additional stock to validate a lock down vested interest.

Profits

The final specific provision of the stockholders' agreement pertains to distribution of profits. Assuming the business is a Subchapter-S corporation, partnership or LLC, the agreement documents that, with the exception of needed working capital, as determined by mutual agreement, annual profits will be distributed to fund the buyout. In recognition of the inevitable need for working capital, the agreement also generally stipulates that either the owner or the manager can dictate that a minimum (usually 20%) percentage of profits can be retained for working capital. If the business is a regular corporation, the agreement would state that profits above minimum working capital needs, would be made available for bonuses.

Any discussion of profits through bonuses dictates the need for employment contracts for all parties. These documents are identical in nature to those we have previously discussed. Also, as previously encouraged, no effort should be spared to document agreement on any and every detail that can impact the ultimate goal.

In keeping with the goal of precluding disagreements, remember that disagreements are usually over money or benefits and rarely occur until the pressure is on, dollars are on the table and character flaws emerge through selective memory.

With respect to the owner, the employment contract confirms the owner's compensation and profit sharing bonuses, giving the manager peace of mind that the owner will not distort profits by inflating his compensation. The agreement also specifies any benefits, such as a car and insurance, that the owner will receive up to the time of the total buyout. In some cases, the agreement will provide for these benefits beyond the buyout as consideration for ongoing consulting.

This agreement also formalizes the owner's responsibilities and specifically acknowledges what is not the owner's responsibility. This formality is important to the owner, who wants to be relieved of the day to day management grind, and to the Buyout Succession Bridge, who does not want the owner sticking his nose where it does not belong.

Generally, the contract states that the owner will serve as chairman of the board and chief executive officer. Unless both parties agree that the manager needs more training and/or experience, the owner's duties are generally limited to management oversight through well organized management meetings and reports that focus on the critical issues that reflect the health and direction of the business.

The employment agreement for the buying manager is more involved. This document stipulates the manager's specific responsibilities as chief operating officer. In addition to addressing the typical day-to-day grind of operating a business, the COO's responsibilities also include keeping the predictably nervous owner informed by personal briefings and written reports that describe the pulse, health and direction of business.

The manager's contract states that the manager is responsible for meeting specific performance benchmarks and complying with the operational parameters and annual business plan as approved by the board of directors. Also stipulated are the manager's compensation and performance incentives. In the case of regular corporations without the capability of passing through profits, special bonuses would be authorized and pledged to the purchase of stock.

This agreement further establishes covenants by the manager in the event of his termination before completion of the buyout. These covenants would state that, in the event of voluntary termination or termination for cause, he will not compete against the owner in the immediate market area. In the event of employment termination, the manager also agrees to the privacy of manufacturing or marketing information and to refrain from recruiting employees from the business. These covenants are fundamental aspects of the Buyout Succession Bridge that give the owner reasonable consideration for the outstanding opportunity being extended to the manager.

As discussed earlier, it is not beyond the realm of possibilities for a strong willed, myopic independent manager to resist these covenants. However, these restrictions should be considered in comparison to the opportunity provided. A buyout Succession Bridge is not chopped liver. It is a once in a lifetime opportunity!

A manager who argues about covenants not-to-compete is usually telling us that the deal is too demanding or that we are dealing with a pinhead.

Trust your judgment on this potentially volatile issue. But do not lose sight of the possibility that the price of the stock, the time for buying out the stock and the probabilities of enhancing earnings are not automatically perceived to be reasonable considerations for career restraint covenants.

In order for these covenants to have substance, the manager must be represented by counsel who can ensure that he understands the impact of these covenants, that they are a logical part of the agreement and that they should not be entered into frivolously. Enforcement of non-compete covenants is always a lose/lose proposition. The most effective use of non-compete covenants is during conceptual discussion on the front end. It is essential that a Succession Bridge not be built around a manager who is not willing to make a reasonable commitment.

In summary, a Buyout Succession Bridge is a win/win strategy designed to satisfy the personal needs of both the owner and a very special key manager. The application for this strategy is unique. However, since only one in four business owners have motivated, capable family successors, there is indeed a reasonable percentage of business owners who should at least entertain this concept. To help you better understand application and structure, here's a case history of a Buyout Succession Bridge that illustrates many of the design considerations that we have discussed.

Case History: Jerry, The Biker

Our client, Jerry, owned a Harley Davidson motorcycle franchise. He was 56 years old, married to his second wife and doing well financially. Unfortunately, neither of his sons were prospective successors.

Both of Jerry's sons were by his previous wife. According to Jerry's own words, "the tattoo dye must have gone to their brains, because both were a few teeth short of a full sprocket." More descriptively, they had spent more time riding with their chums than they had spent paying attention to the business. They also had fallen victim to the hazards of the culture. The oldest had spent time in the "slammer." Both·of them had taken a shot at spending their inheritance on tuition to drug and alcohol rehabilitation centers. The situation was so serious that Jerry and his second wife had adopted his grandchildren (by the oldest son) and were raising them as their own.

I had been referred to Jerry by another Harley Davidson dealer for whom we had implemented a Key Manager Contingency Bridge. Our client had conveyed to Jerry his excitement and satisfaction with a program we designed to protect his young sons.

At our first meeting, Jerry promptly pointed out there was no such contingency in his situation because there was no way his sons were ever going to take over his business. He wanted us to explain how to best posture his business for sale within three to four years. He named the target income he wanted, at which point we did some research on the market value of Harley Davidson dealerships. Subsequently we did a sales proforma, assuming he could get $5 million for the business and maintain the real estate as an investment.

After taxes on the $5 million, he would have about $4 million walking money. Assuming a 6% net cash return, he could have $360,000 per year in combined retirement income. Jerry's response was just as I expected. "What are you, nuts? My current take out of this business is over $500,000 a year. If I sell, you are telling me that I am going to take a $140,000 per year pay cut!"

I responded, "yes, but you will not be required to run the place or guarantee the floor plan debt." A hot debate ensued on a multitude of subjects, including the justification for taking a reduction in income, the benefits of becoming liquid, the price he could get for the business, the taxes he would have to pay and how stupid I was for thinking he would put his money in the stock market.

On his demand, I re-ran the proforma at $7 million, which really pushed the valuation envelope. When, he realized that even at a higher number, assuming T-Bill rates, he would not achieve better cash flow, he released a salvo of "biker words" without malice (it's just part of the culture,) at me, the IRS, the yet to be identified prospective buyer and life in general.

This was an earthy, freewheeling dude who had no trouble sharing how he felt. I ultimately asked what was bugging him so much, because I was just the messenger. I tried to explain that he was not alone, because rarely, if ever, does the investment return on the sales proceeds of a family business exceed the return on business operations. Risk does have some reward.

Unfortunately, he was not impressed with my eloquent illustration so I had to tell him that if he did not believe my numbers, he could retain someone else. I also let him know, as I have on many occasions, that I was hired to help him achieve his goals, not to take his verbal abuse. Then, as though he were just waiting for me to show some backbone, he said, "I know bikes, not investments."

From that moment on, he acted as though I had passed some test and had been admitted to a brotherhood culture. He took on an appreciative attitude, repeatedly offered me shots of whiskey, and continued with some biker lingo I did not understand, but I assumed was a welcome to the hood.

When he started talking English again, Jerry affirmed the obvious; he was just a motorcycle guy, nothing more and nothing less. He had taken on a Harley Davidson franchise when it was not worth a nickel. Motorcycles were his hobby and by blind luck, motorcycles had also become the source of a handsome livelihood. Currently, all of his friends and most of his enemies were in some way involved in his business or the cycling club, The Brotherhood of Leather, which he had formed to promote his business.

He had not paid a dime for the franchise because, 30 years ago, he could not divert any money from his part-time bike repair business. He had obtained the franchise as purely a source of free advertising and had built up such a good relationship with the factory they had honored his loyalty when the franchise began to grow value. He did not consider himself a success, he considered himself a survivor.

Over time, his bike repair business had become prosperous enough for him to give up his day job. Subsequently, Harley Davidson experienced a slow but monumentally impressive revival. He was a biking dude with all the faded tattoos to prove his heritage. In spite of his lack of education, he had become the owner of a vibrant business based on common sense and good character. His idea of a good investment was a used motorcycle. He kept about $10,000 in cash which he called his "attitude money." A speculative investment to Jerry was a bank account.

Jerry had no understanding of the dynamics of stocks, bonds, dividends, capital gains or the risks in the market or the economy. He had no concept or comfort with the prospect of investing $4 million of net sales proceeds anywhere, much less in the stock market.

This was by no means the first time I had seen sales fright. I realized that this was genuine anxiety that was paralyzing Jerry and putting him into the universally perplexing "no-decision" zone. In most cases, having a bad succession plan is better than having no succession plan. I invited Jerry to review his options under the assumption that continuing to make small, affirmative decisions builds positive momentum that can lead to very positive results.

I explained to him that he could sell the business and endure the challenge of becoming a money manager; do nothing and run the risk that the value he had built in his business would be lost in his estate or consider other alternatives. He obviously did not like the prospect of a sale and was not comfortable with leaving his wife and daughter to deal with the business.

As I had hoped, he took the bait and asked what I meant by alternatives. Instead of cashing out in one momentous move, I explained, he could sell the business to one or more key managers and stay involved, essentially for as long as it remained fun.

In our prior assessment interviews, I had learned that he had been struggling to modernize his accounting systems. Ten years earlier, the Harley Davidson vice president of sales had helped him recruit a general manager who literally had pulled him out of the grease with the IRS and floor plan lenders. In contemplation of suggesting a Buyout Succession Bridge, I reminded him that he had a very capable and loyal general manager.

Jerry chuckled as he recalled talking to the VP and asking him what it meant to be out-of-trust. "His answer was beautiful; it means the bank is going to throw your ass against the wall, take your business and what is left of your ass." He continued to laugh saying, "I wish I could talk banker as good as he talked biker. He immediately got my attention. I owe him my butt."

After the chuckle, I suggested to Jerry that there could be a way of establishing a deal with his general manager that would be better than a sellout. This thought grabbed his interest.

The general manager, Zeke, 40 years of age, was essentially running the business. Zeke was not much to look at, being 6'2", 350 pounds, baldheaded, a Fu Manchu mustache, mountainous belly and short, massive legs. However, Zeke had a brilliant mind for numbers and a lovable self-deprecating personality that served as a magnet to both employees and customers.

It was apparent that Zeke loved his job and was totally loyal to Jerry. He earned his CPA on his first pass at the exam, but never went into private practice because "my clients laughed at me more than they listened to me." Jerry made fun of him constantly but it was apparent that he loved the guy and trusted him without question. Behind his macho mask, Zeke was really a sensitive, intellectual eccentric, much like Jerry. He, his wife and daughter lived with his retired parents because "I just need to look after them." You could not help but love the guy, because he laughed at himself more than any other possibly could. Zeke was a perfect candidate for a Buyout Succession Bridge.

Jerry quickly grasped the concept. With a Buyout Succession Bridge, he could stay involved as long as he wanted and, if he died at the handlebars, there would be a guaranteed buyer, thus relieving his wife and children of any risk associated with operating the business. Most importantly, he would not have to burden himself with figuring out how to invest a big wad of cash.

It was the last point that got his attention. However his comments set the foundation for the deal. "Yeah, I'd like to see Zeke get the shop. My two sons would convert any cash to nose candy and my wife and daughter would not have a clue as to how to run this rascal. And if you could set up a trust or something to hold the money for me while I continued to work in the shop, we'll ride this bike."

I proceeded to introduce the opportunity to Zeke. Jerry's issues were not money or control, he just wanted to have a place he could go everyday. When he stayed home more than a couple days, he and his wife would drink too much and ultimately fight like sailors. The one time Jerry had been arrested for spousal abuse, he had to spend the night in the hospital getting repairs before he could go to jail. He wanted a place to go to stay out of his wife's way, enough annual income to support his reasonably conservative lifestyle and financial security for his wife, daughter and adopted grandchildren in the event of his death.

The proposal I made to Zeke involved an immediate purchase of 10% of the stock for $150,000, with a minimum $50,000 down and $100,000 in a note payable from the Subchapter-S earnings off his newly purchased stock. After income tax and 20% retained earnings for working capital, the projected net to Zeke for debt service would be $30,000 to $50,000 per year. After satisfying the $100,000 note, his subsequent profit distributions would be pledged to purchasing incremental stock every year, up to 49% of the equity.

The price for the additional stock purchases, up to 49%, would be set according to the same appraisal technique, which used both lack of control and lack of marketability discounts. This represented a great value to Zeke, equating to only 60% of fair market value. Naturally, protective of Jerry's interest, Zeke recognized the value he was receiving and impressively asked Jerry if he really wanted to sell him the stock at that price.

Jerry's reply was: "Don't you worry Zeke, there will be payback. You are just going to have to tolerate my grimy butt around here when I am too feeble to get on a bike." And with a big smile that showed silver caps on his teeth to match the chrome on his Harley, he said, "Furthermore, I'm going to take a big bite out of your behind when you come to me wanting to buy the 51%. And don't you forget," he added playfully, "I'm the boss until you own the show."

Jerry capitalized on the opportunity to pick on Zeke as he described the third step, Zeke's cash purchase of the remainder of the stock. I explained to Zeke that this purchase would also be at appraised value, which, as Jerry had pointed out in fun, carried a heavy price for becoming the undisputed heavyweight of the business. When discounts were considered for the first 49%, and premiums for the second 51%, Zeke would be purchasing the business for approximately 75% of what we figured it was worth on the open market.

To give Jerry peace of mind about working, the timing for the sale/purchase of the second half of the stock would be no less than 10 years, or when Jerry terminated employment. If Jerry terminated employment for retirement or disability, Zeke could not purchase the second half of the stock until he had fully purchased the first half through the plan. If Jerry died, the corporation would use the proceeds of a $3 million dollar life insurance policy to redeem Jerry's stock.

This redemption was contingent upon the purchase of all of Jerry's remaining stock for cash. Jerry would also have an employment contract, which specified that, in the event he retired or died within 10 years, Jerry and/or his family would receive a $100,000 annual salary, plus benefits, for 10 years.

Zeke's response was classic. "So what you are saying is that I have to pay you $100,000 to hang around here and aggravate me. It looks like all I have to do is come up with 50 grand and keep the gears turning around here until 'cue ball' buys himself out with his own money. Life insurance will probably be a waste because he has proved to us in several accidents that he is hard to kill. Do you even think you can get life insurance on this reprobate? Say, this deal is looking better because I know some brothers who would knock him off for a set of chrome headers."

Neither of these guys gave up a chance to stick it to the other. "And with respect to the covenants not to compete, that is worthless, because after working with this varmint, my reputation has become so bad that I doubt I could get a job anywhere. As far as the salary continuation to Jerry's family, he's too ugly to die. But if he did, I would take care of Connie and Susie like they were mine anyway. The way I read this deal, it is a bargain. No, let me correct myself, this is a gift because I would do everything you are asking without a deal, it is part of my job and friendship."

Zeke was truly a piece of work! I could see why Jerry considered him to be a stepson. He understood and exceeded what this Buyout Succession Bridge was designed to do. All I had to do was confirm his presumption and encourage him to find the $150,000 down payment. Based on my recommendation, Jerry had decided not to finance the initial $150,000 stock purchase. "Words are cheap. I like buy-in." Jerry understood that Zeke was really tight with the dollar, and he knew that if he put up some of his own hard-earned money, he would watch it very closely, to the benefit of all.

Later, after the deal was signed, Zeke told me the story of how he had sold several of his prized bikes, including an "Indian," and had borrowed against his 401(k). When his parents learned why he had sold his beloved motorcycle they became very excited about what was happening and gave their son $50,000 to put *toward the stock purchase. About three weeks after my proposal, he gave Jerry a check for $150,000.*

About 30 days later, we had the documents drafted, refined and executed. As this book was being written, Zeke owned just over 20% of the business and Jerry was content and happy. We had his sales proceeds under very conservative management. The money was simply compounding, because Jerry would not take enough time off to spend it. He and Zeke continued to get along fabulously and the business had grown every year. Profits even increased as Zeke came up with some neat ideas for expansion.

Based upon reasonable objectives, Zeke will reach 49% ownership at the end of the 8th year and will hold at that level, while building cash, until the buyout is consummated in the 10th year. Jerry's 51% share of earnings for those two years should be in excess of $500,000 per year, topping annual earnings before the initiation of the program. The Buyout Succession Bridge goal had been achieved, both of the principles felt they were winners.

11 The Management Company Succession Bridge

We've talked about the various potential classes of strategically important personnel, including key managers, special key managers and very special key managers.

There are special key managers in the business world who are not motivated by a golden handcuff supplemental executive retirement plan. Retirement security is not their hot button. They have high career commitment and an entrepreneurial attitude that seeks special recognition for their exceptional achievements. There may even be several special key managers. Their impressive skills, diverse experience and unyielding commitment account for a substantial portion of the business' competitive advantage.

The proprietary attitude of a special key manager and the profound value he brings to the business create the need for a hybrid form of golden handcuff. Once again, the Succession Bridge initiative begins with the acknowledgement that there are currently no family successors who can provide operational leadership over the next five to 15 years. And, as in many of the other scenarios we have talked about, there usually is an accompanying desire by the owner for more time away from the grind. The best structure to provide the financial and entrepreneurial incentive to lock in one or more special key managers is called a Management Company Succession Bridge.

The attractive aspect of a management company is that an owner can bond several managers into a team to lessen the vulnerability to any weaknesses in the leadership of a single manager.

The management company structure is also attractive when the owner does not have confidence that any one manager has the moxie or leadership ability to assume the reins and be the driving force. The key manager who has the moxie may plan to retire sooner than an owner would like. Furthermore, there may be other, very valuable, supporting key managers who would be deeply offended if they were not included in an executive retention/benefit package. Rather than run the risk of losing them, a Management Company Succession Bridge can be the forum that converts a group into a team and the glue that keeps a talented group in a leadership role while family members are maturing and/or sorting out their careers.

The predominant advantages are twofold. First, the owner has one primary business/contractual relationship with a management company in lieu of several relationships with independent managers. What if this individual falls off his game, or goes through a mid-life crisis, or just becomes an intolerable jackass? What if there is a medical problem or burn-out? Using a management company in the role of the Succession Bridge lessens concerns about health, personality and relationship.

Clearly, the foremost advantage is the achievement of peace of mind regarding the continuity of the management culture that otherwise would not be available. The various members of the management company would represent the values, ambition and commitment of the business. The management company opportunity could satisfy the compelling drive of the special key managers to have a proprietary interest in the business without complicating matters by actually having them become stockholders. This structure allows the special key manager to call the owner "partner." And it allows the special key manager to build net worth through his continuing commitment to quality and profitability. The owner would no longer feel compelled to take on partners to lock in talent or to sell the business because the talent could not be depended upon.

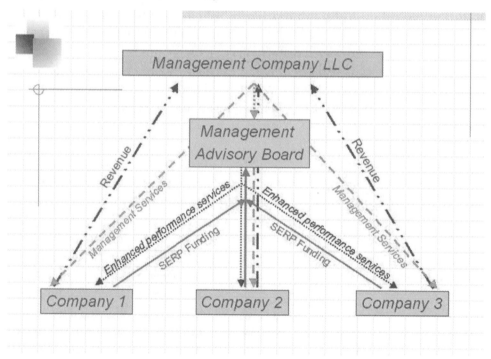

Keep in mind that the Management Company Succession Bridge does not replace the efforts of family successors. It bridges the frustrating gap that may exist between the goals of the owner to reduce the daily grind of management and the inability of his natural successors to relieve him of day-to-day operational responsibility. Furthermore, where unfortunate sibling circumstances exist, the Management Company Succession Bridge can serve as an insulator to the potentially destructive efforts of siblings, cousins or in-laws to undermine each other. With a management company, the leadership of the business becomes a diversified group of capable managers. The loss of anyone in this group should not threaten the integrity of management succession.

Enhanced profitability is also an anticipated advantage, because the nature of the management contract provides a profound incentive to classically entrepreneurial managers.

The members of the management company have a profound incentive to take the business to a new level of profitability.

Another advantage is recruiting. Because of the inherent benefits, a Management Company Succession Bridge is a talent magnet. When word gets out, this Succession Bridge structure will not only retain talent, it will enable you to recruit the best managers in your industry.

The major disadvantage of the structure is its complexity. The formation of an LLC, drafting and adoption of an operating agreement for the LLC and a management agreement for the business is admittedly an effort. However, unless owners are inexperienced with corporations or management contracts, these documents are not complex and are familiar to most business attorneys.

To some degree, owners will have to deal with a group of managers in lieu of just one. As we will discuss later, this is not as complex as it may appear, but from any angle, it is more complex than a Succession Bridge involving only one person. Under extremely rare circumstances, this management group might become a negative union. However, I have never seen it happen, because the entrepreneurial instincts of these special managers tend to override any union instincts.

There are a few fundamental prerequisites for a Management Company Succession Bridge:

- For love or money, the business must be worth the effort and cost to maintain. In other words, the costs and administrative challenges of designing and installing a management company must be justifiable from a family and/or financial perspective.
- The business must meet the criteria for "Succession Success."

- The business must have the marketing momentum and profitability to endure the predictable profit erosion that accompanies a management transition.
- The business must have sufficient size to support a management company. Clearly, the economy of scale for a management company is greater than that of a key manager bridge.
- The business must be large enough to have several key managers who are critical to ongoing profitability.
- The management company must have a recognized, respected leader.

Successful managers are commonly strong-willed and expressive. Owners cannot effectively deal with multiple personalities, each endeavoring to support his own opinion. Therefore, the managers as a group must have a leader who can effectively represent the interests of all those involved.

Most significant is that the owner will contractually delegate control over the business to the newly formed management company.

Documentation is required to specify management responsibilities, revenue sharing, compensation of managers and what the new management company can do with its revenue. Assumptions and promises about compensation and responsibilities will only breed problems later, when the program inevitably comes under stress due to cycles in business or leadership issues. Documentation precludes selective memory.

There are three major agreements that are unique to the Management Company Succession Bridge. First, the employment contracts for the managers; second, the management company organization; and third, the management contract. Close attention to these details is important. Typically, the managers keep their current jobs. They do not necessarily become employees of the management company. However, they do endorse employment contracts that clearly describe their dual roles as an employee of the business and a member of the Management Company Succession Bridge. In order to prevent having to redraft these documents, their specific job descriptions and pay plans are referenced to resolutions of the board of directors, which may change as circumstances warrant.

It is important that the employment contracts contain the covenants not to compete within a reasonable market area, such as a 50-mile radius, and covenants to keep all information about the business and the principles private. The "bad boy" provision would state that the manager would forfeit any vested golden handcuff benefits if he violates these covenants or is otherwise terminated for cause.

The management company becomes a business within a business, involving a variety of contingencies that can impact a key manager or stockholder.

The management company should be a bona fide legal entity. Depending upon the advice of an attorney or accountant relating to the peculiarities of the state of jurisdiction, the structure of the management company should be a Subchapter-S corporation, a limited liability corporation, a limited liability partnership or a limited partnership. All of these legal entities "pass through" the reporting of profits to stockholders, partners or members and avoid taxation at the business level.

This "passing through" is significant for avoiding reasonableness of compensation issues with the IRS, as well as to avoid double taxation on accumulated undistributed earnings. In most instances, a limited liability corporate structure is more compatible with the Management Company Succession Bridge because of greater flexibility.

The actual adoption of the corporation or partnership is relatively simple. The more complex issue is the documentation of the agreement between the partners or stockholders regarding the distribution of profits, the addition of partners, the removal of partners and the repurchase of a partnership interest in the event of the death, disability, retirement or employment termination of a partner.

Arguments and dissension within the key manager group over the way existing members or stockholders will be allowed to withdraw or how new managers can enter can only serve as a counter-productive distraction that erodes the operational effectiveness of the management group.

The management company issues addressed in the operating agreement will vary according to the nature of the business and the makeup of the management group. The stipulations would usually include:

- Only actively employed managers approved by the board of the operating company can be principals in the management company.
- Interest may not be sold, gifted or pledged without first offering that interest to other shareholders.
- In the event of termination of employment for any reason, the terminated stockholder or his representative will sell the interest in the management company and the management company will buy it.

- The terms for repurchase will depend upon the reason for employment termination. Retirement, death, disability or termination without cause would produce attractive terms. Voluntary withdrawal and termination for cause would generate substantially less attractive terms.

- All interests purchased in the sponsoring corporation by the individual members of the management company will be held in escrow by the secretary of the corporation and subject to the transfer restrictions described in the stockholders agreement.

- Operational responsibilities of the management company will abide in a specific individual or group of individuals, with designations of successors and a method of selecting successors.

- Dividend distributions will be made to members of the management company, sufficient to pay the income tax on reportable profits at the highest marginal personal income tax rate. Distribution of after-tax net earnings of the management company will be held or distributed according to specific plans that specify whether to distribute all of the earnings, hold them in a golden handcuff plan or hold them for future acquisitions.

- By a specified percentage vote, a member can be removed or a member can be added according to specified and reasonable financial terms.

The second document is the management contract, which formalizes the relationship between the operating company and the management company. This document is the heart of the Management Company Succession Bridge in that it defines the lifeline between the operating company and the managers who are assuming management responsibility.

This document stipulates the specific operating authority that is being delegated, as well as performance responsibilities and remedies in the event these responsibilities are not fulfilled. It also defines how management fees are earned.

It is important to define performance triggers in terms of profit, customer satisfaction and/or production output that will create management fees.

The performance-triggers management contract will provide the motivation to grow the business. The financial motivators in the contract are generally one of three categories: in the money, growth dependent or a combination of both. An "in the money" contract will generate attractive cash flow from the management contract if the management team simply maintains performance status quo. If nothing goes wrong, the management company is "in the money." This form of management contract is commonly used to create cash flow in the management company that will fund golden handcuff SERP benefits for the managers. The benefits are identical to those discussed earlier.

The "growth dependent" contract will generate cash flow only if the management company grows profits and other performance criteria above historical performance levels.

It is easy to create a management company. Just file articles of incorporation with the Secretary of State. However, it is a formidable challenge to mold two or more dynamically skilled managers into a management team that can reach heretofore unrealistic levels of productivity. The growth-dependent management contract says to a group of managers, "We are not going to pay you just to keep us where we are, but we will share generously (20% to 40%) in the 'ups' if you come together as a team and take us to the next level." The baseline for the 'ups' is usually set at the average profit performance over the last three years, adjusted annually by the CPI. This opportunity to have a proprietary interest in the growth he creates is what gets a special key manager going.

The combo plan has the most appeal. Under this scenario, the management contract has a tiered compensation structure. A base compensation is provided by an "in the money," conservative first tier that funds the SERP. On top of this impressive acknowledgement for the valuable services rendered is a "growth dependent" compensation component that requires the managers to go for the brass ring in order to earn 'folding' money.

In order for managers to take seriously the proprietary opportunity of a Management Company Succession Bridge, they must believe in the security of their achievement.

This security comes in the form of the management contract renewal provisions, as well as the management company buyout and buy-in provisions. The renewal provisions must protect owners from being abused and the managers from being thumped after they have taken profitability to the next level. This protection is commonly provided by giving owners the ability to terminate the contract for cause with 30-days notice if the managers have not been able to respond to written notices of performance that do not meet the standards set out in the contract. Typically, these notices are written in such a way that the manager/s have 90 days to show improvement. Otherwise, the contract requires a three-year cash flow buyout to terminate the contract.

In other words, if the business owner just wants to terminate the management contract so he can get back in the game, a management contract buyout clause would require the owners to pay to the management company a fee equal to the preceding cumulative three years of management fees. If the owners were to sell the operating company, it becomes a win/win. In order for the new owners to assume management control, they would have to divert a portion of the purchase price equivalent to the three preceding year's management fees to the management company. A "growth dependent" management company, it is assumed, has created a portion of the purchase value, so sharing the possible sales proceeds both supports and promotes a proprietary attitude.

As mentioned, a Management Company Succession Bridge can be a very powerful talent magnet. If the organization needs additional special key managers, the opportunity (after a reasonable service requirement) to become part of the management company will be a great recruiting tool. However, if the existing managers have achieved growth and therein created cash flow in the management company, how would they then reconcile giving up a piece of the cash pie to the new guy? The answer is, they don't give the new guy anything. Rather, they sell it to him based upon the same proprietary formula specified in the management contract -- a proportion of the last three year's cumulative management fees, plus any corporate equity.

The Right Attitude

How does the new guy come up with this kind of money? He forks over a modest amount of personal cash (to formalize the commitment) and pledges the earnings off the newly purchased management company interest to pay off a note for the balance of the purchase price. The value of this combination package is what reinforces and promotes this very important proprietary attitude.

Achieving a proprietary attitude is very important for the success of the managers. However, lest we overlook the obvious, this attitude is also very important for the owners as well. The owners have more at risk than the managers, both in terms of business value and the goal of succession. Therefore, the business owner should not only encourage but, if necessary, require the managers to follow fundamental business practices that will enhance the timing and degree of their success.

Therefore, it's critical to develop a strategic plan that outlines acceptable business practices, values and philosophy.

Strategic planning provides a record of the agreement between ownership and the new management regime regarding the direction of the business and how management anticipates getting there.

In any form of Management Company Succession Bridge, the strategic operating plan represents two levels of agreement.

The initial agreement reflects the united goals and operating methodology of the members of the management company. These strategic plans generally come about as a result of an extended, deliberate effort by the management team to amalgamate the talents and experiences into an operating team with clear leadership, strong accountability and reasonable policies and procedures. Because the management company represents a newly organized consortium of strong-willed, ambitious, confident managers, it is imperative that they apply the necessary time and energy to achieve unity of goals, vision and operating methods. In the absence of this unity, the Management Company Succession Bridge is destined for ambiguity and inefficiency that will be very costly both emotionally and financially.

The second level of agreement is between ownership and the operating company. After the management company defines its newly formed culture by establishing its identity, purpose, goals and operating procedures, the owners must work with the management company leadership to develop a strategic operating plan for the business. This agreement, as refined with an operating forecast on an annual basis, provides the baseline for valuation of the management company's performance. It provides ownership ·the peace of mind that there is a clear understanding of the expectations for the management of the business, for the purposes of accountability, as specified in the management contract. This agreement also provides members of the management company peace of mind that the business owners will not be changing the rules in the middle of the game.

Case History: Rick, the pool guy

Here's a case history that illustrates both the application and possible structure of a Management Company Succession Bridge. My client owned a small chain of retail family-recreation equipment stores. About 30 years before I met him, Rick had been employed building oak barrels used in the winery business. Encouraged by his wife and two young sons, he attempted to build an above ground swimming pool in their backyard in his spare time. The completed contraption managed to hold water for one summer season.

Although short-lived, his creation attracted attention within his neighborhood, followed by a request that he build a similar structure for a neighbor. Learning from his mistakes, the following winter he rebuilt his own pool and earned some extra money building higher refinements of the wood-plank structure for his neighbor. By mid-July of the second summer, he had orders to build another dozen pools. After much debate, soul-searching and prayer, he decided to resign from his very comfortable, secure job building wine barrels and risk the few dollars he and his wife, Susanne, had saved in the seemingly crazy business of building above-ground pools. Thirty years later, when I was referred to Rick, he and Susanne owned a chain of nine retail businesses. This lucrative operation now made in excess of $3 million in net *profit per year building and retailing above ground pools, spas, pool tables, gym sets and related merchandise.*

During the process of building his business, in a moment of panic after having to terminate three managers for stealing, he had sold the remaining key manager, Jason, 20% ownership in two stores to hopefully lock him down for a career. Fortunately, Jason, age 45 turned out to be trustworthy, talented and dedicated. Rick's two sons, who were 28 and 31, worked with him as general managers of two of the stores. He wanted to update his estate plans and establish the succession structures that would perpetuate the business for his sons. During interviews, Rick described his sons as sharp, hard-working businessmen and said the family was close.

Susanne was less complimentary and said she thought the younger son, who suffered from severe attention deficit disorder, still had some growing up to do. Nevertheless, both Rick and Susanne believed their sons would be the logical objects of our succession planning.

As a card-carrying optimist, I moved forward to meet with their sons, under the assumption that we would be dealing with a classic family-business succession environment. My first interview was with "Younger." He appeared to be a conscientious young man who loved the family's business and wanted to please his parents. He did not carry any strong goals relating to control or compensation. Alerted by his mom's comments, I did notice that he had an incredibly sloppy office and a compulsion to take every phone call and respond to every employee or customer who walked by his office. He was so involved with what was going on around him that it took all afternoon to complete what would have otherwise been a one and a half hour discussion.

I was about to leave when he said that he was concerned about his relationship with his brother. He made me chuckle with amazement when he said that he could not understand why his brother did not want to work with him. He went on to explain that his brother had transferred out of the corporate headquarters just so they would not have to work together. He resented his brother's separatist attitude and, after being stonewalled on several occasions, had decided his brother could just go to hell -- or some other hot place.

When I visited with Older, he immediately excused himself to shut the door, close the blinds and tell the switchboard operator not to disturb him until we were completed. His office was incredibly well organized.

In contrast with his gregarious younger brother, who was tangentially involved in everything going on around him, Older was a drill sergeant who answered questions very succinctly with obvious reluctance to share any unnecessary feelings. He was wound as tight as an 8-day clock, obviously struggling to hold back emotions. After an hour of marginally productive and awkwardly repetitive questions, I was getting nowhere. Finally, I said, "I hope you are not going to be offended, but it looks like I'm going to have to just sit here and let you work around me until you tell me what's on your mind."

He vigorously denied withholding any information that I should know, and became even more frustrated because he realized I really was not going to leave his office. After I just sat there and stared at him for about five minutes, he finally reached his boiling point. Older jumped out of his chair, came around his desk, put his hands on the arms of my chair and leaned over, with his nose about two inches from mine and said, "I don't have to take this crap from you, and if you don't get out of my office I am going to wipe off the parking lot with your ass."

As the sweat began to pour off my forehead, the phone rang and Rick asked how we were doing. Trying to recover my tongue from my throat, I was most grateful for the relief and a moment to think how I could back down from my position before being tossed to the parking lot. Amazingly, as Older heard his father's voice, he reverted to his other practiced personality and convinced his dad that our discussion was going "just peachy."

After the call, he returned to his seat behind his desk, sat down and returned my stare for a good five minutes without uttering a word. I figured that I had the high ground because he was not going to run the risk of getting his dad involved. Finally he said, "There is no way, and I mean no way, that I will ever work with my brother. I don't want to make any waves, all I want is for Dad to let me have one of these stores and my brother can do whatever he wants to do. He is such a baby, so unorganized and so unreliable that I have zero tolerance for working with him."

"Hold on, I want you to tell me how you really feel."

He was not amused by my levity. Ignoring what I had said, he continued by stating that his father was not aware of his feelings and he did not want him to find out. He was emphatic that I should not develop any succession plan that would require him to work with his brother. He continued to say that I would be doing both him and his family a great service if I developed a plan that would allow him to be in business on his own.

I started to chuckle and he jumped at me with, "this is not a joke, funny man. I am as serious as a heart attack about this."

"Whoa, big boy, let's go for the decaf. Those protruding veins in your neck are a dead give-away that you are not only serious, but also stressed. I am amused because of the absurd circumstances you have created for yourself. You have found yourself incompatible with your brother and this conclusion is in conflict with your father's dream of succession. You want, even demand relief, but you are unwilling to let anyone know how you really feel. In spite of the assistance that I offer, you are content to stand by and wait for the train wreck."

Leaning back in his chair and gazing up at the ceiling he pondered and then responded, "Yeah, I see what you mean. I suppose since I lost my cool and spilled my guts, I am going to have to trust you. But, don't think for even a minute that I am not going to be watching you. Remember, the plan should position me in a business totally independent from my brother."

With these comments confirming the minefield, I proceeded to meet with Jason, Rick's minority partner in two of the stores. He was 15 years younger than Rick and about 20 years older than Rick's sons. As it turned out, he was a partner in two stores, but actually was supervising four, apparently with outstanding results. Impressively, both Older and Younger respected Jason.

He also expressed the utmost respect for Rick. He acknowledged the friction between Older and Younger but did not think it was something that could not be *worked out. He said that, regardless of the boys' differences, he worked well with both. Jason confirmed that he and Rick had discussed on many occasions that, in the event of Rick's death, he would help the boys run the operation. He expressed pleasure with owning a piece of two of the stores, but he realized that, as a minority stockholder of a regular corporation, all he really had were current wallpaper and future value when his stock was repurchased.*

During the subsequent presentation of our Phase I Business Succession Review and Assessment, in addition to an assortment of other important issues impacting business succession, I explained the circumstances regarding their sons. Rick acknowledged that he had suspected there was a problem, but did not want to bring up the issue because his family had never been good at confrontation. He and Susanne had difficulty with the boys as teenagers and subsequently had simply avoided or worked around issues that might create heavy emotions. I told him that his sensitivity to family confrontation was impressive but not necessarily healthy. I asked him how he asserted accountability without confrontation. His response, interestingly enough, was that there was no accountability, he just hoped the boys would comply with his requests -- and apparently they had done so. I told him that the boys appeared to have great respect for him and that's probably why there had been no obvious ugly emotional outbursts.

However, I continued to point out that, in the event of his death and under the current circumstances, Older, who was clearly the more competent business manager, would quickly lose his cool with his brother. Rather than be viewed as a controlling, immature, malcontent, he would just quit. That would leave Susanne in a tough spot, relying upon Younger to run the stores. I further explained that I felt he had two alternatives: change his succession goals to spin off independent operations to each of his sons, or proactively endeavor to enhance communication and find a way that his sons could work together.

After thinking it over for a couple of weeks, Rick, Susanne and I met again. He restated his dream that his sons could carry on his business. I had been doing some creative thinking, but I wanted to determine the strength of Rick's convictions before introducing a plan that could potentially address the issues. Rick expressed a profound desire to keep the stores under unified family management and said he would do anything within reason to achieve that goal. With far less enthusiasm, Susanne affirmed the same goal. Assuming that they were ready to consider ways to get out of this jam, I suggested that we form a Management Company Succession Bridge involving himself, his sons and Jason.

The management company would be contractually delegated the operational responsibility for all stores in exchange for a potentially lucrative revenue-sharing management fee. Jason's participation in the management company would be contingent upon his selling his minority interest in the two stores, thus consolidating all core business ownership within the family. The buy-out and participation in the Management Company Succession Bridge would give Jason a lucrative revenue sharing arrangement from all stores and eliminate management concerns about him having a greater vested interest in two stores.

A smile immediately came to Rick's face as he explained that he had been worrying about what would happen to his partner's stock in the event he died, divorced or just quit. But then he asked how this strategy would help the boys learn to work together and how they could get stock in the businesses?

I explained that the strategic purpose of this Succession Bridge would be to provide a continuation of leadership in the event of a catastrophe or at the point Rick decided to retire. As the successor director of the management company, Jason would provide the management bridge in the event of Rick's death or disability within the next five to 10 years. Not only were Older and Younger not ready for prime time, their rivalry made it impossible to put either in charge. With a management company in place, Jason could be delegated the authority to run the stores for the family, with or without the boys help. Consequently, Rick would not be chained to the business and the good will value of the business could be protected.

I also explained that another important goal of the management company would be to provide a third party, Jason, to facilitate communication and, hopefully, teamwork. As their dad, it was nearly impossible for Rick to begin holding his sons accountable in what appeared to be a classic sibling rivalry. He was just too closely involved. Each of them would take turns blaming "dear dad" for all of their problems. On the other hand, Jason had a good relationship with both of them. Older and Younger had worked for him in the past and, at least up until now, they respected his leadership ability. Jason knew their good and bad traits. His personality was strong enough to tell them to grow up. If he was willing to take on the precarious role of relationship facilitator, he could pinpoint whining and jealousy and stop the "blame game." Most importantly, Jason could very effectively describe to them what they had to lose if they continued to act like brats.

The management company would also offer some exciting opportunities to increase business profitability. The management contract would encourage this by providing lucrative revenue sharing of a portion of profitability in excess of historical highs. Through group problem solving and teamwork, they could take the best practices of each store and develop uniform, optimally profitable operating procedures for all stores. I also forecasted that they could combine redundant activities at each store, such as purchasing, human resources, accounting and delivery and achieve efficiencies from the economy of scale.

Another advantage of the Management Company Succession Bridge would be the recovery of the minority stock owned by Jason. Although he was a special key employee, he was not irreplaceable. Further, if the family owned all the stock, a Subchapter-S election could provide a means of lowering the income tax bite and distributing cash for a variety of reasons, including business expansion, retirement funding and stock purchase by the boys.

Jason was a good guy, but it made no sense for him to have stock in only two stores, because those stores would naturally get his attention. The repurchase of his stock for fair value, plus the lucrative cash flow from a 25% full partnership interest in the management company, would represent fair consideration for the buy-back of his stock.

"Hold on," bolted Rick. "This Succession Bridge gizmo sounds great, but do you really think Jason will give up his stock in two stores for a piece of a brand new LLC that essentially owns nothing?"

"Not doubt in my mind," I responded. Let's role-play and you (as Jason) tell me what you think of this proposal. Jason, I would like to make you a proposition involving your current stock and a management company I am forming. First of all I want to repurchase your stock in those two stores because that stock is not paying you any dividends. Other than sentimental value and possible appreciation, it is worthless to you. Take this cash in exchange for your stock and spend it, put it in the bank or do what ever you do with money. In further consideration of this transaction, I also want to GIVE (emphasis on the word give) you an interest in a management company that will have an exclusive contract to manage all of our stores. You, the boys and I will be the principals. You will be my successor as the controlling member, until your retirement in 10 to 15 years.

"This management company will have some attractive guaranteed benefits and, potentially, some very lucrative dividends. The benefits will be a Supplemental Executive Retirement Plan funded with 15% of your annual compensation. In addition to the retirement benefits, based upon last year's performance, the management contract will direct to you $20,000 per year in additional cash. Even more important, if you and I and the boys can find a way to work together as a team, your share of the earnings growth will be many times that number. And all this will be formally reduced to writing in contracts that you can rely upon."

"Whew, that does sound pretty good," responded Rick. "I would take that deal in a heartbeat. It 's so good, I wonder if I can I afford it? I also wonder if Older and Younger will go along with it?"

"Well Rick, we could have a problem if you feel like you have to ask for your son's permission to provide for the succession of a business that is sure to make them rich."

"But what if they don't go along with the plan," pleaded Rick? I was now gaining a vivid understanding of how Older and Younger became brats.

"If for some bizarre reason they do not like our plan, I would simply ask them to give me a call when they settled into their new jobs and tell me if their new deal was better. Don't worry Rick. They are not going to kick a gift horse in the mouth. When Jason earns those management company dividends, they will too. Your boys may be immature, but they are not dumb."

"Hey, I'm not sure I want to throw a lot of money at them" responded Rick.

"Not to worry, we will be spending this money before they see it. We would have used some of their money to purchase life insurance on you and Susanne to fund your prospective estate taxes. The balance of their portion of the management company distributions for the next five to 10 years will be used to pay down an installment note that we will use to purchase 24% of the company for each of them."

"Leapin' lizards! You are right. They would be dumb as a brick to turn this down. But you never answered how can I afford to give these benefits to Jason?"

"Well Rick, making $3 million net profit per year substantiates that you could afford an additional $50,000 per year outlay on behalf of Jason. However, the more relevant question may be, is this deal worth another $50,000 per year? He is going to serve as a *Succession Bridge* that will put your mind at ease about a premature death and also give you the ability to retire before you are dead from old age. He is going to mentor your two sons and hopefully help them find adulthood. And, finally, he is going to bust his butt to make you more money so he can also make more money. Now keep in mind that, if he does not stay in the saddle, doing a good job for the next 15 years, he will not make $30,000 of the $50,000. Does this look like a good deal for you?"

Rick opened up with a big smile as his face began to light up like a 200-watt light bulb. "Yeah, I see what you mean. If this works out, Susanne and I are the big winners. Jason can do very well, but only if he performs. And if he performs, everybody wins."

Susanne had been silent, but now it was apparently time for her to weigh in. Her expression was swift and concise, "Sell the damn thing, or split it up between the boys. I have no desire to be part of this complex contraption just to placate two overpaid crybabies. I have not understood two cents worth of what you have said, so I just say sell the darn thing. This arrangement is far more complex than is necessary. The only people that will benefit from this mess are the attorneys and two ungrateful daughters-in-law.

Rick jumped in with "Hold on Mama. Don't be so hasty to make that decision. Selling the business may seem simple, but, if you remember, we've been down this road before. Finding a buyer for our stores will not be easy. Also, when is the best time to sell? I don't want to get out now, but what if we wait too long? Then, we are going to have to pay capital gains tax on all our retained earnings and find something else to do with our time."

I acknowledged that, although a *Management Company Succession Bridge* was, at first blush, an undesirable complexity, it did offer a solution to another problem, their daughter. Currently it was undesirable for their schoolteacher daughter to be a stockholder. However, if a newly formed management company became the operating entity, we could transfer stock to Subchapter-S dividend, paying stock to her without concerns that she or her know-it-all husband would want to pitch in their two cents.

Instantly it was apparent that I had pushed the right button. "All right!" said Susanne. "Count me in for anything that will get stock to my daughter. What do we need to do to get this show on the road?" Though she had zero comprehension of how the *Succession Bridge* worked, if it allowed her daughter to become a stockholder, she was for it. Rick and I looked at each other with amazement. We were not sure what we had done, but we were not about to go back and ask Susanne to explain her logic.

We set forth to develop the various pieces of the puzzle. There is so much latitude in the design of a succession bridge that, predictably, the picture changed several times. However, after a deliberate process that began just with Rick, Susanne and Jason, we achieved agreement on the terms of the stock repurchase, the LLC operating agreement, the management contract, Jason's golden handcuff employment contract and the sale of the stock to the boys. The only missing pieces were

Older and Younger. We had yet to explain the program to them and obtain their commitment to participate.

Rick and I agreed to meet with them individually to solicit their endorsement of the succession plan as well as their involvement in the management of the stores. Before we met with them, I asked Rick how he wanted to handle the meetings. He asked my advice, so I suggested that he let me have the meeting and trust me to deal with the boys properly. I promised not to alienate them. Our first meeting was with Older. I did my best to persuade him that the Management Company Succession Bridge was the greatest thing since the paper clip. He listened intently, but I was fearful that he was just waiting his turn. When I said the infamous words, "what do you think," he confirmed my suspicion.

"You may be creative, Mr. Rawls, but you sure do not listen well. I told you that I was not interested in any succession plan that required me to work with my brother, much less own something with him. Dad, I'm terribly sorry, but I have to ask your renowned adviser if he thinks I am stupid?"

I jumped back with "No, I do not think you are stupid for a minute. I am convinced that you are wise beyond your years of maturity. But, as I think you are acting like a five year old, that doesn't give you much credit."

"Loyd," exclaimed Rick, "Please keep your personal feelings out of this conversation." He knew I had little patience for smart mouth kids who had no credibility beyond their own imagination.

"Rick, please trust me on this," I pleaded. Before he had a chance to answer, I turned back to Older and said, "So if I understand what you are telling me, you are looking for a new job beginning tomorrow?"

Older looked over at his dad with a desperate open handed expression but Rick just lifted his arms and shrugged his shoulders as though circumstances were out of his control. "Come on Dad, you are not going to let this smartass with a briefcase split up our family, are you?"

"No son, I am not. The fact is, he is not capable of splitting up our family. Only you, me, Mom and Younger are capable of impacting our family. I have frankly become fed up with your spoiled, whiney attitude. The train is leaving the station son. We are having our first organizational meeting of our management company next week. If you want to be on board, be there with a positive attitude. Otherwise, find that new job that Mr. Rawls was speaking of."

Older looked at me and then his dad in shock. Without saying a word he stood up and started walking out of the room. As he approached the door, Rick hit him with a final remark. "We are having the organizational meeting of the management company next Monday at 5 p.m. Be there, or be scarce."

Older did not miss a step as he faded through the door. I looked at Rick with a big smile, amazed at his newfound boldness. Rick grinned back and said proudly "What do you think? Am I a bad dude or what?"

"Yes. That took some guts and I guarantee you it will pay off handsomely. This is a win/win situation. If he takes his first step toward growing up, he will be at the meeting. If he doesn't, he is going to learn how bad the real world can be."

Our meeting went well with both Jason and Younger. Jason was initially hesitant to give up his stock. However, when he fully understood the opportunity under the management company, he warmed up to the idea. He had some very ambitious growth plans and he quickly determined that this management company not only provided him and his family security, it could also make him wealthy. The cash he received for his stock was the perfect down payment for the new house that he and his wife had been dreaming about. He accepted the proposal contingent upon only one condition, unwavering authority over Older and Younger.

He required that he be vested in the SERP, plus receive an attractive severance package, if Rick or Susanne interfered with his plans for the boys. Having put Older in his place, Rick was ready to go with this restriction right away. It took him all weekend to convince Susanne. Evidently, word leaked out through Susanne to Younger. Being nothing short of an opportunist, Younger proclaimed that the management company was a great idea.

When Monday afternoon rolled around, validating my prediction, Older was at the meeting, at least physically. He was typically stiff as a board and not willing to offer any comments beyond short, curt answers. Sensing what was going on, Rick announced to everyone that they were forming a management company and that Older and Younger would henceforth be reporting directly to Jason. He then looked over to Susanne, and me and said it was time for us to go to dinner. We left lucky Jason, with the two brats, for better or for worse.

We had not even sat down at the nearby restaurant when Rick's cell phone rang. Susanne and I then watched a very interesting conversation. "Oh, I see, Jason has given you a 30 day leave of absence without pay. Hmm. … Well, Older, the last thing you heard me say before we came over here was that you reported to Jason. So, if he gave you a leave of absence then you have a leave of absence. No, Son, I am not going to change my mind.

"Well, Son, it sounds to me like you need to think about your career while you are working on your golf game. My guess is that if you want part of the future of this company you are going to learn to participate in Jason's future meetings."

As we later learned from Jason, Older had refused to talk in his meeting. Jason told him there was no place on his management team for mutes and, if he couldn't find a way to talk after a 30-day leave of absence, he should find another job. As it turned out, Older must have made some profound decisions during his leave of absence. He did return and he did learn how to talk. Actually, I learned during this period that he took my advice and contacted a psychologist I had recommended to him several months earlier. Evidently, this counselor helped him make some progress on a few hang-ups that were blocking his communication with Rick and Susanne, as well as Younger. His brother had a few challenges as well. The second week after our initial meeting Jason had a "brouhaha" with Younger over his disorganization and inability to remember what he had been told the day before. Having kids who also suffered from A.D.D., Jason was familiar with the routine. He also gave Younger a leave of absence contingent upon him seeing an A.D.D. specialist.

To say that everything that subsequently transpired went perfectly would be an overstatement. There were rough spots. The management group began to meet weekly under the leadership of Jason. There were always two meetings: the first with Rick and Susanne and other pertinent managers and the second with Jason, Older and Younger. From what I heard from Jason, there was no shortage of excitement in these meetings. However, over time, Older began to express himself more freely and Younger learned to pay attention and not fall asleep. Seven years later, one would think we had never had these problems. The management company is flourishing. Older and Younger are even hanging out together, once in a blue moon. Jason is 'da man!' He has raised the profitability of the company by 30%, due to a combination of efficiency, innovation and adding two more stores. In addition to the golden handcuff SERP, in which he has accumulated more than $300,000, he is also pulling down an additional $75,000 as his portion of the management fees. As for Older and Younger, through the combination of management company distributions and Subchapter-S dividends, they have both purchased 24% of the company. As for Rick, he is hard to find and his golf handicap is single digit.

12 Management Company Equity Succession Bridge

In Chapter 8 we discussed the Key Manager Equity Succession Bridge that is designed to address the ownership need of a single very special key manager (VSKM). Our next succession strategy, the Management Company Equity Succession Bridge (MCESB) is designed to address circumstances in which several very special key managers (VSKMs) could achieve greater productivity through working together for a common goal. This structure is also appropriate when there are one or two VSKMs who are supported by a group of special key managers (SKMs.)

After reading the previous chapter, you hopefully have grasped a reasonable understanding of the Management Company Succession Bridge. This is an exciting structure that serves as an effective incentive for special key mangers (SKMs) to work together and serve as a Succession Bridge. As previously described, in the absence of a qualified family member, the management company structure empowers a group of special key managers to serve in either a contingency or an active management continuity role. However, some very fortunate businesses have one or more VSKMs who will not be satisfied with ownership in only a management company. Their career commitment is commonly contingent upon achieving an ownership interest in the family business. And unfortunately the potential loss of a VSKM puts the business at risk.

A Management Company Equity Succession Bridge (MCESB) can satisfy the ambition of a VSKM to own stock and the management continuity need of a family without qualified and motivated successors.

This natural progression of the structure discussed in Chapter 11 utilizes a management company to promote teamwork and assure management continuity, as well as provide opportunities for one or more VSKMs to own stock.

There are several business succession advantages to forming a management company and providing stock purchase options to the VSKMs. The non stock ownership advantages of this structure were discussed in the previous chapter. The general benefit of a MCESB (the next progressive Succession Bridge step) is that the owner can be relieved of pressure to sell a business because the most qualified successor managers, the VSKMs, have made a commitment to succession. The VSKMs have exercised stock options and parted with some precious cash to reflect their long term commitment to the success and succession of the business.

The major disadvantage of the MCESB is that, due to the transfer of stock, this Succession Bridge structure is more complex than the non-equity program discussed in the previous chapter. The sale of stock to a VSKM represents a higher level of commitment. The transfer of stock demands more careful planning, more discussions and more documents. In addition to addressing the details of job descriptions and the management company, additional documentation is needed to control and manage the disposition and recovery of stock in a manner fair to all concerned.

As we examine the "Equity Bridge" structure, you will recognize substantial similarities in the construction to the previously discussed management company structure. The major difference is that this structure is designed for VSKMs. Although this terminology may sound like confusing mumbo jumbo, there is a significant difference between these two classes of managers. Notably, a family business simply cannot afford to lose a VSKM without pursuing every retention possibility.

The unique feature of the "Equity Bridge" is that VSKMs are empowered to use management fees to purchase a predetermined block of stock under attractive but mutually beneficial terms.

Chapter 11 discussed the documentation required to spell out management responsibilities, revenue sharing and what the new management company can do with its revenue. The defining characteristic is that the "Equity Bridge" revenue does not fund a golden handcuff SERP for the VSKMs. In lieu of the supplemental executive retirement plan (SERP,) the revenue allocated to the VSKMs is pledged the purchase of stock. The VSKMs are provided the ultimate golden handcuff benefit through the opportunity to use management fees to purchase stock at a bargain price.

For explanatory purposes, let us assume that our group consists totally of VSKMs. However, it is important to recognize equity provisions can be provided for one or more VSKMs who are serving as leaders of a larger group of SKMs. This discrimination in favor of a VSKM can be enacted initially, as we are going to discuss, or subsequent to adoption of a Management Company Succession Bridge. In the latter case, after one or more SKMs have grown and proven that they are, indeed, a VSKM, the bells and whistles relating to the stock options are added as an afterthought. Later in our discussion, we will address these circumstances in more detail.

As illustrated in Chapter 11, the management contract formalizes the delegation of management responsibilities to the Management Company. This document clarifies the specific operating authority that is being delegated, as well as performance responsibilities and accountability in the event stipulated responsibilities are not being fulfilled. From a financial perspective, the management contract is the nexus of the Succession Bridge because this document establishes the potential to earn management fees. Specific to this discussion, the Equity Succession Bridge management contract empowers the VSKM(s) the opportunity to buy stock, build net worth and ultimately enhance income with stock dividends. The opportunity to purchase stock is the golden handcuff motivation for the MCESB. Assuming that earning management fees represents a challenge that will be in the best interest of current and future stockholders, the opportunity for the movers and shakers to purchase a modest allotment of stock with those management fees will further enhance the prospects of Succession Successsm.

Accordingly, as consideration for the opportunity to purchase stock, it is reasonable for the owners who are Seeking Succession to expect the VSKM(s) to meet a reasonable challenge of enhancing historical operations and profits. In exchange for parting with some of the family jewels at an attractive price, the owner should reasonably expect a career commitment for the VSKM(s), as well as enhanced performance. The operative word is reasonable.

If owners force unrealistic profit expectations upon the VSKM(s) the challenge will not be considered reasonable and the golden handcuff will <u>not be achieved.</u>

Creating frustration and failure in highly confident and ego heavy VSKM(s) is no way to establish a long range Succession Bridge strategy.

Further, the management contract of a MCESB is also usually reflective of specific strategic goals that are important to the owner/s. Of course, these goals would include the training, monitoring and accountability of family successors. Other common issues would include maintaining customer satisfaction, minimizing employee turnover and satisfying credit contingencies. More specific to this discussion, when stock options are on the table, strategic goals usually include relieving the owner of some, if not all, of the grinding, day to day management responsibilities. Transferring stock out of the confines of the immediate family is a difficult consideration. However, being tired and worn out with no realistic successor to provide much needed relief can be just the motivation needed to entertain an Equity Succession Bridge.

The details of any performance contract are the most powerful tools available to clearly define the nature of the performance desired. From an asset perspective, VSKMs are undoubtedly the most motivated class of managers. However, from a liability perspective, they can be so focused on becoming stockholders that they lose perspective regarding an assortment of "Succession Success" issues that are critical to the long term business viability. Up front agreement on these issues is critical. The process of achieving agreement on how the business is to be operated is reflected in Operating Covenants, which we will discuss in Chapter 14.

A unique feature of the MCESB management contract is that there are usually two phases of management fees. Typically, the first, pre-purchase phase has more generous revenue sharing. The initial higher revenue sharing percentage (such as 40% of the increases over historical earnings) would create motivation and enthusiasm for the managers to move the business to the next level so that stock could be purchased.

Now you owners should take a deep breath. The concept of the two tiered management contract will not bankrupt your company or put the VSKMs on easy street.

Although the managers may receive a generous percentage of "the ups," keep in mind that the revenue will just be passing through their hands. *The cash stops back in the hands of the owners as payment for stock.*

Voila! The owner achieves more liquidity for fun stuff, such as that retirement home or boat. Furthermore, since the revenue sharing usually applies only to new levels of profitability, dividend distributions to the owners should remain approximately the same, or even grow. As an example, 80% of a $1.2 million profit, assuming 20% of the stock was sold to key managers, would be greater than 100% of a $600,000 profit, even after a $240,000 (40% of the "ups") management fee.

The second stage of the management fee begins after the management team has purchased and paid for their optioned stock. At this time, the management fee steps down (to prevent double dipping) to a less generous, but none the less attractive (such as 20%) revenue-sharing arrangement that recognizes the ongoing operating contribution of the management team. Notably, the continuation of this fee is dependent upon maintaining enhanced profitability. The combination of stock ownership, stock dividends and a reduced, but still attractive, management fee continues to be an outstanding performance incentive to the managers.

Reflecting on this two tiered management fee, near term, the owner gives up a generous portion of the growth in profits to empower the managers to purchase stock. Hopefully, the long-term by-product is that the VSKMs are locked into the business for the balance of their careers. In the optimum application of this concept, the revenue sharing of the management contract will prime the pump of commitment, motivation and teamwork that will lead the company to higher levels of performance and Succession Successsm. It is not unreasonable to anticipate that enhanced productivity associated with a MCESB more than makes up for a future loss of a portion of the profits.

As mentioned earlier, on occasion, a MCESB evolves after the fact. Occasionally, the implementation of a Management Company Succession Bridge exceeds growth expectations because one or more managers illustrate that they are the real deal, a genuine VSKM. Essentially, their leadership ability separates them from the crowd. Recognizing that the organization could not afford to lose VSKMs, stock options are a natural progression for these hot shots.

As an initially designed conversion feature, or as an afterthought amendment, a stock option agreement could state that selected mangers could convert accumulated SERP benefits into a down payment for exercising stock options.

Subsequently, funds that otherwise would have been held in a golden handcuff SERP would be applied to the exercise of stock options according to the stipulated formulas. Of course, this would all be done in pragmatic fashion, assuring appropriate documents were in place to properly manage the any disputation of stock.

Recognizing that there are no secrets in a business, the issuance of stock options to selected managers (verified VSKMs) should be explained to all MCSB managers to prevent bruised egos. It is better for the non-equity managers to hear what is happening from the owner versus the grapevine, which would predictably lead to incorrect assumptions. Specifically, the owner must be prepared to explain to the non-equity managers why they are not being offered stock options. The ultimate revelation is that regardless of the fallout, an owner can afford to lose a SKM but not a VSKM.

Let us now go back to the concept of proactively forming (not backing into) a MCESB. As discussed in the previous chapter, in order for managers to take the equity ownership opportunity seriously, the management contract must provide an element of security. Otherwise, the managers could assume that, as soon as Junior convinces Dad that he has the moxie to sit behind a big desk and give orders, the contract will be voided. The security for both owners and managers comes in the form of the contract renewal and buyout provisions.

A unique and important aspect of the MCESB is the stock purchase and ownership agreement(s), which, according to preference of legal counsel, may be structured as one or two documents. Note that we are not talking about a stock option agreement. Management fees are pledged to satisfy an obligation to purchase stock. As a die-hard proponent of simplicity, I encourage owners to address the stock purchase and stock ownership issues in a single document, which initially stipulates that, assuming management fees are generated, the VSKMs will purchase a specific number of shares in the business.

As one would expect, the striking price of the stock purchase agreement is an important provision that predictably generates very active discussion. This is where the pride of the owner and the ambition of the VSKM's come into focus and bring out the adrenaline and creative thought. The discussion always boils down to determining a mutually compatible striking price. There are a variety of stock valuation methods that call upon both scientific formulas and natural instincts. Most valuations are based upon a mutually agreeable value such as book value. The value can be either fixed as of the date of the agreement (to provide the incentive to purchase stock over a short term) or, in longer term scenarios, the value can float with the performance of the business.

Regardless of the valuation method utilized, the striking price must be agreeable to both parties. Both parties, without undue pressure, should agree that the price is fair. Both the owner and VSKM must believe that the management fees will empower the purchase of stock within a reasonable time frame. Otherwise, we will be facing a big problem down the road, when the last thing anyone wants is another emotional problem.

The amount of stock each manager is authorized to purchase is also a subject of active dialogue. Among managers, there is no reluctance to aggressively express opinions. Each manager has a self-centric view of his contribution to the organization. The senior managers predictably believe that they merit a higher percentage and the junior managers feel that everyone should have an equal percentage. Although I promote my role as a facilitator, I find myself serving more as a referee in valuation and stock allocation discussions.

Generally there are one or two managers within the VSKM group who carry substantially more responsibility, due to experience, training or pure talent. Reconciling this responsibility issue is the first team challenge for this group of strong-willed movers and shakers. Generally, the facilitator (me) offers two or three examples of how the stock could be allocated and steps back to let them have -at it. If someone is getting picked on, the facilitator should step in, cool down the dialogue and offer a few suggestions as a new basis for debate. With the challenge "if you can not work this out, you don't have a chance at successfully managing the company," the group generally comes to a good conclusion.

Other issues of the stock purchase agreement vary with individual circumstances, but you should always preclude stock from being purchased by any means other than management fees. This limitation assures that, in order for the managers to take advantage of a bargain price, they must achieve the performance thresholds that will also benefit the owners. Enhanced profitability supports the best interests of all concerned.

The fundamental reality is that, if there is no enhancement of productivity, there will be no management fees and there will be no purchase of stock.

Mediocre performance will not create an opportunity to be a stockholder. Remember, this is a package designed exclusively for VSKMs who are expected to meet high expectations.

As is customary in closely held and family businesses, the agreement would state that stock options and ownership are not transferable. Furthermore, the agreement would state that the stock can be called in the event of the manager's employment termination.

A combined agreement would also describe any stock option exercise contingencies. These contingencies commonly include provisions such as a minimum accumulation of management fees and the completion of a minimum number of years under the management contract. The management fee accumulation threshold assures that stock will be purchased only as a by-product of success. A requirement that stock can only be purchased in blocks of, say, $100,000, will assure that no stock is transferred unless the managers are significantly moving the profit needle. The time contingency should provide "get-at-it" performance pressure and protection against any breakdowns in judgment regarding the competencies or commitment of managers. Although an owner may think a specific manager is hot stuff, flame out is a concern and a profound pain in the butt. Not only does the time contingency assure success from the management team, but the provision also allows the owner to retain stock longer and continue receiving a higher proportion of dividends.

Most owners feel that requiring a VSKM to make an initial purchase of stock is important to consummate the deal. On the other hand, some owners believe that a management company proving period of two to five years is needed to assure that the managers can back up the hype. I personally prefer to see VSKM(s) put some skin in the game. After generating considerable oratory on the importance of stock ownership, it is satisfying to see them put their money where there mouth is.

There should be no concern about accountability among aggressive managers. Assuming that a reasonable level of team attitude (we-mindedness) has been achieved, VSKMs will not be reluctant to hold their partners accountable. When stock ownership is at risk, a more likely problem is that they will be too critical. No doubt that they will be tougher on each other than the owner ever would. Owners generally are reluctant to really turn the screws on a VSKM because of concern that their star may quit. Management colleagues have no such reluctance. Unfortunately, in some cases, greed may motivate them to trim the ranks. At a minimum, within the team mantra of "we need to be brutally honest," it is not uncommon for a manager who consistently does not meet expectations to be jettisoned.

A Succession Bridge inherently depends upon teamwork.

The greater the incentives provided to the management group, the greater the peer pressure. From the owner's perspective, there is something to be said for no longer having to be the bad guy.

Stock purchase contingencies, such as a minimum number of years under the management contract or a minimum accumulation of management fees, are generally removed in the event the owner is disabled, dies or decides to sell. In fact, that is specifically the moment when the Succession Bridge needs to be locked down. The owner's disability would generally initiate vesting of a portion of the stock options through sale with an installment note. In most MCESB situations, the VSKMs utilize a portion of the management fees to purchase an insurance policy on the owner's life. Those life insurance proceeds would be pledged to fund the exercise of the stock options and immediately create the critical vested interest for the VSKMs. In the event the owner or his heirs decide to sell, the stock option agreement typically stipulates that any unexercised options would be vested to protect the managers' interest and give them a vested interest in the sale process. The managers would realize an impressive gain by simultaneously purchasing the agreed stock at a favorable price and selling to the new buyer at an elevated price.

Relative to the subject of sale, the management contract often provides the management team a first right to negotiate for purchase of the business. Note this is not a first-right of refusal. Unless special circumstances exist, I do not recommend first-right-of refusal because a prospective buyer would view this as a negative contingency, which can hurt the sale price.

Normally, there are two separate sections to the MCESB stockholders agreement. The family member provisions would assure that the family would retain control of the stock (say 80%) that is not subject to stock options. Specifically, the family members would proportionately have the first right to purchase the stock of another family member. Another section would provide the VSKMs similar protection. Specifically, the continuing VSKMs would be provided the first right to purchase the stock of a terminating manager/partner. In the event a manager terminated prior to exercising all of his stock options, the agreement would also transfer the unexercised options to the continuing managers.

The agreement would further state that the manager could only sell stock back to other managers, the family owners or the corporation. Generally, additional management career-retention incentives are provided through the terms for repurchasing the stock. As an example, in the event of a stock buyback due to a manager's voluntary employment termination prior to the specified retirement date, or termination for cause, the agreement would commonly stipulate that the stock would be valued at the manager's original bargain purchase price, or appraised fair market value, whichever is less. However, in the event of a manager's voluntary termination after the specific retirement date, involuntary termination without cause, sale of the company, death or disability, the stock would be valued at the original purchase price, appraised value or sales price, whichever is higher.

The payout terms of the repurchased stock can also be used as an incentive or disincentive. As an example, payout for a VSKM's stock, repurchased due to employment termination prior to retirement, may be considerably longer than the payout period for a buyback initiated upon or beyond the specified retirement date. The combination of an extended payout with a less lucrative buy-back valuation can enhance the impact of the golden handcuff.

Teamwork and Family Business Covenants

Unfortunately, as we discussed in the previous chapter, mere documentation does not make a management company. The making of a management company is a teamwork issue. And unfortunately, the addition of stock ownership to the environment does not make it any easier to achieve the synergy needed to enhance production and profitability. Management companies are not formed, they are built. Although there may be a magic formula somewhere, my experience has proved to me that the critical components of a management team are time, talent, commitment and self-sacrifice for the achievement of unity. Essentially teamwork is all about subordinating the immediate needs of "me," to the more attractive gains of "we." The bottom line is that there has got to be something special in it for everyone or synergy will not be optimized.

Trying to form a team with very special key managers together is an ambitious endeavor. Most of these guys only want to play if they can be the quarterback. They are aggressive, confident, even cocky personalities. One VSKM in the midst of a group of SKMs is much easier. On the other hand, several always aggressive and sometimes demanding VSKMs can create friction that can lead to combustible sparks. The avoidance of costly distractions and the achievement of optimum synergy requires hard work and a reasonable amount of time. Minimally, one year, predictably two and possibly longer is required for a VSKM management group to emerge as a genuine team.

Teamwork requires a combination of God-given talent, selected attitudes and hard work. Unfortunately, some groups never make the cut.

A decision to implement an MCESB should be a by-product of considerable thought. Again, a decision to allow VSKMs to own stock should be followed by appropriate legal formalities to assure that the magic of the Succession Bridge is not ruined by misunderstandings regarding stock ownership rights, employment rights and management rights. Using the same rationale, appropriate management and teamwork formalities should be pursued to protect the business succession aspirations of the family and the stock ownership goals of management from unreasonable expectations.

The management and teamwork challenge of any Succession Bridge initiative is to get owners and operators (VSKMs) on the same page regarding values, goals, priorities and methods.

Management Covenants

- Define management culture and identify a common philosophy
- Define relationship between ownership, mentoring management and family employees for development
- Define a set of standards for communication, problem solving and chain of command
- Not a legal document, but morally binding

This unity is best achieved through developing Management Covenants regarding the "ways and means of Succession Success."

Regrettably, this critically important step in the development and maintenance of a Succession Bridge is frequently finessed. Too often, the owner and/or managers think talking and planning is a waste of valuable time, that "what we need to do is earn some cash." Trust me, business is no different than football, basketball or the Delta Force. Optimum teamwork involves a little "me", a commitment to "we", and a lot of work. In the realm of a Management Company Succession Bridge, the Management Covenants are where the rubber hits the road. To reflect the importance of addressing communication, teamwork and accountability, Chapter 14 has been devoted exclusively to this subject.

Talent Magnet

An invitation to participate in a MCESB is the ultimate compliment that owners can pay to a manager. As affirmation of VSKM status, the manager is receiving the highest possible affirmation of confidence and trust. They are potentially being entrusted with the responsibility of operating the business and providing for the welfare of employees, vendors and customers. But that is not all that is happening with this celebrated event. Managers are being elevated out of the ranks of management and into the hallowed halls of ownership. (Of course it is not that glamorous, but let us memorialize the event with all the glitz we can.)

And here is the good news! There are no secrets in a closely held and family owned business.

> *When owners offer selected managers the opportunity to become partners and lead the business through the next generation, there hopefully will be a formal announcement.*

Even if you try to keep it hush-hush, it will become common knowledge in very short order anyway. If nothing else, an attitude change by an owner or a glimmer of excitement in the eyes of managers will provoke questions: You sure look excited, what is going on? We have not seen you (owner) around as much? What miracle has caused you to relax? What is with all this "we" language? Eventually, the bright minds and long noses will break the code and figure out what has happened.

The impact of this good news (no secrets) is that every manager with a sound mind (and a few of the crazies) is going to want a bite from the apple. Notably, others are going to ask why they were not offered stock. And, of course, they deserve a legitimate answer. The owner is going to have a window of opportunity to explain why some just are not VSKMs and how some can become VSKMs. The fact is, all managers are not created equal. And although some managers may not agree with your rankings, they will ultimately agree that not everyone came to work willing to do whatever it takes to acquire the brass ring.

Predictably, a few very proud and very bold underperforming managers (performance has its price) will not be able to reconcile the comparison and choose to go elsewhere. Equally fortunate, those developing managers who are "giving it up" for the business will be encouraged to hang in there.

After looking around, they will conclude that they will probably never have an employer who cared more about them, individually, as well as the welfare of all who are involved with the business. No doubt word will get out in the community as well. Managers from other less progressive and less succession-oriented organizations will be attracted to join the business.

Case History: Larry and Don, the Seafood Tycoons

Here's a classic example of a management company equity succession bridge involving a company we'll call L&D Seafood. Larry and Don were third-generation owners of a wholesale seafood and restaurant operation. Their grandfather had founded the business right after the turn of the century, starting a fishing operation and opening a restaurant in conjunction with the wholesale distribution. When Larry and, subsequently, Don, became involved, they continued the growth by adding a wholesale truck fleet and by expanding the restaurant operation to eight very popular oyster bars and restaurants.

Larry was 65, very dynamic and outgoing. He had two hard-working sons who worked in the fishing operation and one daughter out of the business who was enjoying a career as a nurse. Larry had been working dark 30 to dark 30 for more than 50 years and was desperately trying to find a way to retire from his chief executive position and put his sons on track to assume leadership responsibility.

However, his two sons, who were affectionately referred to as Tuna 1 and Tuna 2, loved to fish and, with all sincerity, regularly confirmed that they didn't care if the restaurant operation fell into the ocean. Unfortunately as with many vertical businesses, the restaurants had emerged as the cash cow supporting the entire operation.

Don, Larry's cousin and 49% partner, was the numbers man. He was a very competent chief financial officer. However, everyone, Don included, acknowledged that Don was not capable of assuming control when Larry retired. Don had married late and all of his children were still in high school or younger.

One of the profound joys of my profession is meeting really neat people. Larry and Don were two fun-loving, unpretentious, genuine guys who really appreciated someone who took a sincere interest in their welfare. And they had a great deal of pride in their family, employees and business accomplishments. They had very impressively taken advantage of the opportunity provided to them by their parents and had built a business with gross revenues approaching $50 million a year. Although their profits approached $5 million annually, they were strapped for cash due to the capital investment requirements of their restaurant expansion and the truck fleet, as well as the fishing fleet that Tuna 1 and Tuna 2 were building.

Larry and Don were aware of their circumstances and not optimistic about the succession of their business. They had only agreed to see me to get their accountant off their backs. Although disappointed, they had resolved themselves that their business would ultimately have to be sold. During the introductory meeting with Larry, Don and the referring accountant, I learned two critically important facts. First, Larry and Don loved their business and were profoundly depressed at the high probability that the family legacy would come to an end under their watch. Second, the employees were like family. Employees would go out of their way to say hello to them with handshakes, hugs and slaps on the back. Don and Larry knew every one of their 200 employees' first names, and more impressively, most of the names of their spouses and their kids.

Larry and Don were also blessed with a great management team. Both of them spent most of their time talking to employees. Kevin, the general manager, ran the business, attending to every detail in a professional, deliberate manner. When Don wasn't talking to employees he was kibitzing with banks and vendors.

Kevin's forte was financial management, so he had established a support structure for Don that gave him immense free time to stay out front and play the role of godfather and cheerleader.

My interview with other family and managers also confirmed that Larry's boys were memorable characters. At 35 and 31 years old, they were no longer boys, but they did not act like men. They were, most definitely, fishermen, and their idea of dressing up was a set of boots and overalls that didn't smell like the freezer locker of their shrimp boat. Stains, tears and patches provided character to their wardrobe. Tuna 1 was already divorced and Tuna 2 was well on his way, as they would spend three or four nights a week on their boats fishing, fixing and drinking grog with the mates. Barely housebroken, these two likeable chaps loved their work and really didn't give a damn about much else.

On the other hand, Kevin had a Wharton MBA, an impressive big-picture understanding of the business and an iron-fisted control on every aspect of the operation.

After spending a couple hours over lunch discussing management practices and intermediate-term goals, I fully understood Larry and Don's relaxed and even festive approach to the business. I could also better appreciate their description of the frustration, anxiety and pressure they had experienced before Kevin came on board. Very well paid and well appreciated, Kevin enjoyed his work and thoroughly enjoyed working with Lou and Don. His major concern, as would be expected, was the integrity of the business in the event Larry and Don were not around. With no succession plan in place, Kevin shared nightmarish visions of what would transpire if the Tuna Twins and their sister assumed control. Equally impressive, Kevin had assembled a strong support group, including a vice president of restaurant operations, a vice president of wholesale delivery, a comptroller and a vice president of engineering who supervised development and maintenance of all fixed facilities, floating fleet and rolling fleet.

These five guys, led by Kevin, were the heart and soul of the business. My initial report back to Larry and Don was reasonably simple. I first described my fascinating meeting with the Tuna Twins and respectfully expressed understanding why succession planning had not been initiated. As would be expected, Larry and Don received little consolation from my conclusion that there were no viable family successors through whom we could build a succession plan. I then explained my perception of their disposition options: selling the business immediately; selling the business upon Larry's death; or endeavoring to perpetuate the family legacy through a succession bridge mechanism.

Don, who had all the money he would ever need to support his conservative lifestyle, was first to respond with "this is a no-brainer, let's sell this monstrosity before it buries us." Larry, on the other hand, took the bait. He wanted to know more about the Succession Bridge gizmo. It became quite evident that Larry was more sensitive to continuity of the business because he realized that the lifestyle of his two bizarre sons would be on the rocks if the business were sold.

I could offer no argument to counter the expectation that any money the boys received from a sale would be put back into an expanded fishing fleet, which would ultimately suffer the same fate as the Titanic. In response to his inquiry, I agreed to fully explain and evaluate the application of a Succession Bridge. Both Larry and Don acknowledged that Kevin was the key player to any Succession Bridge endeavor. However, they felt that Kevin's long-term success was also dependent upon retention of the other four key managers, as well as each of the restaurant managers. After discussing the various bridge options, they expressed genuine interest in a Management Company Succession Bridge, because it appeared to provide business succession and it also partially addressed Don's desire to sell the business. Larry then requested that I talk with Kevin to find out what he thought.

Kevin's reaction was classic, "I'm not interested in babysitting the Tuna Twins. So, in the event of Larry's death, you can color me out of here. I have several standing offers for higher compensation from lower quality competitors. For the time being, I am not going anywhere because I like working with Larry and Don. They give me the authority to do whatever I think is right and they get out of my way. However, you can bet that the Tuna Twins would be in my way. It's all I can do now to prevent my staff from giving these boys a one-way ticket to the Bermuda Triangle. Just as soon as the Twins started sticking their noses into what I am doing, or second-guessing our managers, we would all find another place to work. No golden handcuff could keep me here if the Tuna Twins started gaffing our restaurants to build stupid fishing boats. They would probably fire me anyway because they know that I know that their fishing is just a boondoggle."

Needless to say, this information did not make Larry, Don, or me feel better. After Larry heard Kevin's comments, I thought he was going to need Prozac. His big Italian face lost all its joy and sparkle. His emotional swings were hitting all-time lows. Don just became more resolved in his "sell the sucker" attitude. Our discussions began to lean more to when, how and for how much the business should be sold.

I suggested another run at Kevin under the assumption that he would become a stockholder. I said that I thought Kevin could get excited about this opportunity if, as a result of a stock purchase by a management team, the Tuna Twins would be out of control. Larry naturally expressed that he wasn't sure he wanted to take control out of his sons' hands.

I responded that his family would have control through his daughter's involvement. I also pointed out that his daughter's conclusion that her brothers were a couple of over-sized adolescents was not too far off base. Her disrespect for them could provide the accountability we needed. Moreover, if he wanted to keep Kevin, and probably at least two of the other key managers, the Tuna Twins could not be in control. Otherwise, a sale of the business was probably the right thing to do.

Larry wanted to think it over. He understood that control would be maintained as long as his family and Don's family agreed on strategic issues, regardless of cooperation from his daughter. However, in the event they were divided, the management team would cast the deciding votes.

All was quiet for about six weeks. Larry gave me a call and said that the concept of an Equity Bridge was not his idea of succession, but it might be better than a sale.

He asked me to discuss the concept with Kevin and the key managers. Later, I heard through the grapevine that what had prompted Larry's decision was a rumor that the Tuna Twins had entered into an agreement with one of the local organized families to use their fancy boats to begin providing transport for square grouper (bales of marijuana).

Evidently, Larry sent his boys on a surprise two-week vacation to the Caribbean while he took his hat in hand and went to the family leader, whom he had grown up with, and humbly asked to be relieved of the agreement. Presumably, Lou even wrote a big check to get his sons off the hook.

When I explained to Kevin that he and his managers could own a third of the company and, more importantly, that the Tuna Twins would not be in control, I got his attention. Actually, Kevin began to resemble a heat-seeking missile. When he understood that he and his management team would be contractually delegated day-to-day management control and that the management contract would provide them one-third of profitability increases with which to purchase the stock, he became a deal-making machine.

He contended that the company was not half as profitable as it could be. If he were given the unencumbered ability to make day-to-day management decisions, he could double the profitability in short order.

Over the next six months, the deal was done. Not only did we adopt a Management Company Equity Bridge with the five managers, we also organized a Management Advisory Board with 12 middle managers. These managers were provided a golden handcuff supplemental executive retirement as motivation for participating on the management Advisory Board (MAB) and maximizing the team-related profitability of the individual restaurants and wholesale operations.

Interestingly, the first year with this new infrastructure was not particularly productive. Actually, profitability dropped by a third as the principals of the Management Company began to implement new ideas and the MAB offered suggestions for eliminating some bad programs and enhancing some good ones. It was simply too much to do, too little time and too few bodies to get it done.

Nor was the second year any bonfire, as the Management Company diverted some of its otherwise productive energy to jettisoning one of its members, whom they felt was not setting the proper example for work ethic and character. During the second year, the MAB also reorganized itself and elected a new leader. As the program entered its third year, Larry and Don were getting a bit antsy. Both had elected to work only half-time and were becoming fond of more freedom. Larry was enjoying fishing with his boys and really doing well as a cheerleader for the employees and a politician with the community. Don was serving primarily as an auditor to review control procedures to make sure the sharpies in the Management Company were not running off with all the money. After they saw no growth in profitability, they expressed concern about the viability of the whole idea and about complying with the five-year buy-in window.

I had my doubts as well, but Kevin was offering a mid-year forecast for a profit increase of $2 million above the profit threshold. During the first year, he said, he and his colleagues had to learn how to be a team. That had taken some of the focus off the bottom line. He continued to be confident that everyone would reap the rewards of these organizational efforts. As history proved, Kevin was impressively conservative, bringing in profits $5 million above the profit-sharing threshold of $4 million. Needless to say, Larry's demeanor changed. I was personally transformed from an eccentric consultant with a crazy idea to a genius and Kevin was a walking candidate for businessman of the year. At the year-end party, all the members of the Management Company were feeling "large and in charge" as they had their picture taken with a 6-foot check showing their $1.25 million management fee.

The fourth year, things got really exciting, as the very special key managers realized that, although they had done very well the prior year, they were significantly behind in their 5-year forecast. It called for $6 million, after taxes, to purchase stock.

In early January the group went on a retreat to examine ways that they could further optimize profitability. They returned with many good ideas, but one blockbuster: Dump the fishing fleet.

Evidently, the underground information pipeline was working well, because the Tuna Twins were waiting in Lou's office after the presentation meeting. Without time to absorb the Management Company's proposal, Lou was besieged, first by his sons, and then by a seemingly endless parade of local town officials, union stewards, longstanding employees and even family, who contended that the fishing fleet was the heart and soul of T&T Seafood. No one went to see Don, because they knew he was a numbers man and that he thought the fishing fleet was only an in-house tax shelter. Actually, his contention was that any venture that consumed cash was not a tax shelter but just a dumb business.

I could hardly believe the ruckus that was created by the proposal to shut down the 15-boat fishing fleet. There were calls from congressmen and even picketing at the restaurants. My reaction was that anything that caused this much attention would have to be some form of welfare program. Evidently I wasn't too far off. But Lou had an emotional attachment to the fishing fleet. That's where he had begun his career. However, unlike the Tuna Twins, he ultimately grew weary of long trips and rough weather.

A routine began where Larry would meet with Kevin and his manager/partners every Monday morning. As a result of their discussions, he would get all excited about the opportunity to make everyone's life simpler and increase profitability by $3 million a year. However, by Friday, the pro-fishing pressure would have taken its toll and Larry would become an ornery and confused paisano.

This back-and-forth stroll continued for six months. Larry was unable to make a decision and all of the employees were taking sides. The most unfortunate development was that Kevin's four partners in the management company began to lose confidence that they could generate the needed profitability to purchase stock, because they had concluded that Larry was going to continue to subsidize the fishing fleet. So, to make things worse, they began thinking that the stock purchase escrow fund should be distributed and everyone should go their own way.

My advice to Larry was, as always, protect the golden goose. My concern was not for the current $3 million per year subsidy, but for the future capital investment that would be required to keep the fleet modernized. The bulk of the current loss was due to antiquated equipment. The $3 million per year subsidy was chump change compared to the cost of an equipment update.

Larry shut me out as another lobbyist until the annual fishing festival. In conjunction with the festivities along the harbor, the company traditionally hosted a shrimp feast on one of their trawlers. As always, it was a great time with friends, visitors and dignitaries showing up for beer and shrimp.

However, after Larry, Dave, Kevin and the managers called it an evening, the Tuna Twins and some of their rowdy friends stayed on board to clean up the mess.

According to a well-known tradition, they kept drinking and deferred the cleanup until the next morning. Unfortunately, as a result of being preoccupied with beer and babes, they failed to turn off one of the gas grills. In a of a course of events that no one really understands, a fire started and the flagship of their fishing fleet burned to a crisp tied up to the dock. The media arrived just in time to get video of the Tuna Twins and their girlfriends running around on the dock in their skivvies, acting like keystone cops trying to put out the fire. A video of these antics made the local T.V. news. Evidently, this fiasco took Larry over the top. He called me a couple days later. I bit my tongue not to laugh as he described how his sons explained what happened. Larry could hardly hold back a chuckle himself when he said something about doing shots and strip poker. One of the girls in the video was the Mayor's daughter, who just happened to be married to the son of union heavy. The notable statement was that there would never be a better time to dump the fleet. "Sonny boy may be as business minded as a stump. However, his wild and crazy antics have done this family and business great service."

Kevin and his management team went to work right away to take advantage of the embarrassed power brokers in the city government and the unions. About 120 days later, they closed a socially acceptable deal, merging the fishing fleet with a comparable sized competitor. Prior to the merger, Larry loaned the Tuna Twins the money to purchase the fleet from the holding company, terminating their employment with L&D Seafood.

As expected, profits immediately grew, but not quite as fast as expected because of the tax sheltering impact of the fishing fleet. Unfortunately, the five-year $3 million accumulation goal was not within reach. However, in light of the circumstances, Larry and Don extended the stock purchase opportunity for three more years. Seven years after the initiation of the Management Company, equity ownership was achieved and we proclaimed L&D Seafood as Succession Certified.

This was a proud day for Larry and Don. From their perspective, L&D was now on autopilot under the outstanding management of Kevin and his colleagues. The Management Company, under Kevin's direction, had so enhanced profitability that they were able to make a $6 million down payment on one-third of the business. The $4 million they borrowed to complete the purchase was projected to be paid *off in an additional two years. The Tuna Twins, Larry's daughter and Don's oldest child sat on the Board of Directors and expressed unwavering contentment with Kevin and his management company colleagues. They may not have been the sharpest hooks in the box, but they were not stupid.*

Although they had sold one-third of the company to a Management Company Succession Bridge, its value had tripled. It took Tuna II a month to do the math and another month to explain the concept to Tuna I. When the light bulb came on, they were both very pleased with a program that freed them to pursue their fishing, generated better profits than previously realized and had created twice the value with only two-thirds the ownership.

13 The ESOP Succession Bridge

Our final Succession Bridge option represents a departure from the fundamental structure of the previously discussed Succession Bridge concepts. Up to this point, all Succession Bridge "golden handcuff" career retention incentives have been "non-qualified benefits." As we have discussed in chapter 3, a business owner can utilize a benefit that does not have to qualify according to the Employment Retirement Income Security Act (ERISA) to discriminate in favor of a select group of more highly compensated key managers.

In the realm of our discussions, a business owner can offer non-qualified benefits as consideration and incentive, exclusively to key managers who show the competency, commitment and character to serve as a Succession Bridge. By definition, only the highly compensated managers may participate in non-qualified plans, because they are presumed to have the sufficient education and experience to represent their own interest. Non-qualified benefits, as the name implies, do not qualify for tax-deductible contributions. However, being exempt for the restrictions of ERISA, non-qualified benefits can be highly versatile tools in the construction of a Succession Bridge.

In stark contrast, an employee stock ownership plan, more commonly referred to as an ESOP, is a "qualified" plan. Qualified plans such as pensions, 401(k) and ESOPs are not utilized as a primary incentive for Succession Bridges architecture because there is very little ability to discriminate in favor of the small group of managers who can handle the responsibilities inherent with management continuity.

However, the significant and unique business ownership opportunities provided by an ESOP, dictate inclusion in our Succession Bridges discussion. With due respect to the inherent limitations and administrative burdens of a qualified plan, let's cautiously review how an ESOP can also provide the support needed for a Succession Bridges.

It is beyond the purpose of this discussion to make you an expert on the technical aspects of an ESOP. You will have to rely on your personal advisors or other text to nail the detail. My goal is to make you aware of the major features of an ESOP and to stimulate your consideration of this unique tool in a Succession

Bridges strategy. As we are going to discuss, there are some exciting features to an ESOP. However, there are also some significant disincentives from utilizing this relatively complex structure in a business succession strategy that we want to keep as simple as possible.

It bears mentioning that an ESOP can be utilized as an exclusive Succession Bridges incentive or, as creative minds will quickly recognize, in combination with any of the previously mentioned Succession Bridge options. In fact, most commonly, the ESOP is utilized as an "add-on" to other non-qualified benefits, due to the significant impact upon either the owner or the managers. However, ESOP regulations specifically limit the use of non-qualified benefits, referred to as synthetic equity, to abusively dilute an ESOP's ownership.

Before we get too creative, let's review the fundamentals.

An ESOP is a qualified retirement plan specifically designed for funding with the stock of the corporate sponsor.

Public corporations developed the concept of funding an employee benefit plan with their stock as they pursued creative methods of conserving cash, funding employee benefits and providing employees with a vested interest in the welfare of their employer.

Although initially hesitant to approve anything with so many potential conflicts of interest, the IRS and the Labor Department eventually signed on to this concept because stock in a public company was easily valued and readily liquid. To appease their inherent lack of trust, very specific regulations were implemented to ensure that stock valuation and allocation were fair. As time passed, additional regulations were implemented to provide participants with the right to diversify their interests as they approached retirement.

When the creative minds of private enterprise requested approval for ESOPs in closely held businesses, the Feds were less responsive, due to the valuation and liquidity challenges inherent with stock that is not actively traded. Eventually, with the support of a few zealous congressmen, the private business lobby prevailed. Because the IRS approved ESOPs for private companies reluctantly, a continuum of legislative reforms was incorporated to prevent employers from taking advantage of their employees. But then those zealous congressmen got involved again and behold, significant employer incentives were enacted. Currently, both the IRS and the Labor Department have accepted that an ESOP can be a very attractive business liquidation tool for the employer.

The Feds have responded with tight regulations that define structuring parameters and administrative compliance procedures. Trust me! The IRS is hyper-sensitive to the prospect that an employer may take advantage of his employees. Therefore no doubt, legislative tinkering will continue.

It bears mentioning that a profit-sharing plan and 401(k) plan can own stock in a sponsoring employer, but the amount of stock that the plan can own is substantially limited, relative to a formal ESOP. Furthermore, since an ESOP is specifically designed to own employer stock, it is exempt from several compliance issues to which other qualified plans must comply.

An ESOP has several other unique features that can be a distinct advantage from a Succession Bridge planning perspective.

As a qualified plan, an ESOP is subject to full regulatory scrutiny of both the IRS and the Labor Department. In other words, an ESOP is a serious business endeavor and you had better have your technical support team on board before you start stepping on land mines. In addition to the customary administrative and compliance hoops of any form of qualified plan, an ESOP also carries the requirement of an annual appraisal of the employer's stock. And to ensure objectivity, the regularly employed accountant cannot perform this appraisal. This appraisal is needed to determine the value of the asset (stock) contributed and the resulting income-tax deductions received by the corporation. This appraisal determines the value of the employees' retirement account, the amount of the employer's tax deduction, the price the employee would be paid for the stock and the personal income tax that will ultimately be due. Recognizing the weight of the issues riding on the appraisal, it is prudent to understand that the appraisal of the stock is the primary ESOP audit magnet. There is nothing to be gained by cutting corners here. The business owner should hire a qualified appraiser and get out of their way. Any valuation pressure exerted will only mean that the employer will share in the appraiser's liability.

My personal description of an ESOP is "going semi public." In fact, an ESOP creates a market for closely held stock.

In contrast to the regulatory gauntlet of an IPO, an ESOP creates various forms of liquidity by providing the funding to make stock available to <u>current, future and, sometimes, even past employees.</u>

The administrative demands and implementation costs of an ESOP are lesser evils than those associated with an IPO. However, if independent trustees are utilized, the adoption and administrative cost can become substantial. In contrast, an IPO is funded with third party money. With an ESOP, ultimately the business will have to generate the money or stock to fund the plan and then provide additional money to buy back the stock when the employee retires. The "buyback liability" is easily over-looked but never forgotten once the employee retires and says, "I don't want this stock, where's my money?"

The legislative intent of an ESOP has the lure of capitalism and the aroma of socialism. Through this unique form of retirement plan, our legislators have provided the owners of lucrative businesses an incentive to spread the benefits of ownership among the employees. The incentives are both real and imagined. With respect to employee motivation, there are endless numbers of ESOPs that have enhanced employee commitment and improved productivity. Unfortunately there are also resounding failures, some of which have made national headlines. No doubt, the effectiveness of an ESOP depends upon the motives of the owner(s), the unique nature of the business, the quality of the ESOP initiative and the culture of the employees. Like most things in life, the realistic business succession rewards of an ESOP are directly proportionate to the time, effort and conviction of the initiative. Unfortunately, from an incentive perspective, having a vested interest in the employer's stock in a retirement plan does not necessarily mean that employees are going to have the proprietary attitudes of business owners.

An ESOP will not make an apathetic, self- centered employee any better.

As an incentive to share the profits of ownership with labor, an ESOP provides a business owner with the ability to create a valuable corporate income tax-deduction for contributions of treasury stock to the <u>*employee's retirement plan.*</u>

Depending upon the nature of the corporation and the stock purchase circumstances, the business owner and employed family members can also participate in the ESOP. Within the parameters established by the IRS, the amount of the stock contributed is at the discretion of the business owner. Cash that would have otherwise been committed to funding retirement benefits is conserved for other uses.

The contributed stock is held in a trust under the fiduciary responsibility of a trustee. Each participant does not have stockholder rights. It is the trustee who has the stockholder rights. The participants would be given access to the corporate valuation through the trustee. However the employee would not have access to the intimate books and records of the corporation.

In this way, the trustee connects the owner with the employees. The trustee can be any reasonably qualified party willing to accept this responsibility, including the business owner, key employees, an independent party, an independent institution or a combination thereof. In order to achieve technical compliance and practical buy-in by the employees, the trustee must act like a legitimate representative of the employees. Due to the fiduciary liability implications and business control implications, selecting a trustee is always an important planning issue. Due to the inherent conflicts of interest, the IRS is most comfortable when the employer is not the sole trustee. Unfortunately, there are few highly qualified third parties who are equipped to serve as independent sole trustees.

The business can receive a tax deduction for contributing stock to an ESOP in lieu of cash. This feature can represent a substantial cash savings by conserving cash that would have otherwise been contributed.

The business can also contribute cash to the ESOP, which is intended to purchase stock from the existing owners. Depending upon the circumstances, needs and immediate goals of the business owner(s), the ESOP can incrementally purchase stock, amortize debt that was incurred to purchase stock or accumulate cash for the anticipated purchase of stock at a point in time when the owner is prepared to sell. The actual structure of the stock purchase is usually dominated by taxation because the potential deferral of capital gains tax on the sale of stock to an ESOP represents a substantial benefit. However, in order for an owner to qualify for capital gain tax deferral, the ESOP must own at least 30 percent of the corporation's stock. This tax deferral is not available for the sale of S-Corp stock to an ESOP.

As mentioned above, the business owner can also empower (usually with the corporation's and the owner's guarantee) the ESOP to borrow cash to make a significant stock acquisition. The business owner can then cause the corporation to make annual tax-deductible cash contributions to the ESOP to amortize the loan. In light of the ability to defer tax on significant transactions, ESOP contributions are usually applied to amortize a loan or to accumulate until sufficient funds are available to purchase 30%.

It bears mentioning that, in order for a business owner to defer capital gains tax on the transaction, the proceeds of the stock sale must be reinvested into stock or bonds in another business, either public or private.

In other words, the business owner could defer tax by investing in another private business. Or the business owner could achieve liquidity by reinvesting the proceeds of the ESOP sale into publicly traded stocks or bonds. Tax would be paid on the gain, incrementally as the reinvested stocks are subsequently sold. If securities with this deferred gain are passed through an estate, under current law the capital gain can be totally avoided. From an estate planning perspective, either an individual or a family partnership owning stock can qualify for this tax deferral.

Either a regular C-corporation or a Sub Chapter-S corporation can sponsor an ESOP. However, funding and administrative parameters vary according to the structure of the corporation. The maximum tax-deductible cash or stock contribution to a C-corporation's is 25% of the corporate eligible payroll. In addition to the 25% of payroll, the ESOP deduction can also include the interest on an acquisition loan.

Participants of a C-corp ESOP cannot be required to sell their stock back to the corporation or the ESOP. In other words, there is a possibility that a quirky participant may want to hold on to his stock in lieu of converting the stock into retirement funds. Fortunately, terminated participants of a S-corp ESOP can be required to sell their stock, back to the corporation due to the vulnerability of Sub Chapter-S status to stock transfers specifically prohibited by IRS regulations.

However, both S-corps and C-corps with ESOPs should be prepared to repurchase a retired participant's stock. What good would the stock do a participant anyway? The common motivation is for cash. This is further supported by the fact that participants will have to pay tax on the value of the stock when received from the ESOP.

Other interesting differences include the opportunity for a C-corp to realize an income tax deduction for dividends paid to stock held in an ESOP. However, S-corp distributions on stock held in an ESOP are not technically considered dividends and therefore are not tax deductible. Again, there is no tax deferral opportunity for S-corp stock sold to an ESOP.

As you ponder the above technical nuances, try to restrain the conclusion that I have lost my mind promoting a Succession Bridges program that draws so much attention from the Feds. How could an ESOP be of any use to a business owner who already has a belly full of government regulation, declining energy and kids who are not ready for prime-time business management. Admittedly, an ESOP, independent of any other key manager initiatives has only limited Succession Bridge application. Key managers will not be sufficiently motivated by the non-discriminatory allocations of a qualified ESOP. The IRS allocation and participation regulations that protect rank and file employees, will not motivate key managers.

Actually, if the owner announces the adoption of an ESOP to a VSKM and offers no other supporting qualification or explanation, the response may be "adios." Being the most ambitious key manager species, a VSKM may have very little tolerance for dealing with the administrative demands of the IRS and the Department of Labor. Furthermore, these driving managers may be repulsed by the assumption that they will be required to nursemaid a group of half-hearted employees with unrealistic benefit expectations.

Advice: if you have a VSKM, do not even think about an ESOP Succession Bridge without his involvement from the beginning.

Using an ESOP as a Succession Bridge

Nevertheless, in specific situations, an ESOP does have Succession Bridges applications. The first would be as an enhancing component of a Golden Handcuff Succession Bridges. Let us assume that the business owner has important key managers (KM) or even special key managers (SKM) and has taken the initiative to lock them into a career commitment with a supplemental executive retirement plan (SERP.)There could even be a functioning Management Advisory Board (MAB) complete with Management Covenants, through which the managers were taking an active role in management.

Let's further assume that these key managers are pressing to be stockholders and, for legitimate reasons, the owner does not want partners. These are not very special key managers (VSKM), so the owner has set reasonable limits as to what he is willing to do. Yet, in the absence of a VSKM and deference to the disdain for adding partners, the owner feels obliged to do something with stock to nail down the Succession Bridges. Furthermore, the owner is a few pesos short of the cash needed to fulfill retirement security. But, the owner does not want to require the children to mortgage their souls to the bank to support his retirement. Equally important, although the owner recognizes the value of the managers, he does not want to leave the next generation handcuffed to relatively light-weight (KM and SKM) partners.

ESOP as a KM/SKM Silver Bullet

Under these unique circumstances, an ESOP Succession Bridge could be just the ticket. Although no automatic answer to all succession challenges, an ESOP does offer profound opportunity. As an example, the owner could advise the managers that their request for stock ownership will be honored by giving them the opportunity to participate in an ESOP. To sweeten the pot, the owner would stipulate that this form of stock ownership would not be costing them (KMs and SKMs usually have marginal uncommitted income) a dime. If you have not figured it out, a very special key manager would probably not accept this indirect form of ownership. A VSKM wants to personally own a piece of the rock and is willing to spend personal funds to get it.

But back to this example, as the highest earning plan participants, the key managers should receive the highest allocations of stock. Further, if the SERP does its career retention job, the reallocation of ESOP buybacks and forfeitures should ultimately position the majority of the allocated stock in the accounts of the KMs and SKMs.

Consequently, the SERP would have created a golden handcuff security benefit for the managers and the ESOP will provide these same managers <u>a vested interest in the growth of the company.</u>

From the owner's perspective, he would have dispersed business ownership without adding lots of new stockholders and the complications that naturally arise. This would especially be the case if the business was Subchapter-S. The owner would have the option to be the trustee and continue to represent the interest of all stock.

Furthermore, the owner would have a rare opportunity to utilize funds that are currently being contributed to a qualified 401(k) plan or a pension plan for the owner's benefit. More specifically, the owner could sell some of his stock to the ESOP and use the prior 401(k) contribution to pay for his stock. The owner could liquidate his stock with tax deductible corporate funds without creating a cash flow challenge for his kids. And, notably, if appropriate prerequisites are met, (sell 30 percent or more of his stock) the owner could defer tax on the transaction. In summary, he sells stock on a tax deferred basis, pays for the sale on a tax deductible basis and uses funds that were previously paid to the employees (401(k)) to fund the transaction.

The kid's would be relieved of the pressure of personally purchasing their Dad's stock. Furthermore, the cash from the sale to the ESOP would make their Dad less financially dependent upon the business. Therefore Dad would be more inclined to get out of their way and allow them to learn how to run the business. As a trade off, the kids would have to learn to live with an ESOP for at least five years.

They could be the successor trustees and maintain unencumbered control of the business. The tax savings from this transaction could be utilized to fund a life insurance policy to underwrite estate taxes on the balance of their parents' stock or buyout/terminate the ESOP.

An ESOP Succession Bridge can also be a dynamic planning tool when the owner already has a Key Manager Equity Succession Bridge in place, <u>and there are no family successors.</u>

The owner may not want to sell any more stock that would give one or more VSKMs the control of the business. The owner may be concerned about how notoriously aggressive VSKMs will behave, or just not be ready to hang up his spurs. The owner may not want to pay any more capital gains tax on the sale of stock to the VSKMs. And, equally plausible, the owner may be feeling the financial pressure of retiring managers and may not want to be personally involved in the repurchase of stock.

Under these circumstances, an ESOP could be utilized as a hybrid Control Equity Succession Bridges. Since the VSKMs are already stockholders, the owner could be more aggressive without concern that they may revolt. The owner could advise the VSKMs that, in addition to the minority stock that they already own, they would vest into another block of stock at no cost through an ESOP. The initial sale to the VSKMs and the second sale to the ESOP would together constitute a majority of the business. Again, assuming stockholder criteria are met, the VSKMs, as the highest earners, would receive the largest allocations of stock both from contributions, buybacks and forfeitures. So now the owner is in a minority and the employees, led by the VSKMs, indirectly own the majority.

However, the owner or his family can remain in control of the business. Although they retain only a minority position, as both minority owners and trustee of the ESOP, the family remains in control. Further, the sale of this minority block of stock to the ESOP, as opposed to the sale of stock to the key managers, could be tax-deferred, assuming the proceeds were reinvested in a portfolio of common stock. And, because the owner technically would be giving up control, a higher sales price could potentially be justified on this sale. Without the pressure of repurchasing the stock of retiring managers and, with a deadlock vote as at least an ESOP co-trustee, the business owner or family members could continue to enjoy the benefits of minority stock ownership without the concern that the controlling position of the VSKMs could put their financial interest in jeopardy.

Another application of an ESOP Succession Bridge is a hybrid of the Buyout Succession Bridge.

An ESOP can facilitate a succession plan if a business owner wants to defer tax on a portion of the buyout or if he recognizes that key managers will never individually generate the financial resources to buy <u>him out.</u>

Under this option, he would not be concerned about the administrative headaches that an ESOP may be creating for his successor owners because, with the commitment to sell the business, neither he nor the family members will be around to worry about it. And for security purposes, he could retain the trusteeship of the ESOP until the owner was fully paid out. Although the key managers would not individually own 100% of the company, they would have total control as successor trustees of the ESOP.

If they agreed that control was nine tenths of ownership, the designated-successor VSKMs could become large-and-in-charge. Furthermore, if the VSKMs are unhappy with administration of the ESOP, after five years they could terminate it. Of course they would have to find some serious money.

The business owner could become a retiree, with his cash reinvested into a diversified portfolio. The major question under this scenario is: Will the sale to the ESOP generate sufficient cash for the owner? As emphasized earlier, the IRS recognizes that stock valuation is a hinge pin of an ESOP. The owner would not be able to just pick the price. In order to satisfy the "arms length" criteria, the value of the stock would have to be determined by an independent appraiser. Needless to say, the opinions of qualified arms length appraisers can be influenced, but unfortunately there is no guarantee that the owner will like the price. Of course, if an owner doesn't like the price, they don't have to sell.

Case History #10 - Mr. Rose, late bloomer

One of the neatest examples of an ESOP Succession Bridge was back in the mid-1990's with a late blooming automobile dealer. Mr. Rose was 66 years old and owned two car dealerships saddled with mediocre performance. He had worked hard all of his life, but seemed to specialize in taking one step forward and two steps backwards. When the cycling economy or factory strikes were not burning his backside, he would independently find creative ways to make business blunders. With the combination of too much work and worry, Mr. Rose had experienced a mild heart attack in 1989. His son, Bud, had quit his job as an engineer with a public company and had come home to help his mom and dad save the security that they had accumulated within the business. A couple of years later, Bud called to say business was great, but they had a dilemma. The manufacturer/franchiser had given them an ultimatum due to overcrowded market conditions.

As they were the oldest dealer in the area, with the highest customer satisfaction ratings, they were given the option to buy out their two closest competitors and reposition their store in a new facility equipped to handle the increased volume from the consolidation. The manufacturer had even agreed to put some money in the deal, in exchange for an agreement that Bud would not put any other make of automobile on the site.

He continued to say that much of their recent success was due to his father's renewed enthusiasm for the business. Bud's return had relieved his father's stress by providing assurance that his security would not be at risk.

The good news was that his father was working harder than ever. The bad news was that, if he did not get him out of the stores, he was concerned that his father was going to have another heart attack or Bud was going to murder him. In short, he needed money to buy out his parents, assure their security and prevent his Dad from driving him crazy. However, he did not see where he could find enough cash.

So, pen, paper and calculator in hand, I began to consider the various angles to raise enough capital to deal with a three-headed challenge: buy some of dad's stock, build a new building and buy out competitors. Having frequently stated, "the difficult we do right away, but the impossible takes a little time," I encouraged Bud to optimistically search for avenues through which we could raise approximately $7 million. Calling on all sources of financing, we ultimately hit a brick wall. The math just would not work. We could address two out of the three needs but, beyond that, we were running on empty. I saw no way, short of Divine Intervention, for Bud to come up with enough money to make the deal work.

Finally, as I was perfecting the art of hemming and hawing, Bud asked if I had ever considered using an ESOP. Trying not to look stupid or naive, I told him that I was aware of the technical parameters of an ESOP but had never really taken a closer look because I did not like the administrative implications. Not only was an ESOP an administrative load, I was concerned that Congress could change the rules whenever the mood stuck. And that could seriously impact assumptions that had been initially critical to the compatibility of the program.

Bud explained that his previous employer had an ESOP. As neither of us could come up with any viable alternative, he wanted me to join him in a meeting with the attorney who had handled the ESOP adoption. My response -- if someone could turn water into wine, I was all ears.

The truth was that I had not even considered an ESOP because I had no idea how an ESOP could be our "silver bullet." Far from being an advocate, I categorically believed that all ESOPs were administrative beasts, as well as management nightmares because employee participants would have stockholder rights

To my surprise, Jonathan, the attorney was not an analytical worm. He was both a realist and, in addition to being very bright, an impressive creative thinker. After hearing about the demands on Bud's cash flow, he agreed with my conclusion that there wasn't enough money sitting around to achieve all these objectives.

However, Jonathan thought Bud might be able to pull it off through an ESOP. He got my attention by sharing impressive data published by the ESOP Association that contended that ESOP businesses were more productive than their counterparts.

Bud expressed confidence that he understood the administrative complications, but was concerned about the legislative vulnerability. Jonathan acknowledged that an ESOP was a legislative creation and therefore the rules could change with the ebb and flow of politics. Yet, he believed traumatic legislation was unlikely because Congress was a proponent of ESOPs. He emphasized that Bud should not consider an ESOP a short-term solution to his capital need. In the unlikely event this potential silver bullet became an administrative beast, IRS regulations provided for "safe harbor" termination after five years.

Trying to show how smart I was, I stated, "but we do not want the hassle of all these employees becoming stockholders."

"Interesting point, Loyd, but the fact of the matter is that employee participants of an ESOP are not stockholders."

The attorney then continued to graciously ignore my lack of sophistication and explain, "just because a qualified retirement plan owns stock, does not mean that the plan participants are stockholders. The stockholder of record on behalf of the ESOP is the trustee. The trustee is the only party who has access to the corporate records or who has a right to vote the stock. Now, in the rare event a retired stockholder wanted to pay tax on the value of the stock and then hold on to it, you could have an outside stockholder.

"You cannot make them sell it back to you but you can put in place an enforceable first right of refusal if the retired participant tried to transfer the share(s) to a third party."

Before I could be concerned about getting my foot out of my mouth, the attorney grabbed a magic marker and began drawing on an easel. His recommendation was that Bud and his dad convert the existing profit-sharing plan into an ESOP. Bud would be the trustee, along with a key manager, so employee meddling would not be an issue. With the approval of the franchiser, Jonathan suggested Mr. Rose sell 30% of Rose Automotive Inc. to the ESOP.

We all felt the business would justify a $10 million value, so Jonathan projected that Mr. Rose would receive $3 million for the sale.

He then suggested Mr. Rose take $1 million of the proceeds and invest it in a blue chip stock portfolio. He contended that this invested capital, independent from the business could give Mr. Rose a head start on a retirement fund. He subsequently suggested that the remaining $2 million be combined with $3 million that Bud would borrow from the bank, along with cash thrown in by the manufacturer, to buy out the competition. With a confident smile on his face, the attorney also pointed out that if Mr. Rose and Bud purchased the the competitor's existing corporations, capital gains tax could be totally deferred on the sale of stock to the ESOP.

With a confused look, Mr. Rose asked if the attorney was sure that he could defer the capital gains tax with the purchase of both public and private stock. The attorney responded that tax deferral was one of the unique features that could make this plan work. He continued to explain that, in order to defer tax, the seller must reinvest into common stock. There are no requirements that the reinvestment be in either private or public stock. He concluded by stating that, through deferral of the capital gains tax on $3 million, Mr. Rose would be receiving a substantial interest-free loan from the IRS that would be instrumental in making this deal work.

"Where is this ESOP going to get $3 million to buy Dad's stock?" Bud asked.

"Well, no doubt you are going to have to borrow some money. But I do not think getting this loan will be all that difficult. The company's profit-sharing plan can be converted into an ESOP. The plan can borrow money using a guarantee from the business that sufficient contributions will be made to the ESOP to service the loan. If we assume that we make ESOP contributions comparable to the expanded (much bigger organization) profit-sharing and 401(k) contributions, you should be able to retire an ESOP loan of $2 million in approximately 10 years. I estimate that you personally are going to need to borrow approximately $3 million to join your dad in buying out your competition.

"Assuming $$2 million of the reinvested ESOP proceeds, $3 million from you and the manufacturer's $2 million line of credit, we can raise the $7 million and make this deal work. What makes the deal work now is that we are getting $2 million from the ESOP that will be amortized by cash flow already committed to retirement plan fund. You have already convinced the floor plan lender that you are worthy of the $3 million personal loan."

"So, I've got the money for the deal. Dad's got a million bucks in the bank and the profit sharing pays off the debt. That is slick."

An impressed spectator up to this point, I no longer wanted to make bold statements from what was a limited understanding of ESOPs, but felt I would not embarrass myself with a few respectful thoughts and questions. *"Mr. Rose what do you think of all this technical mumbo jumbo? I understand your passion for the business, but I also understand your hatred of unnecessary complication and the government sticking their nose in your business. Can you live with an ESOP?"*

"Obviously Loyd, you know me well. To be perfectly honest, an ESOP would not be my preferred answer to our dilemma. No government administered program is a silver bullet. But, on the other hand, I do not have a better idea and we have to do something or watch this opportunity pass us by. I am ready to pull the trigger and get on with it, but I am not the one who will be married to this babe.

"As soon as Bud does not need me I am going to start seriously working on my handicap. I just want to say that before we move forward, I want Bud to fully understand the implications. Jonathan made mention of a safe harbor termination but that sounds to me like legalese. I have to believe that a termination could be a cat fight. I just want Bud to be careful."

"Thanks Mr. Rose," I responded, *"You have expressed my sentiments perfectly."* I then proceeded to say that an ESOP, much like a marriage, is easy to get in to, challenging to live with and expensive to terminate. But I didn't have any better

ideas. Furthermore, time was not on our side. We had to either put-up or shut-up. The opportunity to buy out our competitors was short lived.

"Listen," responded Mr. Rose, "You are absolutely right and as much as I hate to get in bed with both the government and our employees, I am loving an ESOP if it is the only way to put-up. If we were the ones to sell the $5 million in walking money would enable Judy and I to play golf to our heart's desire. But as you guys understand, I have not been in this crazy business to get rich or fund a run at the senior tour. I am a 'car man,' not a professional golfer. We have enough money now to fulfill our simple ambitions. My number one goal in life is to see this dealership continue under Bud's management. And it would be no surprise to any of you that I would get bored with no place to go and start getting under Judy's feet."

"Not to worry Dad," injected Bud. "We would need a lot of help around here for the foreseeable future."

Supporting Bud, I added, "you need not be concerned, Mr. Rose about having enough to do. Your primary challenge would be transitioning from grind of being the general manager to being a leader and coach. Your primary responsibilities would appear to be convincing the manufacturers that an ESOP is not Satan incarnate and giving the managers, employees and banks the confidence that this plan is in the best interest of everyone. Assuming we proceed, as soon as you have worked things out with the manufacturers and made all the senior managers comfortable with what we are doing, I think you should take some time off. If Bud needed you, he could contact you. Otherwise a 30 to 60 days off would provide Bud a good transition period for becoming the answer man, give you and Judy some well earned time to relax and allow you to recharge your batteries for your return."

The room became noticeably quiet as everyone looked to each other for questions and comments. After a few moments, the attorney looked over at me and Mr. Rose and offered, "it looks like you guys are warming up to this tool of socialism."

Mr. Rose quickly returned the volley with, "I would not call me comrade just yet. What I see here is a unique and risky avenue through which one of three marginally profitable dealers can become a healthy store. All three of us dealers are in the same boat, with insufficient capital to make the deal work. Through having the "cajones" to utilize a sophisticated, profoundly complicated and relatively expensive employee stock ownership trust, we could be the one who pulls this deal off. What I want to know from you is what happens 10 years from now when Bud is large and in charge and tired of dealing with an ESOP? What are his options at that time?"

The attorney responded simply, "we can just terminate the plan. That is not as easy as it sounds but, if circumstances dictate, we can deep six the sucker after a minimum five years. However, there is some negative fallout. Notably, all participants in the plan will be vested and assets, which of course will primarily be stock, would be distributed to the participating employees. What that really means is that Bud would have to be prepared to buy back the stock that you are currently selling. Now that may not seem like a big deal today, but remember he would be buying back the stock based on more or less the same formula that you are currently selling. Predictably, the stock will be worth considerably more."

"Hold on Jonathan," responded Bud pausing a moment to reflect on what the attorney had said. The gears were obviously turning behind troubled eyes. After a few quiet moments that acknowledged his thinking, he continued. Oh yea! I get it! The ESOP will be my partner and if I move the needle on valuation, buying back the stock is going to cost me more money. I'll have to keep that in mind as I consider buying other franchises. I suppose I could do that in another business that did not have an ESOP."

"Exactamundo," replied Jonathan! A sister business would have to have comparable benefits but it would not have to be participate in the ESOP. You may also want to reconsider your Subchapter-S election because of the limitation on ESOP contributions and restrictions on your ability to participate. But, losing cash flow is not a big deal because you do not have to make dividend distributions. Of course, after five years, if and when you bought out the ESOP, you could make another S-Corp election."

Although I was by no means sold on on the concept for everyday use, this experience had profoundly illustrated how an ESOP could serve as a Succession Bridge. There were costs, but there were circumstances where the price was worth the benefits.

"I would rather be driving the survivor in this face off. I think staying in business is preferable to cashing out and worrying about where you are going to reinvest your money. Allow me to extend my compliments to Jonathan for his excellent presentation. Count me in, but remember that I am going to be relying on Jonathan every step of the way."

In retrospect, circumstances developed almost exactly as the Jonathan had projected. As we speak, they are five years into this plan and are steadily whittling down the debt. After moving up on the learning curve through my own research, I actually had to coach Bud to accelerate the repayment of the the ESOP debt. He was creating equity too fast for the ESOP participants. Mr. Rose, the late bloomer, has been quite the stockmeister, growing his stock portfolio to about $2.5 million. And, at 67, he is more excited about the business than ever. He is like a kid in a candy store. After taking out their competitors, they are now looking to buy another franchise and are dealing with the issue regarding stock appreciation. I am arguing against the acquisition because I think he should keep his nest egg out of the automobile busi-

ness to assure his retirement independence and facilitate equitable distribution of his estate to his two daughters.

The administration of the ESOP is a little pricey and we have survived an audit from the Department of Labor. However, Bud has no second thoughts because he readily admits that, without the ESOP, succession of the Rose Automotive Group would have been a fleeting dream. Needless to say, as happens every day in my exciting career, I learned something new. An ESOP Succession Bridge can be a very effective business succession planning tool.

14

Succession Bridge Covenants

The Succession Bridge concepts we have discussed provide potential avenues of management continuity when family members are not able to do so for any of several reasons. The preceding chapters have described the primary avenues through which one or more key managers bridge the Succession Gap by assuming various levels of extended management responsibility. The viability of the Succession Bridges theory rests upon the presumption that current or prospective key managers have both the aptitude and the attitude to temporarily serve as steward of a family business legacy.

As we look back on the various structures, and even consider other equally innovative Succession Bridges ideas, I acknowledge that there are inherent risks to this concept. As my father frequently shared, "the fruit does not grow close to the trunk. If you are looking for something sweet, you had better be prepared to go out on the limb." Any time an owner relies upon a manager to lead his business, there are inherent risks that the quality of the manager's aptitude or attitude has been miscalculated. There is also the unfortunate possibility of changes in competency, commitment or character along the way. In either of these events, we can search for excuses, play the blame game or just kick something. Yet, when the emotions have been vented, we have to pursue a replacement and just reconcile that "stuff happens."

I have seen the vulnerability of succession initiatives and - earlier in my career- I chalked up the flame outs to the inherent risks. Frankly, the first time I had to rebuild a Succession Bridges, I did not know what had gone wrong. I attributed the unfortunate circumstances to an inherent risk, a manager "gone stupid."

Later, I came to recognize that a Succession Bridges is much like a marriage. I realized that the reason a plan did not work, like most failed marriages, was because fundamental covenants could not be achieved or maintained. The agonizing review of several less than stellar Succession Bridges experiences revealed that there was more to bridging a Succession Gap than the implementation of an organizational infrastructure.

When the Succession Bridges concept failed, it often was due to the inability of owners and managers to achieve agreement on fundamental concepts. And, as we have talked about throughout the book, it often was due to the parties' inability to learn to communicate in a truly authentic way.

It became very apparent that effective communication between owners and managers was the foundation upon which a Succession Bridges must be constructed. And the key was to identify which issues - and which values - must be communicated.

This is not easy. The inherent emotions, risk and reward make the closely held family owned business the perfect test-bed for developing extraordinary and innovative methods of communication breakdown. We, who deal in this bizarre environment, quote the phrase "facts are stranger than fiction." Owners, family members, senior executives, managers and prima donna employees have a surprising assortment of fears and concerns about their security, fulfillment of individual goals, owner relationships, rival manager relationships and the welfare of the business.

Important human values can easily be distorted by the subjective interpretation of circumstances. And the attitudes of owners and managers regarding these values can result in perceptions of threat or temptation that overwhelm logic.

There can be grievous lost productivity due to the inability of owners and managers to learn to communicate effectively.

Communication about emotion-laden issues takes some practice. In a routine setting, the perceived risks of business by owners and managers can create emotionless machines and "suck-ups" who would rather die than show their vulnerability or express their feelings. They avoid expressing anything that may impact their livelihood, security, goals or recognition. Only when and if these individuals reach positions where they feel unconditionally accepted, or where there is no risk of being misunderstood, do they begin to express who they really are or how they really feel.

In the preceding chapters, I have emphasized the importance of documents and structures to the development of a Succession Bridge. Now I must break the news that the details of documents and the versatility of business structures alone cannot be relied upon to guarantee Succession Success. These important documents formalize individual property rights of operating agreements, stock ownership, business management and employment that are developed by attorneys according to prevailing business law.

The simple legal philosophy is that you only put in a contract what you expect a court of law will address and uphold as an enforceable right. Esoteric, spiritual or non-legal issues within a contract are known to confuse and weaken the ability to enforce property rights. However, documents and structures are only a means to an end. A Succession Bridge is not fulfilled by reliance upon legal commitments or jurisprudence.

Some of the strongest Succession Bridges structures I have witnessed had zero documentation. Interim management continuity was secured by unwavering personal commitments and maintained by open, unencumbered communication. The golden handcuff arrangements were based solely upon good faith verbal understandings.

In most management continuity arrangements, however, after documenting agreements on responsibilities, rights and finances, there is an assumption that owners and managers also agree on goals, priorities, methods and values. There are many smoking craters across the business succession landscape evidencing flaws in this rationale.

Do not make assumptions regarding business agreements that will be fulfilled years later, when memories may weaken and personal preferences may override character.

I feel strongly that there is too much at risk in business succession to assume agreement on management issues that will be the substance of <u>continuing unity, harmony and teamwork.</u>

Fundamentally, what good are documents that formalize everyone's legal rights, if there is no agreement on business values, ethics, protocol, goals and priorities?

This brings us to another kind of agreement, a Succession Bridge Covenant, which sets down in black and white the operating and management beliefs that are fundamental to achieving and maintaining the harmony and synergy essential for long term Succession Success.

Some might view this final step as unnecessarily complicated. Unfortunately, my conclusion that there is no room for spiritual assumptions in a family business only came after substantial frustrations from several failed Succession Bridges. My partner, Don Doudna, and I were scratching our graying heads trying to figure out why a Key Manager Equity Succession Bridge with a son-in-law would periodically begin to unravel.

This was an ideal Succession Bridge situation involving a famously successful automobile dealer with two daughters, neither of whom was seeking a career in the business. The oldest daughter was married to one of the brightest, most promising young managers I have ever encountered. Even the father-in-law said he was the best he had seen in his 40 year career. The number of managers the "ole boy" had worked with should have been a clue to what we were going to experience. In spite of our nurturing and coaching of this potentially very powerful duo, every 90 days or so, Don or I would be called to go cross country and restrain these two adults from acting like infants squabbling over a toy. After a particularly frustrating day with these guys, while asking the "genie of the wine glass" to show us the way out of this predicament, behold, we were simultaneously run over by the answer: unreasonable expectations.

It was apparent that each of these articulate and successful businessmen had profoundly unreasonable expectations of the other. As an example, the father-in-law believed that, although he disrespected all employees -- and especially his son-in-law -- everyone, including his son-in-law, should revere and esteem him like royalty. Although he was very reluctant to give compliments, he would act as if he did not want recognition while all along coveting praise. Go figure! He also believed every rumor he heard and never grasped the fact that at least half of his employees and friends were outrageously jealous of his son-in-law. Notably, my client expected his son-in-law to express gratitude for the opportunities he was being provided. My client commonly referred to his son-in-law as the as "the ungrateful little bastard."

But, before you throw the rope over the limb, consider that the son-in-law was no choir boy. He was a control freak and couldn't understand that he was working for "el controlo supremo!" To prevent his father-in-law from looking over his shoulder and second guessing his decisions, he would not tell him what he had done, what he was doing or what he planned to do. Furthermore, he prohibited his managers from divulging information.

He also needed affirmation and recognition for what he was doing. He resented that he had to constantly justify his extraordinary, but well-earned compensation and he resented that his father-in-law took all the credit for the dealership's accomplishments.

Consequently, they were constantly offending each other. Irrespective of good intentions, both were fully capable of setting the other off at any given time. As a byproduct of the continual emotional roller coaster neither trusted the other. There was no good faith to draw upon when business circumstances did not go according to expectations, which, in the car business, is about every other month. Both of them, but most notably the Dad, received a daily diet of disappointment. And, regardless of the predictably unmerciful family fallout from both of their wives (the Queen and the Princess), they could only restrain their feelings for so long and then one of them would crawl down the other's throat. Poor communication would then evolve into open disrespect, and ultimately the son-in-law would tell Dad to "stick it where the sun does not shine." Then both would withdraw.

As if these circumstances did not have enough excitement, the daughter would take sides with either her father or her husband with no predictable pattern. In either event, this ultimately impacted grandmother's access to her only grandchildren, taking all the fun out of being dysfunctional. Irrespective of our coaching, brutal grandmother implications and significant financial rewards, the Succession Bridge expectations were good in name only. The prospect of becoming Succession Certified was a joke.

As you might imagine, this complex situation had little compatibility with a succession strategy that relies so heavily upon trust, harmony and unity. Ultimately, we recognized that we had been unrealistic to assume that this ship was going to float. Since that time, with additional insight from another creative partner, Ricci Victorio, we have learned that any Succession Bridges cursed with unreasonable expectations just won't fly!

Simultaneous unreasonable expectations between two highly critical parties are not common. When this occurs, those unreasonable expectations can usually be reconciled. Most of time, each side has an individual experience and a realistic view, however, the varying filters of each group create a different understanding of the same event or challenge. Insecurities and self-centric assumptions are indeed a handicap to productivity and harmony, but can usually be overcome by achieving an understanding of the other's perspective.

Harmony and unity among team leaders is essential to save any business from the morass of mediocrity and vulnerability to meltdown.

Otherwise, Succession Success, as described in Seeking Succession, is at best a struggle and at worst a fleeting dream.

Teamwork

The greatest risk associated with a Succession Bridges, or any team management undertaking, is unreasonable expectations on the part of owners and key manager(s.) As a byproduct of our Adamic nature, we are naturally "me-minded." Consequently, we must be divinely changed (gifted) or work beyond our natural inclination to become "we-minded." When confronted with a team challenge, the unreasonable expectations of me-mindedness will destroy trust. In the absence of trust, there is no interdependence. You cannot depend upon someone that you do not trust. In the absence of interdependence, there is no synergy, more commonly referred to as teamwork.

In long-standing situations, some highly compatible groups have evolved into successful teams by astutely learning from the mistakes of unreasonable expectations. In others, the impact of an extremely effective leader affirmed reasonable behavior by diligently dispatching unreasonable expectations and eliminating uncooperative participants. Ultimately, through constant affirmation and the process of elimination, a team culture becomes second nature.

Unfortunately, the majority of group initiatives, whether little league, business or politics, never achieve optimum team status due to a variety of circumstances including: incompatibility of the members; lack of continuous affirmation; lack of a decisive leader to eliminate incompatibility or lack of time.

The variety of time-sensitive excuses would include, but not necessarily be limited to: The season was too short, the coach (leader) was inept, the enemy was too strong or the boss was a wuss. Those groups/teams fill the loss columns and fade into obscurity. Some may feel teamwork is not complicated or difficult. You may believe that, given enough incentive, managers, ball players and soldiers will find unity and harmony to get the job done. Yet, just look around at all the losers who had the motivation of megabucks, notoriety and even survival

I also suggest that you reflect upon the legacies of renowned, but more important, proven teamwork experts, such as General Dwight Eisenhower, Coach Jim Valvano and Bill Gates. These gentlemen, like countless other successful leaders, built their teams on the foundations of reasonable expectations that included an agreement of accountability among teammates.

Put another way, there is surprisingly little direct correlation between how hard individual members of a group are working towards a stipulated goal and the likelihood the group will achieve outstanding productivity.

Mediocrity is well within the reach of hard work, but extraordinary performance is a spiritual issue. In the realm of business succession, the focus is not on how hard members are working/trying, but on how much is getting done. In fact, due to wear and tear, the advantage goes to the team that can achieve the highest level of productivity with the least strain.

There are no do-overs in the world of business. A typical business group learns to work together and meet profit expectations and growth needs or there are casualties. However, in a family business there is limited capital and there are circumstances and exceptional needs, like estate taxes. Just working together and competing against each other for higher performance will not cut it. Through 30 years of family-business team coaching I have concluded that family business succession critically depends upon teamwork to achieve and sustain a competitive advantage over larger, better capitalized competitors. Reliance upon non family managers creates an even greater dependence upon teamwork. Business succession has a price and the price is teamwork.

Fortunately, I do not believe that teamwork is a cosmic or mystical state of productivity that only Tibetan Monks can achieve after a lifetime of self sacrifice and spiritual enlightenment. To the contrary, regardless of the venue (business, sports, community) I believe that teamwork is the byproduct of a choice to be part of a collaborative group.

The foundation for making that choice is the formal acknowledgement of critically important, reasonable expectations and goals. And that is the essence of Family Business Covenants.

As you may have gathered, I believe there is limited room for assumptions within the infrastructure of a business succession plan. There is just too much at risk to take on the role of a mind reader or to assume that bosses, partners, subordinates and team members will remember old agreements. Continuing this structured logic into the realm of synergy, I contend that there is little capacity for the assumed conclusions regarding teamwork.

Family Business Covenants transcend the capabilities of legal contracts. Covenants are written confirmation of the expectations that formalize a team culture. Specifically, we are talking about the evolving spiritual agreements that establish the foundation for working together. Covenants predictably evolve as time passes. When a group comes together as a fledgling team, there are fewer expectations of behavior and attitude than there will be as the team matures and seeks greater power and influence. As goals change, covenants change. Covenants represent awareness by team members that, when the stakes are high, mutual trust should not be assumed.

Family businesses have a head start. The family unit, whether active or passive, has an inherent potential team advantage. However, this is only a potential advantage because, like everyone, family members also have the choice of "we" over "me." Achieving the benefits of this advantage requires hard work. Any assumptions regarding teamwork will lead to a struggle to break out of mediocrity and, at worst, a meltdown. There is little tolerance for mediocrity in business today, and less tomorrow.

How do family businesses begin capitalizing on the inherent teamwork advantage?

Confirm commitment to continuing the legacy. Examine expectations regarding behavior and attitude at three levels: owners, managers and employees. Through deliberate interaction at each level, identify and dispel unreasonable expectations. Over time, select against any family manager, manager or employee who is unable or unwilling to subordinate "me" for "we."

How do the owners, managers and employees of a business begin achieving team synergy?

Confirm the desire of all members of a group to seek fulfillment of personal goals through group efforts. Confirm reasonable expectations of all group members. Adopt covenants at each level, and then between levels, for the way team members will operate and how group goals will be achieved. Abide by the Primal Covenant, to "hold one another accountable."

How do the owners, managers and employees of a business push team synergy to higher levels of productivity?

Having confirmed covenants, promote harmony and unity through non-business interaction. Meet frequently, three to six times per year, to review Covenants, encourage team members and affirm goals. Annually reconfirm Covenants by addressing new or refined reasonable expectations. Continue to abide by the Primal Covenant, to hold one another accountable.

There are three potential levels of Covenants within organizations aspiring to optimize Succession Success: Operating, Management and Organizational.

Operating Covenants among the owners, directors and very special key managers are appropriate in all business succession circumstances. Management Covenants among the owners, operators and managers are appropriate in all Succession Bridges circumstances. Organizational Covenants are appropriate only for those businesses that are endeavoring to capitalize on all team synergy opportunities and are willing to go the extra mile to achieve the highest levels of productivity and efficiency.

Let's look at some details.

Operating Covenants

Operating Covenants formalize reasonable expectations regarding the ownership rights and operating rights that are critical to the achievement of long term strategic goals. Under ideal circumstances of mutual trust and clear, open communication, Operating Covenants are not needed. In 30 years of family business consulting, I can count those situations on one hand. Operating Covenants are appropriate to assure unity within any multi-owner/operator environment. The adoption of Operating Covenants is a critically important step in the process of dealing with stressful multi owner/operator circumstances, such as: addition of new stockholders, addition of a Board member (assuming the Board is active,) change of operating control, neutralizing a control freak or bringing an "heir-do-well" stockholder back to reality.

The purpose of Operating Covenants is to take the first step in "familizing" the business: which I define as assuring that the values and goals of ownership are reflected in management policy.

This process also pursues unity, harmony and ongoing effective dialogue regarding the goals, values and direction of those who have a vested ownership or security interest in the business. Operating Covenants affirm the reasonable expectations of owners, special Directors and operators. Covenants seek confirmation of agreements regarding anticipated growth, income, fringe benefits and performance expectations. Equally, if not more important, agreement is formalized on the operating authority of management, communication expectations and communication procedures.

It is important to mention that, depending upon circumstances (a history of bad communication habits,) Operating Covenants may also express reasonable expectations of what the owners, Directors and the CEO will not do. The necessity for the "will-nots" is caused by some family members who lack understanding of management dynamics and expect to do what ever they want to do, whenever they want to do it, without any understanding of the impact of their entitlement attitude. Although some may feel this is crazy, let me assure you that I have been told on many occasions "this is my business and I will do as I please."

My common response is "and you see what that kind of behavior has got you; a wonderful sandbox, but a very mediocre business." Consequently, some Operating Covenants express that owners covenant to refrain from second-guessing executive decisions; disrupting the chain of command, impulsively distracting management; asking rhetorical questions or drawing down working capital below specified minimums. The specific nature of these "will-nots" depends upon the unique nature of the owners, who may only understand the hub-and-spoke concept of management. The CEO also typically agrees to some "will-nots" that, depending upon the sensitivity of the owners, could include an agreement not to take various forms of action without prior Board approval. That could include refraining from spending above a specified level, terminating any manager; terminating any employee with more than 10 years service or changing banks.

Notably, Operating Covenants formalize the mission, leadership techniques and general operating practices of the company to remove wonderment and unnecessary distractions that are common to over-active family in family owned business.

The Foundational Covenant is the willingness to accept 360-degree accountability from superiors, colleagues and subordinates.

This is a major challenge to pride, but this exercise in humility is a team building exercise that creates the performance foundation for the Management Covenants that will be discussed later.

The common expression within the Covenant approximates "we have agreed that these are reasonable expectations and we expect to be reminded when we are not fulfilling these expectations."

The process of adopting Operating Covenants begins with private meetings with each operator, which includes owners, active directors and the CEO. With prior notice to encourage thought, each operator is asked: What are your expectations of owners, directors, the CEO, employees and the business? Family dynamics always make this a very interesting and potentially exciting exercise. It bears mentioning that much of what I have learned about the dynamics of family business, I have learned through exciting experiences, such as mediating reasonable expectations between siblings and cousins.

Early on, I learned that soliciting expectations in a group forum had two common results, neither of which were particularly desirable. Usually, in the face of immediate accountability from their colleagues, operators were reluctant to express their genuine feelings. On the other side of this equation, when uninhibited feelings were expressed, there was a high potential for negative consequences (excitement.) The fact is that some expectations of family members, directors and CEOs, are profoundly bizarre, ridiculous or even stupid. Rawls' planning theorem number one: Never presume that money breeds sophistication. If feelings regarding competency, reporting order and character were expressed without appropriate refinement, these off the wall comments could set back family/organizational harmony/unity to the half-life of uranium 235.

The facilitator's role (yours truly) is to gently but firmly lead a process of refining, restating and even eliminating expectations that are crazy or destructive without disenfranchising anyone from the Covenant process.

The indelible memory of a pitcher of water launched across a conference table is a constant reminder that the first expressions of expectations should always be in private.

Historically the first highly effective filter for unreasonable expectations is to reduce them to writing. The process of converting thoughts to writing always leads one back towards reality. Furthermore, review initiates editing and refinement as the facilitator reminds each operator in private that the goal is to confirm reasonable operating expectations. The expectations predictably become ready for public viewing as each operator seriously considers that, in due course, their personal expectations will be shared with the other operators.

The second major filter for unreasonable expectations is brought about by examining the expectations of others. Again, this initial review of a partner's, sibling's or CEO's expectation is a private affair to provide emotional insulation. The facilitator, who has been going through this process with all the operators, gives background and foundation for what may initially appear to be shocking expectations. If any expectation is profoundly rejected as unreasonable, it is the facilitator's role to serve as an intermediary to find common ground for compromise.

Based upon the facilitator's judgment, the operators eventually come together to personally stand behind their expectations. Based upon the preparation and counsel of the facilitator, these face to face meetings are generally immediately productive at defining a mutually agreeable business mission and business succession methodology. This discussion seeks agreement on business organizational structure, executive authority, business ownership purpose, business operating mission and effective means of communicating between family members, family members and owners and between owners and the Chief Executive Officer. The owners and operators make a commitment to the Operating Covenants or conclude "this is more complicated than I want" and decide to sell.

Operating Covenants also confirm that the operators are dependent upon management and clearly express the values and character that owners expect management to represent. And they formally agree upon the Succession Bridges structure that will be utilized to motivate and retain management. From start to finish, in a series of three to six meetings -- depending on the number of operators and preexisting personality issues involved-- reasonable business operating expectations are confirmed, reduced to writing and adopted as Operating Covenants.

On many occasions, as my partners and I have embarked on Operating Covenants with notoriously hard headed owners, someone (usually a frustrated manager or family member) has attempted to reminded us that you can't teach an old dog new tricks.

My patented reply is, "we may not be able to teach old dogs new tricks, but with everyone's cooperation, we can make it very awkward for old dogs to practice inappropriate behavior."

History has indeed affirmed that some micro-manager control freaks will never change. However, history has also proven that, with sufficient motivation and regular reinforcement, many old dogs that specialize in "seagull management" (fly in; crap all over everything; and then fly out) can be led away from a crisis management style. However, there is no doubt that persistence is the key.

We also must recognize the reality of "attitude creep," the natural return of powerful personalities (old dogs) to their natural (dysfunctional) management attitudes. The avoidance of attitude creep relies upon a passion for Succession Success, an understanding that we are embarking on a never-ending process (not a project) and a long term commitment (persistence) to review and reinforcement.

The passion supports a commitment to the Foundational Covenant to hold one another accountable. No owner/operator should just go along with the development of Operating Covenants. Unenthusiastic participants must be converted or eventually eliminated from the leadership group. If owner/operators are not willing to genuinely seek unity of purpose and goals, they must be genuinely encouraged to stay home. In the absence of passion for succession, harmony and unity, owner/operators will not honestly express expectations and will weaken in their accountability. They will not have the gumption to speak up when an overbearing founder, unreasonable partner or arrogant family member falls off the covenant wagon and expresses an unreasonable assertion. The power of the covenants relies upon everyone buying into unity for succession and practicing accountability.

Management Covenants

The next step in synergizing a closely held or family owned business is the adoption of Management Covenants. This is the spiritual focal point of family business covenants that empowers and ordains the Succession Bridge. Management Covenants endeavor to do something extremely important and profoundly challenging -- achieve agreement between the unequal parities (owners, senior managers and middle managers,) who have responsibility for leadership of the business. Although owners are often not involved in day to day management, they are always included in the Management Covenant process because of the profound impact ownership has upon management. Up front buy-in from ownership is essential to give managers confidence that their reasonable expectations regarding management policies and procedures can and will be fulfilled. Participating senior management could include all three classes of managers, but would vary depending upon the size of the operation and the form of the Succession Bridge being implemented.

Management Covenants go beyond the purview of a legal contract. Management Covenants are an aspect of strategic planning that pursues the spiritual synergy that can be achieved when a diverse group learns that it can work together for a common goal. This initiative seeks a we-minded attitude that will remove the limits to their productive capability. If they can agree on it, they can achieve it.

Management Covenants establish the reasonable expectations regarding mutual respect, communication, goals, accountability and how the business will be managed.

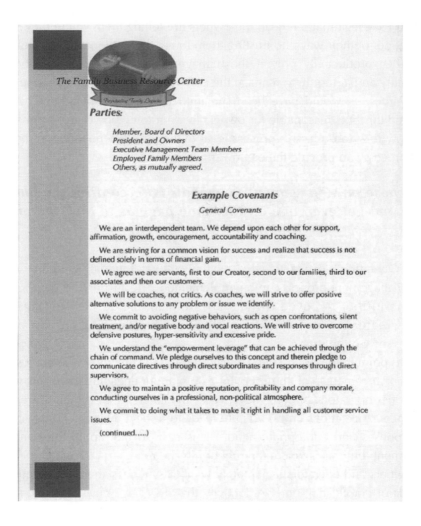

The Family Business Resource Center

Perpetuating Family Legacies

Parties:

Member, Board of Directors
President and Owners
Executive Management Team Members
Employed Family Members
Others, as mutually agreed.

Example Covenants

General Covenants

We are an interdependent team. We depend upon each other for support, affirmation, growth, encouragement, accountability and coaching.

We are striving for a common vision for success and realize that success is not defined solely in terms of financial gain.

We agree we are servants, first to our Creator, second to our families, third to our associates and then our customers.

We will be coaches, not critics. As coaches, we will strive to offer positive alternative solutions to any problem or issue we identify.

We commit to avoiding negative behaviors, such as open confrontations, silent treatment, and/or negative body and vocal reactions. We will strive to overcome defensive postures, hyper-sensitivity and excessive pride.

We understand the "empowerment leverage" that can be achieved through the chain of command. We pledge ourselves to this concept and therein pledge to communicate directives through direct subordinates and responses through direct supervisors.

We agree to maintain a positive reputation, profitability and company morale, conducting ourselves in a professional, non-political atmosphere.

We commit to doing what it takes to make it right in handling all customer service issues.

(continued.....)

The purpose of Management Covenants is to establish vertical (owner/manager) and lateral (manager/manager) clarity for the way the business will be managed. Through open, unrestrained dialogue, Management Covenants pursue a cohesive bond between owners and managers and begin the process of building a single vision of the family's management culture. And, specifically from a Succession Bridges perspective, Management Covenants give owners the peace of mind that empowered management is going to follow policies and procedures that are compatible with their feelings, goals and values.

Before we go any further, let us pay due respect for the above mentioned concept of empowered management. The pursuit of Management Covenants depends upon the managers being legitimately empowered to manage the company.

And when I say legitimate, I mean the owners are telling them where they want to go, getting out of their way and trusting them to get there. Management Covenants can enhance productivity only if the managers have been delegated both the responsibility and authority to manage the company, within reasonable boundaries and guidelines, as would have been specified within the Operating Covenants. Having said this, it is reasonable for owners to want to empower management, but not to know how to do it. This process is, at minimum, dependent upon the "want to." This process can provide the empowerment "how to."

The purpose of Management Covenants is to confirm the business mission and get everyone on the same page as to how the mission is going to be achieved.

The Operating Covenants serve as the cultural foundation upon which a winning management process can be implemented. The larger the organization and/or the further removed owners are from the actual day to day operation, the greater the impact of formally affirming, defining and developing Management Covenants.

At this point in the discussion, I always remind my clients -- who are just crazy for team enhancement -- of an important axiom about engaging managers in planning: Owner/operators should never ask managers about their career and performance expectations unless you are ready to respect their reactions with legitimate responses and appropriate action. It is easy to talk about the concept of empowerment, but this is where the rubber hits the road.

If owners and operators legitimately want to synergize their organization and seek levels of gratification and productivity that they have never even considered achieving, they had better not have any hang-ups about subordinates reminding them that they are not fulfilling reasonable expectations.

History has repeatedly shown that empowered, respected and recognized managers will take a proprietary attitude towards the business that predictably takes owners/operators out of their comfort zones. The guts it takes to empower managers will ultimately be validated with performance beyond expectations.

The Management Covenant process is the first step in strategic planning that establishes the team structure through which ambitions strategic plans can be achieved. The pursuit of Management Covenants is always a subsequent endeavor to the Operating Covenants. It is futile to pursue unity among managers if there is no unity among owner operators. Development and implementation of Management Covenants is a less emotionally challenging endeavor because there is more humility among managers. They have earned their positions (versus those born into the family) and are comfortable validating their value on a daily basis.

The process of achieving agreement on how the business is going to be operated (Management Covenants) affirms what is being done right, facilitates the introduction of what is not being done and discourages what is being done wrong. This process requires self examination of management techniques, attitudes and procedures. Initially the facilitator presents the Operating Covenants to the management group, requesting their confirmation that the expectations of the owner/operators are indeed, reasonable. Although it is not necessary to disclose intimate family details of the Organizational Covenants, it is necessary that all business related covenants are presented, because the managers must understand all the rules of the game they are going to try to win. This especially applies to the "will-nots," because, unless the managers have been exiled to the Siberian Division, they have had first hand experience with the bad attitudes and habits of the owner/operators. Any formal agreement to improve attitudes and behavior of the owner/operators will only help motivate key managers to serve as a Succession Bridge.

The facilitator subsequently meets with each of the managers privately to determine their true feelings, as well as to ask each manager his reasonable expectations regarding the owners, colleagues and subordinates. The first goal is to identify any Operating Covenants that the manager does not understand or that he feels are unreasonable. Further, the facilitator solicits from each manager his career aspirations and expectations of owners, supervisors, colleagues and subordinates. The facilitator plays an important role in providing the managers with feedback regarding their written expectations. The deliberate process provides needed filters with the operators.

The managers then come together as a group to discuss the Operating Covenants and their individual expectations as a collaborative Succession Bridge. Through what would conservatively be classified as active dialogue (they don't pull any punches with each other), the managers discuss and eliminate unreasonable expectations and agree on how they believe the business should be managed for optimum productivity, addressing exciting subjects such as: communications, reporting order, compensation, advancement, accountability, affirmation, goals and benchmarks. As a group, they also review the Operating Covenants and offer refinements they feel are critical to Succession Success of the business. Subsequently, the facilitator coordinates interaction between the owners and managers to achieve agreement on the Operating Covenants.

In this initial stage of synergizing an organization, the facilitator moves back and forth between the two groups because, although the managers have been told to honestly express their opinions, they still do not really believe they have this power.

There is also reasonable concern from owners that their honest opinions may disrupt the Succession Bridges or alienate critically important managers. The assumption is that, in initial face to face interactions, neither owners nor managers would be forthcoming with their true feelings. When the timing is appropriate, the owners join in the meetings with the managers to debate and ultimately confirm reasonable expectations. Now we have the foundation for teamwork and leveraged productivity, Management Covenants.

With a philosophical agreement among owners and Succession Bridges managers, regarding the character, values, policies and priorities of the business, grass roots strategic planning begins. The assumption of this endeavor is that business performance is in the hands of management. Therefore, within the value and priority boundaries of the owners, the only effective roadmap to success is one that is developed and powered by management. The owners are involved at this level to confirm their dependence upon management and formalize management's empowerment to establish and achieve mutual goals. As a team, the owners and managers confirm goals, operating strategies, performance benchmarks and develop detailed implementation checklists. Follow up meetings are scheduled for accountability and refinement of direction.

Immediately upon conclusion of the strategic planning, implementation checklists and draft Management Covenants are circulated for review and refinement. This is another deliberate step to achieve buy-in for the way the business is going to be operated and the goals of the management team and Succession Bridge. At the first follow up meeting, the facilitator determines progress on the implementation checklists and confirms that the Management Covenants are ready for adoption. The Foundational Covenant, "to hold one another accountable to the agreed upon communication policies and business values," is reaffirmed both in theory and in practice.

The Critical Covenant, "to review regularly," is also honored by scheduling the first semiannual refresher meeting. Subsequently, as soon as can be scheduled, the owners and managers come together in a festive environment (dinner, cocktail party) to formally adopt the Management Covenants. As an outward and admittedly corny representation of unity, all owners and all members of the Succession Bridges sign the Management Covenant document and receive original copies, complete with photographs. The formalities represent the higher level of commitment required for teamwork that provides the foundation for achieving a sustainable competitive advantage.

Organizational Covenants

The teamwork benefits of Management Covenants can have a significant impact on the success of a Succession Bridges. However, as we all know, teamwork does not find fulfillment with management. Management alone cannot provide a sustainable competitive advantage. Major advances in productivity occur through the application of teamwork with rank and file employees.

The adoption of Organizational Covenants is the ultimate initiative to bring teamwork to a closely held or family owned business, down to the <u>newest hire.</u>

The focus of this book is on the commitment and productivity of management as a Succession Bridge. Therefore, Organizational Covenants are beyond the scope of this book.

However, a brief overview is worthwhile, The Organizational Covenant initiative asks all employees to take an active role in establishing reasonable expectations for the organization, ownership, managers and employees. Due to the classic tense relationship between managers and employees (Do what I say because I am the boss,) Organizational Covenants are not an easy undertaking. It is not a project. It is a never ending process that from time to time appears to be a profound waste of effort.

But not to worry, if you are striving for optimum productivity and gratification that you are impacting the lives of every employee and the mission of every vendor and customer, this is not a waste of time. Synergizing an organization is a serious undertaking that predictably creates distractions from immediate issues. This is an endeavor for visionaries and by no means a condemnation for owners, operators and managers who say "We are not going there. We are confident we know how to get where we are going without asking our employees the best way to get there."

To give perspective, the development of Operating Covenants generally takes 30 to 60 days and the adoption of Management Covenants that secure the implementation of a Succession Bridges, generally requires four to six months, depending on the size of the organization. However, synergizing an organization with 50 to 100 employees will require a year. Organizations with 200 to 500 employees could require two to three years.

Synergizing an organization is ideally suited for family businesses with 500 employees or less. The process of bringing all employees into the family team establishes the teamwork that can provide a sustainable competitive advantage with any product in any market.

I presume the process could work for larger organizations, as reflected in Ken Blanchard's book, "Gung Ho." However, I admittedly have not been to that party. My focus is on the moderate-sized closely-held family business. The process of synergizing a large organization would, no doubt, be more challenging and more protracted. My point is that the adoption of Organizational Covenants at any level is a formidable undertaking.

Although we are not going into the weeds regarding "how to," the process of establishing Organizational Covenants follows the same general pathway as the implementation of Management Covenants. Beginning with groups of 10 to 15, members of the management team serve as facilitators and meet with the most senior employees. The senior employees are asked their expectations of owners, management and colleagues. A working draft of the previously adopted Management Covenants and strategic plans are shared with these groups. In small groups, reactions, opinions and recommendations are solicited. When agreement on operating direction, values, methods and goals is achieved, each of these senior employees is asked to lead/facilitate a similar group. If you want to make sure managers and employees get it, ask them to teach it.

The employee response to this team initiative is initially skeptical and, depending upon history, even cynical. After time and repetition has proven sincerity, employees will begin to understand that they are being given the opportunity to determine the character and productive capacity of the business. Over a prolonged development and regular reaffirmation, employees will gain an understanding of what management science has always known, they are in control and their individual commitments and standards will determine the success of the organization and the individual benefits received.

Optimum productivity is not about competing with other employees; it is about competing with your own productive capability.

Over a period of months or years, everyone in the organization signs on to the direction, values, methods and goals of the organization.

After formal implementation of Organizational Covenants, regular refresher classes are organized for new hires and hard heads. If you snooze you will lose. Constant reaffirmation is critical. These refreshers provide opportunities for owners and managers to continue to express their enthusiasm for these otherwise esoteric standards, procedures and goals. Refreshers also provide the opportunity for ongoing refinement and progressive buy-in. Gotham City was not built in a day and the synergizing of a business will not happen overnight.

So there you have the spiritual backbone of a Succession Bridge, Management Covenants. The process of assuring Succession Success, begins with establishing a foundation of Operating Covenants. And after the Management Covenants are adopted, the process can continue with Organizational Covenants. The deeper into an organization we go, challenging everyone to express and affirm reasonable expectations and the empowerment to hold each other accountable, the greater the potential benefits. The ultimate fate of a Succession Bridge initiative relies on a commitment to Management Covenants.

15

<h1 style="text-align:right">Summary</h1>

The family business is a great place to pursue a career, both for family members and others who are endeavoring to get the most out of their career. The family business is not a place to ride in the wagon or just hang-on. It is impossible for your good, your bad or your neutrality (still bad) to go unnoticed. No doubt, the family business offers the greatest opportunity for talented, highly motivated employees to grow, achieve recognition and realize rewards for achievements. The fact is that there are just not enough motivated and capable family members to oversee the many moving parts of an aggressive ambitious business. Furthermore, in support of this book's theme, there are not even enough family members to satisfy the demand for successors.

Anyone who has had contact with a family business above the mom and pop level understands the importance of management support for day-to-day survival and long-term success. A talented and motivated entrepreneur can create magnificent business but he cannot run complex, challenging enterprises by themselves. Also it is amazingly common to find highly motivated, modestly talented, over-achieving entrepreneurs who can grow a business beyond their own leadership and/or technical capability. Family is the first and most natural resource for management support.

However, based upon my experience, only about one in four closely held businesses have a ready, willing and able family successor who could offer executive management assistance or ownership succession. Another 25% of the prospective family successors are willing, but not, as yet, ready or able. They lack the maturity and experience to assume responsibility for the family's most precious asset. Another 25% are just average dudes, good citizens, responsible and well-meaning family employees. They are solid contributors but not capable of providing leadership through the next generation. And finally, at least 25% of the family business never scratched in the sperm lottery. They have no prospective family members working in the business for any number of reasons including freedom of choice or no offspring.

In light of the above, from a pure statistical perspective, if a family has fewer than four children there appears to be a high degree of luck involved in the succession of a vibrant family business. Unfortunately, the odds are a little better than one in four, because it is amazing what families will do when their backs are against the wall. Widows who had previously never darkened the door of the business will pitch their civic volunteering and evolve into determined leaders. And some under-talented children will be so committed that they will over achieve.

But, no doubt, the succession of all family owned businesses are dependent upon the support of key managers. Even the determined widow and the over-achieving offspring cannot do it by themselves.

But here is the chin music, the succession of least three out of four family businesses, the bedrock of our economy and the foundation of business ethics, faces a formidable gap of succession candidates.

And far too many of these dynamic businesses are becoming victims of this succession gap. Some recycling of opportunity is OK as other private entrepreneurs step in to seize the opportunity of failed succession. However, the free enterprise, open competition, capitalistic nature of our society suffers due to the lack of suc-cession plans for family owned businesses. It is in everyone's best interest to recognize that Key Managers can play a significant role in the succession of family owned businesses.

Having read this book, it should be no news to you that I believe the succes-sion prospects of a business are not much better than the quality and commitment of the key managers who make things happen on a day to day basis. My primary contention is that Key Managers can also be the critical succession connection. Rec-ognizing that only 25% of the closely held business currently have, or will ever have, a capable and committed successor, the Succession Bridge concept is very important to the continuity of an important aspect of our culture and our economy.

Hopefully this book has provided you have a better understanding of key man-agers, their role in the family business and the various ways they can bridge the gap and serve as a Succession Bridge. My hope is that you also better understand how to identify, motivate and retain key managers. And most important, hopefully this introduction to the Succession Bridge concept has enhanced your expectations of business succession under less than optimum circumstances.

I wish that everyone could take from this book my specific intent: Seeking Succession is a worthwhile, laudable endeavor, regardless of your circumstances.

However, what you take from this book will be determined by your point of view. Your position as a manager, family member, advisor or owner will substantially impact your perspective.

For Managers

As a manager, hopefully you now understand that there is upward opportunity. Just being responsible for a department or area is not all you have to look forward to. Your attitude is going to be more important than your aptitude. Yes, competency is important. That was what opened the door of management for you. But, where you go now will be dependent on what is in your heart, not what is between your ears. You can distinguish yourself through your character, commitment and your sense of community.

Hopefully this book has helped you understand your potential value in the total scheme of succession planning. Be encouraged that you can play an important role in both the management and the perpetuation of the business. And who knows what kind of opportunities will lie ahead? Although you are not in a Succession Bridge decision-making role, you are in control of your own destiny. It will be your actions and your attitudes that will determine if you are a line manager or a key manager. And you will have the opportunity to further distinguish yourself as a special key manager or even a very special key manager.

"Forsake not humble beginnings," and worry not about the achievements of others. Take care of your responsibilities. Be trustworthy. Be prepared at all times to make the tough decisions. Decide how "key" you want to become and get at it, leading with a positive unassuming attitude. If you strive to showcase your commitment, character, community and competence, you will be noticed.

Unfortunately, being noticed does not necessarily mean that you are going to be given the opportunity to participate as a Succession Bridge, but it does mean that you are going to be in a better position. And dispel your frustration that you are not being noticed. There is no such position as an unnoticed key manager. Sometimes your colleagues and competitors know you better than your boss. If a colleague moves up faster or moves on to another business, do not worry about those things beyond your control. If your represent the right stuff, chances are that your boss will use you to fill the gap or your departed colleague will be back to hire you away, because good people are hard to find.

If you are selected to participate in a Succession Bridge, you will have a unique opportunity to take your career to the next level. You must be prepared to come out of your comfort zone, adopt new attitudes and take on more responsibility. You must be prepared to sit down with colleagues and the owners and develop Management

Covenants that will be the foundation of teamwork. You must be prepared to give before you receive.

No doubt, as a participant in a Succession Bridge, you will be under the microscope. Someone will be watching at all times. If it is not the owner wondering if he made the right decision, it will be other envious employees and managers just watching for you to take a shortcut. Appreciate whatever you have been offered and don't hold back. Unless you feel you are being placed in a position that is contrary to your character or goals, give this opportunity your best shot. Continue to seek the excellence that has gotten you where you are and you will do fine. Recognize that there are always better ways of doing a job and you will excel. Do not jump to hasty decisions. Give the new opportunity time. Recognize that, in spite of appearances, the only dead ends in business are self-imposed.

If, after a reasonable period of time, the job is not meeting your expectations, step back and evaluate where you are going and how you and your family feel. Gather your thoughts and conclusions and express them to the owner or your supervisor. Consider the feedback. Then affirm or modify your thinking and take any action that you feel is necessary for your peace of mind and the welfare of your family.

As I am sure you are aware, the renowned philosopher, Dirty Harry, said, "every man should know his limitations." It is wise to understand this philosophy if you are considering a career in the NBA or rocket science. However, Dirty Harry was not talking about a family business. There is nothing to be gained by dwelling on your limitations in your business career. Business opportunities are created by common folks doing uncommon things.

You cannot create talent that is not there, but you can dress up hard work and character and make them look pretty sexy.

A positive, encouraging, never-say-die attitude can make common sense and hard work look like extraordinary talent.

If you are not selected for a golden handcuff or to serve on a MAB or to serve as a Succession Bridge, collect your thoughts and restrain your emotions before you approach your boss and/or the owner. In the face of rejection, your attitude will have a profound impact on your future. And remember, if you go straight to the owner, you are going to provoke your boss. The selection of participants should not have been a casual thought. Your boss and/or the owner thought long and hard about the selection of Succession Bridge candidates and they have reasons for not choosing you, either legitimate or illegitimate. Regardless, listen and think before you react. If you expect to continue to work in this business and earn your way on the team, you must respect the reasons you were not selected.

However, you do not have to agree with their reasons. As you consider the circumstances, calculate what will be required to enhance your skills and attitudes to align with their expectations. In this calculation, do not overlook humility. There is a chance, even though remote, that your boss and/or the owner are right. There is nothing more notable, more impressive and more prized than a management turn-around. Also, do not overlook that they may just be pinheads. If, after a reasonable amount of time, you conclude that they are short on grey matter, you may have to go elsewhere to fulfill your expectations. Even then, do not burn any bridges because, more often than not, management grass is not greener on the other side.

For Advisors

If you are a consulting professional, hopefully I have stretched your thinking about business succession and given you reason to believe that you can expand the services you can provide business owners. Although the Succession Bridge concepts may at first appear new and innovative, you have or will recognize that there is relatively little new technology involved in this concept. Beyond the spiffy terminology, I have applied long standing, executive benefits and proven management philosophies to specifically enhance the succession of closely held and family owned business.

If you are not familiar, or if you are uncomfortable with the multiple, interdependent issues of family business succession, welcome to the deep end. Not to worry if you feel overwhelmed. You have lots of company. I would suggest that you read my earlier book, "Seeking Succession."

You can also feel free to give me a call and I can share with you life as a professional duck: looking calm on the surface but underneath, treading water like crazy just to stay afloat.

Family business succession planning is a great profession, but admittedly very challenging. I encourage you to do your research and consider joining us.

From a Succession Bridge perspective, if you are not familiar with non-qualified structures or pass-through business entities, not to worry; this is not rocket science. You can get up to speed quickly. Otherwise, you surely have colleagues who are familiar and they can cover your back. Otherwise, give us a call at The Rawls Company and we would be delighted to make our resources available. You may also be concerned about the management issues. The same applies. There are resources out there that can make you wise beyond your years. Feel free to contact our management consulting company, The Family Business Resource Center, and our management gurus can give you specific direction. This isn't quantum physics, but, experience sure helps.

My simple purpose is served if you just acknowledge that there are always succession options; in the absence of a family successor, sale is not inevitable. I will be gratified if you are motivated to personally get involved in succession planning and, by virtue of this book, feel better equipped to do your job. I would be honored to learn that you are expanding this body of thought. Succession Planning is a rewarding endeavor and career field.

For Owners

If you're an owner, I hope you are not confused or overwhelmed. This was probably new material and you could reasonably be spinning with wonderment: "Do I have any key managers? What are the key manager criteria? Do I want to be qualified or non-qualified? Who does the qualifying anyway? Which Succession Bridge is right for me?"

Not to worry. At first pass, confusion would be normal. Even the simplest Succession Bridge is a multidimensional strategy involving reasonably technical structures. With no training in accounting and law and no experience with golden handcuffs, you will have to give these strategies time to sink in and make sense.

I will feel very pleased if this aggressive concept has expanded your thinking and given you reason for optimism and hope. I certainly understand any depression and frustration that may have surrounded your considerations of business succession. If you have not read "Seeking Succession," you should, as it will affirm that you are not alone. Others have shared your depression and frustration and prevailed.

My profound hope is that you now recognize that the answers to your succession questions are no longer limited to "pass it to Junior and pray for the best" or "just, sell the sucker."

I present these expanded succession options because I understand that your family business is a precious commodity. The price (you, your family, your forefathers) for the development of your business is beyond calculation in terms of time, money, and the less noticeable sacrifices relating to personal interest, family time and health. Your new responsibility, as well as mine, will be to determine if the money that buyers throw in your direction is worth the termination of your family's legacy.

I will also be pleased if you recognized that, in addition to enhanced financial security, a Succession Bridge can provide great satisfaction through helping key managers achieve career opportunities that otherwise would not be available. My purpose is served if you just pause or, better yet, give serious consideration to the concept that there are viable succession options that you otherwise would not have considered.

Does a Succession Bridge have risks? Sure it does, but what else is new? The risk involved with key managers assuming more responsibility, and even equity ownership, are no greater than the risk you have had to undertake in the normal course of business. Yes, you are older and you have less time for recovery. However, you are also more experienced and you know your key managers better. The risks taken with key managers, who you recruited and mentored, are usually less than the risks taken with the reinvestment of the proceeds from a sale.

The perpetuation of your family's legacy is worth a little risk. If the Succession Bridge does not meet your expectations, you still have the option to sell. Give this concept your prayers and consideration and I am confident you will do the right thing.

IGWT, Good luck.